Contemporary American Drama

Edinburgh Critical Guides to Literature
Series Editors: Martin Halliwell, University of Leicester and
Andy Mousley, De Montfort University

Published Titles:
Gothic Literature, Andrew Smith
Canadian Literature, Faye Hammill
Women's Poetry, Jo Gill
Contemporary American Drama, Annette J. Saddik
Shakespeare, Gabriel Egan

Forthcoming Titles in the Series:
Asian American Literature, Bella Adams
Children's Literature, M. O. Grenby
Eighteenth-Century Literature, Hamish Mathison
Contemporary British Fiction, Nick Bentley
Contemporary American Fiction, David Brauner
Victorian Literature, David Amigoni
Crime Fiction, Stacy Gillis
Renaissance Literature, Siobhan Keenan
Modern American Literature, Catherine Morley
Scottish Literature, Gerard Carruthers
Romantic Literature, Richard Marggraf Turley
Modernist Literature, Rachel Potter
Medieval Literature, Pamela King
Women's Fiction, Sarah Sceats

Contemporary American Drama

Annette J. Saddik

Edinburgh University Press

In memory of
my mother, Gila G. Saddik
and my father, Dr Meir Saddik
with overflowing gratitude and love

© Annette J. Saddik, 2007

Edinburgh University Press Ltd
22 George Square, Edinburgh

Typeset in 11.5/13 Ehrhardt
by Servis Filmsetting Ltd, Manchester, and
printed and bound in Great Britain by
Antony Rowe Ltd, Chippenham, Wilts

A CIP record for this book is available from the British Library

ISBN 978 0 7486 2493 5 (hardback)
ISBN 978 0 7486 2494 2 (paperback)

Contents

Series Preface   vi
Acknowledgements   vii
Chronology   xi

Introduction   1
Chapter 1   Experimental Innovations After the Second
            World War   17
Chapter 2   Revisiting the American Dream   40
Chapter 3   African-American Theatre: Voices
            from the Margins   72
Chapter 4   Avant-Garde Theatre Groups:
            Revolutions in Performance   108
Chapter 5   Postmodern Presentations: Questioning
        ,   Boundaries of Representation   129
Chapter 6   The Politics of Identity and Exclusion   151
Chapter 7   Fragmented Representations of American
            Identity in the Theatre of the Vietnam War   174
Chapter 8   The 'NEA Four' and Performance
            Art: Making Visible the Invisible   190
Conclusion   207

Student Resources   212
  Glossary   212
  Guide to Further Reading   215
Index   222

Series Preface

The study of English literature in the early twenty-first century is host to an exhilarating range of critical approaches, theories and historical perspectives. 'English' ranges from traditional modes of study such as Shakespeare and Romanticism to popular interest in national and area literatures such as the United States, Ireland and the Caribbean. The subject also spans a diverse array of genres from tragedy to cyberpunk, incorporates such hybrid fields of study as Asian American literature, black British literature, creative writing and literary adaptations, and remains eclectic in its methodology.

Such diversity is cause for both celebration and consternation. English is varied enough to promise enrichment and enjoyment for all kinds of readers and to challenge preconceptions about what the study of literature might involve. But how are readers to navigate their way through such literary and cultural diversity? And how are students to make sense of the various literary categories and periodisations, such as modernism and the Renaissance, or the proliferating theories of literature, from feminism and marxism to queer theory and eco-criticism? The Edinburgh Critical Guides to Literature series reflects the challenges and pluralities of English today, but at the same time it offers readers clear and accessible routes through the texts, contexts, genres, historical periods and debates within the subject.

Martin Halliwell and Andy Mousley

Acknowledgements

I would like to acknowledge the many colleagues, artists, students, and friends who have enriched my understanding of the complexities of contemporary American performance during the years that I have been researching material for this book. Countless conversations with my friends, colleagues, and students at Eastern Michigan University – particularly Annette Wannamaker, Jessica 'Decky' Alexander, Michael Page, Scott Still, Eric Abbey, Khalilah Watson, Rodney Pratt, Monica Williams, and Jim Meade – were very helpful throughout the various stages of my research. At New York City College of Technology (CUNY), I owe thanks to my research assistant Rachel Wilson and the students in my EG 202 Drama courses for valuable insights and lively discussion during the later stages of manuscript preparation.

My former department heads, Russ Larson and Marcia Dalbey at Eastern Michigan University, along with Dean Pam Brown, Dean Sonja Jackson, and Provost Bonne August at New York City College of Technology, were wonderful at finding grant money to aid with course release, conference travel, and research, and the amazing Jocelyne Castro was always on hand to assist with my frantic questions at the eleventh hour. Thanks also to Brian Keener, Nina Bannett, and George Guida at New York City College of Technology for helping me organise my teaching schedule to allow for small pockets of writing time, and to Lily Lam and Elayne Rinn for always knowing where to find the answer to any question.

Although we have not worked together directly for some time, I continue to be grateful to my mentors at Rutgers University, Thomas Van Laan and Elin Diamond, for helping me find my voice in twentieth-century drama; to Michael Shafer, for nurturing my interest in Vietnam veterans' theater; and to Peter J. Swales, for many years of friendship. Another Rutgers veteran, the dynamic and brilliant Patricia Tobin, sadly passed away in 2005, but we were in contact until then and I am confident that she knew how much she meant to me.

I am very grateful to Richard Schechner, Philip Kolin, and Robert Bray for helpful comments and suggestions when portions of this book were at the essay and proposal stages, and to performer Reggie Gibson and professors Mel Peters and Charles Simmons at Eastern Michigan University, who helped me gain insight into the social issues surrounding popular art forms, such as hip hop, in African-American communities. Much thanks goes out to Ozzie Rodriguez and Ellen Stewart at La MaMa E.T.C. for providing me with rare photos from The La MaMa Archive/Ellen Stewart Private Collection. I am also indebted to Michael Paller and Janette Gallegos at the American Conservatory Theater, and Peggy Fox and Thomas Keith at New Directions for giving me their time, assistance, and photos.

My gratitude to Thomas Keith for so many things – reading the manuscript and offering suggestions, putting me in contact with some wonderful people who helped with this book, inviting me to performances, and being my friend – is ongoing. Jackie Jones, James Dale, Máiréad McElligott, and Nancy Marten at Edinburgh University Press, along with Series editors Martin Halliwell and Andy Mousley, were always on hand to assist with my seemingly endless queries, and I heartfully thank them. Special thanks to Martin Halliwell for carefully reading my work throughout its many stages, and for his inspiration, patience, intelligence, and friendship.

Humble thanks goes out to my friends who have offered insightful observations and kept me entertained during preparation of this book: Kathleen H. Formosa, for taking on what seems like a part-time job responding to my emails with her sage advice and for refreshing me with food and wine; Michael Formosa, for initiating the 'Annette J. Saddik Lecture Series' and for many hours of animated venting at DTUT and The Palm; and Todd B., for just being Todd. Much gratitude to Shari Punyon and Mark Noonan for letting me drag them to performances of varying quality; Fitz Holloway, for letting me drag him to some very strange performances, sometimes in Polish; Annette Wannamaker, Steve Krause, and Will Krause, for being my Michigan family; Walid Younes, for emergency late-night phone calls; my colleagues at New York City College of Technology for their good wishes and support; and all my friends in the Eastern Michigan University English and Theatre departments – I am very lucky to have had the privilege to work with them.

The support and love of my family is a light in my heart that I wouldn't know how to live without. My uncle and aunt, Aaron and Tikva Murad, and my cousins Morry Murad, Renee Murad, and Eileen Murad, gave me joy at a time when there seemed to be none, and continue to make my days happy. A great debt of thanks falls to my sister, Orly Saddik, for her unconditional love and support in all things, and for being my most enthusiastic fan.

Finally, my endless gratitude goes to my mother, Gila G. Saddik, whose sudden passing in 2002 left a void in so many lives. She was the definition of beauty, kindness, strength, and grace, and I don't know how I go on without her. Her spirit and my father's spirit are with me everyday, and I am unbelievably fortunate to have had them in my life to guide and love me. They deserve the credit for everything that I accomplish. This book is for them.

I am grateful to both the City University of New York and Eastern Michigan University for their generous support during the years of manuscript preparation, particularly through the following grants: PSC-CUNY 37 Research Grant (2006–2007), PSC-CUNY 36 Research Grant (2005–2006), PSC-CUNY 35 Research Grant (2004–2005), Eastern Michigan University Spring/Summer Award (2000), Eastern Michigan University Provost's New Faculty Award (1999).

Portions of this book first appeared in academic journals in revised form: '"Blueprints for the Reconstruction": Postmodern

Possibility in Tennessee Williams' *Stairs to the Roof*,' *Tennessee Williams Annual Review* (2007); '"You Just Forge Ahead": Image, Authenticity, and Freedom in the Plays of Tennessee Williams and Sam Shepard,' *South Atlantic Review* 70:4 (Fall 2005); 'Rap's Unruly Body: The Postmodern Performance of Black Male Identity on the American Stage,' *TDR: the journal of performance studies* 47:4 (Winter 2003); 'Performing the American Dream: Postmodern Blurrings of Myth and Reality in the Work of David Mamet and Sam Shepard,' *Études Théâtrales/Essays in Theatre* 20:2 (May 2002).

Chronology

Date	Political/Cultural events	Theatre/Arts
1945	Second World War ends.	European and British playwrights such as Jean Genet, Samuel Beckett, Eugène Ionesco and Harold Pinter introduce a style of theatre that dealt with the anxieties of living in a postwar society, which Martin Esslin eventually terms 'Theatre of the Absurd' in 1961.
1946	House Un-American Activities Committee (HUAC), created in 1938, becomes a permanent committee of the House of Representatives to investigate 'Un-American' activities.	
1947	Bertolt Brecht is called to testify in front of HUAC to account for his Communist	Julian Beck and Judith Malina establish the Living Theatre.

Date	Political/Cultural events	Theatre/Arts
	allegiances; he testifies, then leaves the US to settle in Europe.	
1950	US Senator Joseph McCarthy begins his Communist 'witch-hunts' by investigating US citizens, many in the theatre industry.	Eugène Ionesco's first play, *The Bald Soprano* [*The Bald Prima Donna*] premieres in Paris.
1953		Arthur Miller's *The Crucible* and Tennessee Williams's *Camino Real* premiere; both are reactions against Senator McCarthy's 'witch hunts' and oppressive tactics. Beckett's *Waiting for Godot* premieres in Paris.
1954	McCarthy and HUAC lose credibility after McCarthy accuses the US Army of Communist infiltration.	
1956	Arthur Miller called to testify in front of HUAC and refuses to 'name names'.	Beckett's *Waiting for Godot* produced in the US. John Osborne's *Look Back in Anger* initiates a 'stage revolution' in Britain.
1959		Jack Gelber's *The Connection* is one of the first off-Broadway plays to achieve mainstream critical attention. Edward Albee's *The Zoo Story* premieres off-Broadway.

Date	Political/Cultural events	Theatre/Arts
		Lorraine Hansberry's *A Raisin in the Sun* is the first play written by a black woman to be produced on Broadway.
1960s	Political and cultural movements such as Gay Liberation, the Women's Movement and the Black Power Movement take shape and flourish.	The off-Broadway movement flourishes, with theatre venues such as Café Cino and La MaMa E.T.C., as well as performance troupes such as the Living Theatre, the Open Theater (1963), and the Performance Group (1967).
1962	The first US combat troops are sent to South Vietnam.	
1964	US involvement in Vietnam escalates.	Sam Shepard's first plays, *Cowboys* and *The Rock Garden*, produced at Theatre Genesis. LeRoi Jones's *Dutchman* and *The Slave* premiere. Adrienne Kennedy's *Funnyhouse of a Negro* premieres.
1965	Malcolm X is assassinated in New York.	The NEA (National Endowment for the Arts) is established. The Black Arts Movement (BAM), led by playwrights such as LeRoi Jones, Ed Bullins and Ron Milner, begins to take shape.
1966	The National Organization for Women (NOW) is established.	The first plays to deal with the Vietnam War, Megan

Date	Political/Cultural events	Theatre/Arts
		Terry's *Viet Rock* and Jean Claude Van Itallie's *America Hurrah*, are produced.
1968	Martin Luther King is assassinated.	The 1927 theatrical censorship laws in the US, which prohibited the depiction of 'sex perversion', including homosexuality as it was classified at the time, are repealed. Similar laws (the Licensing Act of 1737) are repealed in Britain. The Performance Group produces *Dionysus in 69* under the direction of Richard Schechner.
1969	'Stonewall Riots' in New York City, where gay and transgender patrons fought back against police oppression, fueling the Gay Liberation Movement.	
1973	US troops are withdrawn from Vietnam.	
1975	Vietnam War ends when Saigon falls to the North Vietnamese. HUAC abolished.	
1976		BAM, as an organised movement, breaks up. David Mamet's *American Buffalo* premieres.
late 1970s		The rise of rap and hip hop culture in the South Bronx.

Date	Political/Cultural events	Theatre/Arts
		The rise of postmodernism in the arts.
1980	Ronald Reagan elected President of the United States.	Shepard's *True West* premieres.
1981	AIDS is officially reported by the Centers for Disease Control and viewed as a 'gay plague'.	
1983		Mamet's *Glengarry Glen Ross* premieres.
1987	President Reagan finally acknowledges AIDS.	
1989	The fall of the Berlin Wall, as communism crumbles in Eastern Europe.	
1990		The NEA is attacked when controversial awards for 'indecent' performance artists are questioned.
1991	The Soviet Union collapses.	Tony Kushner's *Angels in America, Part One: Millennium Approaches* premieres.
1992	Pat Buchanan's 1992 Republican Convention speech initiates the 'Culture Wars' of the 1990s.	Anna Deavere Smith's groundbreaking performance piece, *Fires in the Mirror*, is a runner-up for the Pulitzer Prize in Drama. Kushner's *Angels in America, Part Two: Perestroika* premieres.
1993	Performance artists Karen Finely, Holly Hughes, Tim Miller and John Fleck (the	Anna Deavere Smith's *Twilight Los Angeles, 1992* is disqualified for the 1993

Date	Political/Cultural events	Theatre/Arts
	'NEA Four') sue the US government and win reinstatements of their NEA grants, which had been awarded by a panel of their peers, then rescinded on 'moral' grounds.	Pulitzer Prize on the grounds that it was not fiction and could only be performed by Smith. Kushner's *Angels in America, Parts One and Two*, opens on Broadway and wins the Pultizer Prize for Drama and the Tony Award for Best Play of 1993 and 1994.
1998	President Bill Clinton appeals the 'NEA Four' court decision, winning a Supreme Court ruling that the NEA can use 'general standards of decency' in making funding decisions.	Paula Vogel's *How I Learned to Drive* wins the Pulitzer Prize.
2003		Off-Broadway alternative theatre begins to increasingly receive mainstream attention. *Russell Simmons' Def Poetry Jam on Broadway* receives a Tony Award for Best 'Special Theatrical Event.' *Avenue Q* opens off-Broadway at the Vineyard Theatre; it moves to Broadway in 2004, winning the Tony Award for Best Musical.
2004		Doug Wright's *I Am My Own Wife* wins the 2004 Tony Award for Best Play

Date	Political/Cultural events	Theatre/Arts
		and the Pulitzer Prize for Drama. Lisa Kron's *Well* opens at the Public Theater; it moves to Broadway in 2006, earning two Tony nominations.
2005		Will Eno's *Thom Pain (based on nothing)* is a finalist for the Pulitzer Prize. August Wilson dies at the age of 60. The Virginia Theatre on Broadway is renamed the August Wilson Theatre, the first theatre to be named after an African-American.
2006		Sarah Jones wins a 'Special' Tony Award for *Bridge and Tunnel*. Will Power's hip hop drama, *The Seven*, a reimagining of Aeschylus' *Seven Against Thebes*, premieres at the New York Theatre Workshop.

Introduction

In the US there was this myth of American character formed
on the frontier. This myth was destroyed by industrialisation,
massive immigration at the beginning of the century, and the
resulting urbanisation. Now the question seems to be, what
experience constitutes being an American?

Carol Martin, interviewing Anna Deavere Smith, 1993

In his 1976 treatise, *An Anatomy of Drama*, Martin Esslin writes,
'The theatre is the place where a nation thinks in public in front
of itself.'[1] He adds, 'Hamlet speaks of the theatre holding a mirror
up to nature. I think in fact it is society to which the theatre holds
up the mirror. The theatre and all drama can be seen as a mirror
in which society looks at itself.'[2] Esslin's reference to the theatre
as a 'mirror' relies, of course, on Aristotle's classical theories of
dramatic representation, which laid the foundation for Western
dramaturgy. Aristotle's notion of mimesis – dramatic action as an
imitation or 'mirroring' of reality/nature – was fundamental to his
conception of the function of the theatre. Yet theatre and all forms
of representation are, ultimately, where society not only 'looks at
itself,' but imagines itself and its identifications.

This dialectic of mirroring/imagining, or reflecting/creating
social reality, clearly plays itself out in various modes in which
American identity has historically been represented on the stage.
Since the Second World War, the ways in which America has

thought 'in public in front of itself' through drama and performance have taken various forms, from the conservative conventions
of domestic realism that typically reassert the dominant social
order, to more anti-realistic, anti-mimetic dramatic modes that
question and resist these restrictive definitions of what it means to
be, or to actually count as, an 'American' on the stage in terms of
ethnicity, social class, gender, sexuality and race.

Esslin's questioning of the *subject* of realistic theatre's mimetic
function fails to address the problematic issues inherent in the very
idea of a mimetic theatre and its connection to dramatic realism, the
form of theatre based on Aristotelian theories of representation that
dominated the American stage during the 1940s and 1950s. Along
with the style of acting known as 'the Method', with its emphasis
on the creation of psychologically consistent characters from
'within', realism as a dramatic style sought to reproduce the surfaces of reality, with stage settings that reflected a specific place and
time, and characters who aimed to mirror the speech, dress and
behaviour of their middle-class audiences engaging in readily
believable social and domestic situations, in order to present 'Truth'
as fixed, stable and knowable.[3]

By the late 1950s and 1960s, however, a more anti-realistic theatre
emerged in the United States to take on the job of questioning the
conventional ideologies of realism in order to reveal the gaps in such
limited constructions of identity and Truth. Anti-realism is concerned with eschewing the reproduction of surface reality, distorting
these surfaces through stage settings that are not faithfully specific of
a certain time or place, and presenting characters who, rather than
representing a psychologically consistent identity, play with the
boundaries between actor/character/real person, the blurred line
between 'acting' and 'being'. Anti-realistic theatre can offer a degree
of freedom from the constrictions of 'reality' in order to access a truth
that is not readily apparent. Politically, anti-realistic theatre is usually
anti-Aristotelian in the sense that it resists the (re)presentation (to
present 'again') of a singular, dogmatic idea of how the world should
be, and instead presents multiple views of reality that are not necessarily consistent with the hegemonic dictates of the powers-that-be.

One of the most articulate discussions of the political aims of
Aristotelian drama is to be found in Augusto Boal's *Theatre of the*

Oppressed (1974; English translation 1979). As Boal – an innovative Brazilian director, writer and political activist – argues, despite Aristotle's declaration that art is independent of politics, he constructs the first 'poetic-political system for intimidation of the spectator'[4] with the aim of purging those tendencies, thoughts and emotions that oppose the aims of the dominant ideology of the State. The conventional wisdom tends to equate Aristotelian theatre with realism, primarily in relation to his theory of mimesis outlined in the *Poetics*. However, as Boal clearly explains, this equation with realism or mimesis does not involve the copying of a nature that already exists, but instead implies a 're-creation' of 'nature' in terms of movement from the imperfect towards the ideal, an ideal which was, of course, defined by politics, by the State. For Aristotle, 'imitate' meant:

> To recreate that internal movement of things toward their perfection. Nature was for him this movement itself and not things already made, finished, visible. Thus, 'to imitate' has nothing to do with improvisation or 'realism,' and for this reason Aristotle could say that the artist must imitate men 'as they should be' and not as they are.[5]

This emphasises a specific model of human behaviour rather than its reality. Aristotelian drama is therefore involved in (re)presenting the status quo for the purpose of re-establishing the dominant social order, things 'as they should be' according to the lawmakers, or the ruling class.

For Aristotle, the theatre achieved its function through catharsis, typically defined as a 'purging' of negative emotions, thereby purifying and strengthening the spectator. Audience members arrive at catharsis through their reaction to the play, experiencing both terror (sometimes translated as 'fear') and pity in connection with the action and their identification with the protagonist. The *Poetics* primarily analyses the function and structure of Tragedy, which Aristotle describes as an imitation of an action, representing characters who are to be taken seriously (that is, those of noble or aristocratic birth). He explains that the tragic flaw of the protagonist leads to a reversal of fortune and a recognition of the truth of the situation that marks the protagonist's downfall. The tragic flaw is primarily a socially discouraged behaviour (pride or 'hubris', for instance), involving a transgression or social taboo. Witnessing this progression on the stage is most satisfying for the audience members, Aristotle claims, since in their identification with the protagonist they experience terror at his fate (as he is ultimately punished for his transgressions), along with pity (a feeling of superiority, often accompanied by a relief that one has escaped this victimising fate). Essentially, Aristotle's argument is that since the audience members do not directly experience the pain and humiliation of the protagonist – it is merely a representation on the stage – they can learn the lessons of his transgressive behavior without being subject to its punishments, receiving and, hopefully heeding, its warning. The satisfaction of simultaneously witnessing and escaping the protagonist's fate, along with the fear that the social transgression that caused it must be avoided, ultimately leads to catharsis, or the purging of any 'negative' impulses, which is Aristotle's goal for the audience. Boal reads these negative impulses as revolutionary ones. For Boal, Aristotelian catharsis ensures that any potential for revolution has been left behind in the theatre, correct social behaviour has been reinforced, and the good of the State is preserved.

This insistence that the audience's antisocial, revolutionary impulses – those that would question and threaten the dominant social order and potentially force political change – are 'purged' is, as Boal points out, precisely at the core of Aristotelian theatre's socially and politically coercive nature. Along with Boal, European theatre practitioners in the twentieth century, such as Bertolt Brecht and Antonin Artaud, would offer political, ideological and structural challenges to Aristotle, opening the doors for a dynamic theatre that would ask audiences to engage with difficult existential, epistemological and ontological questions – issues regarding the nature of experiencing, knowing and being in the world – to inspire thoughtful considerations of who we are and how we fit into our various communities.

When I refer to 'anti-realistic', 'anti-mimetic' or 'anti-Aristotelian' drama in this volume, I am therefore not only referring to dramatic form (differences in the representation of character, language and action), but also to the political aims of realism – the coercion of spectators who are manipulated into purging tendencies that oppose the dominant ideology and conforming to the existing social order. The anti-Aristotelian forms of theatre discussed in this book are anti-realistic not only in form, but in their socio-political goals of challenging hegemonic political representations and presenting identities outside the established social ideal of how Americans 'should be', identities that speak to and complicate who we in fact are.

This division between realism and anti-realism in the theatre, however, is certainly not absolute and uncomplicated. Realistic plays (such as Ibsen's *A Doll House* (1879) or *Ghosts* (1881)) often do imply the need for social change in their representation of oppressive social realities, and therefore can serve to question, rather than reinforce, the status quo. In this way, the political concerns of anti-realistic theatre were prefigured in much of the realistic drama that reacted against the mindless entertainment of styles such as nineteenth-century melodrama, and realism as a dramatic form continues to survive and evolve in interesting ways in the contemporary American theatre. I employ this distinction in order to provide a context for examining plays and performances that have been stylistically and politically experimental, and certainly many complex plays simultaneously make use of both realistic and anti-realistic conventions. It is primarily plays that depart from realistic tradition, however, that I am concerned with here, as I explore the ways in which superficial reality has been distorted on the stage in order to reveal the truth(s) beyond it.

For the generation(s) that lived through the devastating effects of two world wars, instability, uncertainty and a severe sense of alienation from other human beings as well as from one's home, work and even oneself began to define the conditions of a new world order. The primary literary response after the First World War was part of a broader wave of cultural modernism, which strove to destroy the old forms and 'make it new', in the words of American poet Ezra Pound. Yet the modernists were still searching for absolutes, the codes of a fixed and immutable reality that would give order and meaning to the world through concepts such as 'human nature' and a unifying religious or spiritual sensibility. After the violence and atrocities of the Second World War, however, the fragile foundations of meaning and truth were shaken even further. As a result, a more fragmented and dislocated individual emerged to usher in what from the mid-1970s onwards became known as postmodernity: a historical phase where there were no certainties, no origins and no absolute position from which one could safely view the world. The term postmodern refers to both a particular historical era that is generally considered to have begun after the Second World War and the cultural or artistic products that mark this era. Critics often make a distinction between the terms post-modern*ity* and postmodern*ism* on the basis that the first implies the social or historical period that involves a transition from mod-ernism, while the second is associated with the specific ideas, styles and cultural formations that came out of this historical period. In contrast to the elusive search for essential and fixed truths that define the quest of the modernists, in the postmodern world truth and illusion are often indistinguishable, identity is not fixed, and differences co-exist in the same sphere. And although there is a certain degree of nihilism and instability to this philosophy, many would define it as liberating in its realisation that 'Truth' is often politically motivated rather than fixed, and reality can be dependent on the person or group that is viewing it. Characteristics of post-modern literature and drama include a focus on the instability of meaning and the inadequacy of language to completely and accu-rately represent Truth, along with an irony and playfulness in the treatment of linguistic constructs; an acknowledgement of the past and a sense that literary creation is never truly original, but owes a debt to what has come before; a lack of any hierarchy or boundaries in the treatment of 'high' and 'low' culture; and an eschewing of the notion of an origin or essential 'core' in terms of identity, as identity becomes a series of layers or 'masks' with no distinction between the artificial and the real.

The complex and varied dramatic texts that grew out of this world view and began to gain prominence at the end of the 1950s in Europe, and throughout the 1960s in Britain and the United States, are the plays and performance styles that gave rise to the contem-porary American theatre. This volume is concerned with the roots of contemporary drama in the United States and its development from the 1960s to the present day, addressing the cross-cultural impact of postwar British, European and Latin American innovations on the American theatre. It begins with an exploration of the influence of Brecht and Artaud on the experimental plays that Martin Esslin in 1961 termed 'Theatre of the Absurd', and explores a series of plays and performances that have been representative of a contemporary postmodern theatre, primarily in Europe, Britain and the United States. Rather than attempt to offer a complete history of contemporary American drama in these pages that would remain inevitably superficial, I focus mainly on plays and performance texts regarded as representative of this period's interest in experimentation with both form and content, as contemporary drama typically employs anti-realistic conventions that resist mimetic representation and distort the surfaces of reality in order to access a truth beyond superficial appearance. The chapters are therefore organised theoretically in order to offer a historical, sociopolitical and aesthetic view of the development of contemporary American theatre as an experimental theatre of inclusion and diversity that, in postmodern fashion, questions the nature of reality, presents multiple versions of truth(s), complicates the notion of an origin or 'essence', and destabilises the illusion of fixed identity by blurring the boundaries between role-playing and authenticity, or acting and being. Inevitably, my particular theoretical focus and the limitations of space have made it necessary to exclude several important playwrights of the period, but their rich and complex work has, of course, been covered elsewhere in numerous volumes.

Most anthologies of drama and literature locate the beginning of 'contemporary' drama at the end of the 1950s, with the increasing prominence of post-Second World War experimental plays that resisted traditional narrative plot and discursive language in favour of strikingly non-rational structures and a more minimalistic style of dialogue. These anti-realistic experiments focused on experience beyond rational understanding and, as a result, tend to be more theme- or conflict-centred rather than plot- or character-centred, a factor which constitutes the most marked break with the nineteenth-century tradition of the well-made play and early twentieth-century realism (which I discuss in some detail in Chapter 1). Contemporary drama is primarily a drama of postmodernism, one that is concerned with innovations in both the form and the subject of representation.

Yet while anti-Aristotelian experiments with form generally characterise contemporary drama, traditional realism has certainly survived into the twenty-first century. Even those plays that remain traditional in terms of their dramaturgy, however, are often revolutionary in terms of their subject of representation. By the 1960s, 1970s and 1980s, postmodern drama in America had extended representation to socio-political groups that had formerly been denied a voice, primarily on the basis of social class, race, gender or sexual orientation. These groups resist the dominant version of how the world should be according to those in power, who stand to gain by perpetuating the myth of one valid and stable reality for all – the Platonic 'ideal' that Aristotle strove to maintain. Postmodern performance has expanded the representation of identit(ies) to those who have been marginalised in society, and focuses on the subjectivity and multiplicity of truth and experience. These concerns with multiplicity, socio-political identity and experimentation in form are ones that have continued to mark contemporary American drama at the end of the twentieth and into the twenty-first century, albeit through a different lens, as we move from postmodernity into a phase of increasing 'globalisation' and its concerns with a more imperialistic sense of experiencing both difference and sameness simultaneously, yet – it could be argued – on a quite superficial level.

At the end of the 1940s and throughout the 1950s, playwrights in Europe, influenced greatly by the theories of Bertolt Brecht in Germany and Antonin Artaud in France, were developing a new kind of drama that deliberately questioned the nature of truth and reality primarily through exploring the notion that language interprets and constructs – rather than simply represents – reality. Eugène Ionesco and Jean Genet were causing controversy throughout the 1950s with plays such as *The Bald Soprano* (1950), *The Lesson* (1951) and *The Balcony* (1958), and Samuel Beckett's *Waiting For Godot* shocked Paris in 1953 with its world premiere. While not an immediate success, *Godot* gradually became known throughout Europe for its highly unorthodox form and its controversial presentation of the futility of human existence. It was produced in London in 1955, and reached the United States in 1956. At this time, British and American playwrights were beginning to embrace the styles of experimental drama dominating the European theatre scene. In

England, John Osborne initiated what has been called a 'stage revolution' on 8 May 1956 when *Look Back in Anger* was presented at the Royal Court Theatre. Although *Look Back in Anger* was essentially traditional in terms of style, its themes were bold and controversial, depicting the 'angry young man' working-class hero, and during the late 1950s and early 1960s writers like Harold Pinter and Tom Stoppard introduced their innovative work to London. Pinter's *The Caretaker* (1960) eventually reached the United States in 1961, and in the meantime Edward Albee was busy creating a place for the 'Theatre of the Absurd' in American drama. In 1959, the director Herbert Blau returned from Europe determined to introduce American alternative theatre to the new directions that he had seen. Blau's consequent productions of Beckett, Ionesco and Genet in the United States, the translation of Antonin Artaud's treatise *The Theater and Its Double* into English in 1958, and the powerful emergence of off-Broadway and off-off-Broadway in 1959 with the premiere of Albee's *The Zoo Story* and the Living Theatre's pivotal production of Jack Gelber's *The Connection* (one of the first off-Broadway works to receive mainstream critical attention) promised drastic changes in the American theatre that would apply burgeoning theories of the postmodern to dramatic representation.

By the 1960s and 1970s, the off- and off-off-Broadway theatre scene (comparable to 'off-West End' and 'Fringe Theatre' in Britain) was increasingly becoming the venue of choice for dramatic experimentation, offering an alternative to the economic pressures of expensive Broadway productions. As early as the 1950s, traditional Broadway playwrights such as Tennessee Williams were moving off-Broadway for both economic and artistic reasons, and newer playwrights such as Sam Shepard, who began his career in 1964 downtown with Theatre Genesis, were avoiding Broadway altogether. The off-Broadway movement was primarily interested in exploring the period's concern with personal freedom and authenticity apart from political and social oppression, and with avoiding realism's representations of superficial appearance in favour of more abstract presentations of an inner reality. In much of the work that was produced off-Broadway at this time, the elusive search for an individual essence or reality outside social conformity is acknowledged alongside the inevitability of role-playing or performance, marking a tension that would characterise contemporary postmodern drama in the United States.

This volume begins by setting up the background for what would become contemporary American drama during the latter half of the twentieth century. Chapter 1 discusses the historical, social and aesthetic development of experimental theatre that grew out of a post-Second World War world view and gained prominence at the end of the 1950s and into the 1960s in Europe, Britain and the United States. Instability, uncertainty and contradiction dominated these dramatic forms, as the unreliability of memory/history and the struggles of human connection and communication became dominant themes to be explored. Key playwrights discussed include Jean Genet, Eugène Ionesco, Samuel Beckett, Harold Pinter and Edward Albee, as well as the theories of Bertolt Brecht and Antonin Artaud.

Focusing on the work of major American playwrights Arthur Miller and Tennessee Williams, Chapter 2 explores the construction of American identity in the context of a changing world order after the Second World War. Miller and Williams gained prominence in the late 1940s, and throughout the 1950s they were responding to the social anxieties of the McCarthy era regarding both private and public identity (Miller, of course, appeared before the House Un-American Activities Committee in 1956). Primarily in terms of content but also in form, their work began to illustrate the contradictions of the American dream, as late capitalism's ideological failures left behind those betrayed by promises of self-determination, wealth and power. As the political upheavals of the 1960s continued to struggle with definitions of what it means to 'be American', these playwrights increasingly questioned its representation on the stage. They explored the hypocrisies of social and 'moral' exclusion and exposed its inherent dangers.

The disappointing promises of the American dream were possibly most evident in the struggle of African-American playwrights for a place in the contemporary American theatre. The success of Lorraine Hansberry's *A Raisin in the Sun* in 1959 – the first play written by a black woman to reach Broadway – is usually hailed as the beginning of a successful contemporary black theatre in the United States. Although Hansberry's success is marked by her Broadway inclusion, throughout the 1960s playwrights such as Amiri Baraka (formerly LeRoi Jones) were more interested in developing a black aesthetic that would stand apart from the mainstream in keeping with the artistic and cultural revolutions of the period, and focused on producing work off- and off-off-Broadway. Baraka, along with Ed Bullins and Ron Milner, was pivotal in using drama to bring attention to the specific concerns of racial identity and social reform in American culture. His role in the Black Arts Movement, an artistic movement of the 1960s that focused on black nationalism and self-determination in promoting an art which would speak directly to and from African-American experience, led to the founding of the Black Arts Repertory Theatre and School in Harlem in 1964, and to the general promotion of African-American theatre in the United States. Black women playwrights such as Adrienne Kennedy during the 1960s and Ntozake Shange in the 1970s reached critical success with their more expressionist, poetic attempts to unmask racism and gender discrimination. These accomplishments led the way for black playwrights such as Suzan-Lori Parks and August Wilson, who reached a turning point in his career in 1982 with *Ma Rainey's Black Bottom*, and continued to enjoy both critical and popular success until his death in 2005.

African-American theatre has relied on both realistic and anti-realistic dramatic modes to express complex cultural and personal experiences, and will be addressed in Chapter 3 as a crucial component of contemporary American theatre, both in terms of form and social content. Key playwrights discussed will include LeRoi Jones/Amiri Baraka, Ed Bullins and the Black Arts Movement, Adrienne Kennedy, Ntozake Shange, Suzan-Lori Parks and August Wilson. Despite the great success of artists such as Parks and Wilson, however, the late twentieth century still provided only limited mainstream opportunities for African-American playwrights. The growing popularity of hip hop/rap in American culture during the 1980s and 1990s increasingly influenced contemporary American dramatists such as Ishmael Reed, Glenn Wright, Raul Santiago Sebazco and Robert Alexander, who incorporated hip hop style and rap dialogue into their plays. As hip hop was becoming the dominant style of African-American cultural expression, its highly dramatic character allowed black artists such as Ice Cube, Tupac Shakur, Biggie Smallz and Chuck D, for example, to move beyond the boundaries of traditional theatre and use hip hop performance to comment on the complexities of racial identity and the hypocrisies of the American capitalist system. I address this influence of hip hop culture on contemporary American drama, taking into account the history of African-American performance and the tradition of 'rapping' as part of a continuum of cultural expression.

During the 1960s and 1970s, the American theatre was becoming increasingly political, and performance groups developed mainly in New York City to challenge the primacy of the written text in the theatre and serve as a protest to realism's strict boundaries between audience and performer, actor and character. These theatre groups were revolutionary in both form and content, often serving as venues for political dissent during turbulent times, and focusing on breaking realism's 'fourth wall' – the invisible wall that separates the stage action from the audience – in order to encourage live encounters between spectator and performer. They challenged the very idea of what constituted 'theatre' in their disregard for authoritative texts, traditional representation, and a reliance on language. Instead, performance groups embraced spontaneity and improvisation in performance, along with a more physical presentation and reconception of classic plays. Often these physical and spontaneous spectacles were referred to as 'happenings', and were a central part of avant-garde revolutionary theatre during the 1960s and 1970s, especially in New York and other US cities, but certainly also in Europe as well as in Latin America. Chapter 4 will cover performance groups and playwrights such as Julian Beck and Judith Malina's Living Theatre, Joseph Chaikin's Open Theater, Jerzy Grotowski's Polish Laboratory Theatre, The Bread and Puppet Theater, The San Francisco Mime Troupe, Luis Valdez and El Teatro Campesino, Richard Schechner's Performance Group (and 'environmental theatre'), The Wooster Group, Charles Ludlam's Ridiculous Theatrical Company, Richard Foreman's Ontological-Hysteric Theatre, the work of Robert Wilson, and key playwrights associated with these theatre groups: Jack Gelber, Jean-Claude Van Itallie and Megan Terry.

By the 1970s and 1980s, the performance innovations of the 1960s had made their mark on the American theatre, as more and more new plays were regularly employing anti-realistic devices in order to avoid the facility of realistic illusion, seamless narrative plots, representations of psychologically consistent characters, and the notion of rational language as a means of accessing truth. Instead, a self-consciousness of performance, experimentation with narrative form, the deconstruction of character, and fragmented language that focused on the gaps in constructing meaning were common features of plays that are now considered part of contemporary American drama. These postmodern experiments that characterised much drama from the 1970s to the end of the millennium tend to differ widely, sometimes remaining essentially realistic in terms of form, yet employing anti-realistic devices to address the complexity of contemporary social and political issues. Many artists, however, were radical in their rebellion against traditional realism, with its focus on surface representation and insistence on rationality and order, offering more subjective, flexible interpretations of reality. They were interested in testing the limits of drama and exploring the issue of how 'meaning' was created through language and performance, and so experimented freely with theatrical conventions. Although the work of this period, discussed in Chapter 5 and Chapter 6, differs in terms of the degree of experimentation, what these texts tend to offer in common is an awareness of representation as performance and a sense of 'play', highlighting a postmodern sensibility that questions the stability of truth by blurring the boundaries between the 'natural' and the 'artificial' – being and acting, actor and character, authenticity and role-playing – in order to address the construction of social and political identity. Chapter 5 covers the work of key playwrights Sam Shepard and David Mamet, who explore the instability of identity in terms of the central myths of American culture. In Chapter 6, I address the complexities of constructing identity around the politics of gender, ethnicity, sexuality, citizenship, power and inclusion to determine who will 'count' in American society. Playwrights discussed in this context include Lanford Wilson, David Henry Hwang, Tony Kushner, Paula Vogel, Maria Irene Fornes and Lisa Loomer.

As the American theatre was exploring the blurred boundaries between authenticity and role playing in relation to identity during the 1970s and 1980s, the full impact on American culture and identity of one of the nation's most traumatic historical events, the

Vietnam War, was becoming apparent. Vietnam is arguably the American war most vulnerable to 'revisionism' in the areas of politics and media, but the theatre points to another very key form of revisionist myth-making in this context. Besides serving as a way to come to terms with and give meaning to temporal, excessive situations that were traumatic and unfamiliar, the metaphor of war as theatre had a tremendous social and psychological impact on negotiations of identity during and shortly after the Vietnam War. Chapter 7 examines how the memory of personal experience in Vietnam was revised and translated into public art, particularly in the kinds of 'psychodramas' (such as John DiFusco's 1980 play *Tracers*) presented by Vietnam veterans, the well-known 'Vietnam plays' of David Rabe, and David Berry's *G.R. Point* (1980), in order to explore the Vietnam War as a central myth in the American imagination and its recreation in American drama. I look at how the Vietnam veterans writing, producing and performing in the theatre make meaning out of experience (art out of war) and address shifting representations of American identity after the war. The compatibility of theatre and modern war seems obvious, as soldiers serve as actors playing temporary parts. For the soldiers, seeing themselves as actors playing the parts of characters who act in a capacity that is separate from the values, morals and cultural identifications of the self was a psychological survival tactic. The psychic fragmentation that this splitting of theatrical 'character' and 'real' self created, however, fuelled contradictions of identity that held especially true in the case of Vietnam veterans. Whereas in the case of past wars, veterans had come home to warm receptions and parades – signs of national recognition and approval – for Vietnam veterans there was usually only hostility and accusation. The ultimate acknowledgement that self and other were one and the same, and that the self was responsible for the actions of the actor, blurred the boundaries between acting and being that needed to be explored. The difficulty in resolving these contradictions of identity fuelled the need for representations of a newly negotiated American identity that had to be formed and expressed by and for Vietnam veterans after the war.

As the complexity of representing American identity grew during the 1980s and 1990s in the United States, solo performance texts gained increasing attention as theatre, often under the heading of 'performance art' ('live art' in Britain). These politically charged performances were primarily interested in challenging the dominant power structures of society, exposing the language, values and assumptions about gender, ethnicity and social class set up by patriarchal constructs. Rather than creating a theatre of seamless illusion or a realistic 'slice of life', these artists directly addressed the audience and used unconventional and sometimes controversial techniques in order to expose the invisible power structures surrounding identity, often generating political attention. In 1990, the National Endowment for the Arts (NEA) was attacked when controversial awards for performance artists Karen Finley, Holly Hughes, Tim Miller and John Fleck (later known as the 'NEA Four') were questioned, resulting in a Supreme Court case. Feminist performance art, such as the work of Karen Finley and Holly Hughes, was especially focused on the deconstruction of enforced gender identit(ies), while the character creations of Danny Hoch and Anna Deavere Smith's reflections of the community members involved in the Crown Heights and Los Angeles riots were more interested in exploring what constitutes 'character' and exposing the hegemonic structures surrounding identity. These solo performances often are less of a reflection *of* society in the realistic tradition than they are reflections *on* society, commenting on complex social and historical experiences. In the tradition of anti-realistic theatre and performance, these reflections are often deliberately fragmented or distorted in order to illustrate a reality that exists beyond the surface. While the roots of performance art rest firmly in off- and off-off-Broadway, more recently this genre has gained mainstream critical attention, with several productions moving to Broadway and accumulating Tony award nominations. Performers discussed in Chapter 8 include Karen Finley, Holly Hughes, Tim Miller, John Fleck, Deb Margolin, Lisa Kron, Anna Deavere Smith, Danny Hoch, and the performance groups Split Britches and The Five Lesbian Brothers.

Finally, I conclude this volume with a brief discussion of the more recent directions in theatre and performance in the United States, returning to the question of what it means to perform American identity. Twenty-first-century American drama has been focused on the continued exploration of national identity through questions of being, knowing and meaning. These questions are often framed through an examination of the cross-currents in our socially constructed identities and a consideration of the concept of the individual in relation to politically determined representations of character. And, as in the past, contemporary drama continues to address the pertinent issues of our time – social justice, the complexities of war and the meaning of patriotism, the negotiation of individual human rights and collective responsibility. These new directions in contemporary performance emphasise their reliance on the theatrical innovations that have emerged during the last forty years or so, providing a comprehensive sense of the continuity and development of contemporary American drama during the late twentieth and early twenty-first centuries.

NOTES

1. Martin Esslin, *An Anatomy of Drama* (New York: Hill and Wang, 1976), p. 101.
2. Ibid. p. 103.
3. Throughout this book, when I refer to 'Truth' with a capital 'T,' this signifies a concept of truth as absolute and singular, a unity that remains timeless and unchanging ('fixed, stable and knowable'). By contrast, 'truth' or 'truth(s)' with a lower-case 't' indicates a more relative sense of truth, or a multiplicity of truths that can depend on several factors, such as cultural, historical or even personal circumstances.
4. Augusto Boal, *Theatre of the Oppressed*, trans. Charles A. and Maria-Odilia Leal McBride (New York: Theatre Communications Group, 1985), p. xiv.
5. Ibid. p. 8.

CHAPTER I

Experimental Innovations After the Second World War

> A work of art is the expression of an incommunicable reality that one tries to communicate – and which sometimes can be communicated. That is its paradox and its truth.
>
> Eugène Ionesco, 'The playwright's role', 1958

Shortly after the First World War, German playwright Bertolt Brecht began influencing the direction of twentieth-century drama with his plays and innovative theories. By the 1940s and 1950s, he had revolutionised the European theatre, developing a style he called Epic Theatre, a term attributed in its modern sense to the German director Erwin Piscator and his dramatic experiments that espoused strong Marxist convictions and advocated a theatre that was a catalyst for social change. The phrase 'epic theatre' was originally used by Aristotle and implied an 'episodic' style of presentation, or a series of distinct episodes that are connected through a central theme but disregard theatrical convention and resist the seamlessness of narrative illusion. Brecht used the term for the first time in 1926 to emphasise a style of drama which resisted the conventions of a mimetic, realistic theatre that relied on illusion and an identification with character. Instead, Brecht insisted that the audience members remain constantly distanced, or 'alienated', from the action on the stage, aware that they are watching a performance rather than becoming seduced by the illusion that they are experiencing reality. Therefore, a primary goal of realistic drama, suspension of disbelief, or deliberately ignoring improbabilities and inconsistencies in a work for the sake of enjoyment, runs contrary to Brecht's intentions for his Epic Theatre. He rejected the theatre as mere entertainment, and believed instead in its social function and the spectators' power to change the world. According to Brecht, the function of theatre is not to make audiences *feel*, but to make them *think*. Brecht's Epic Theatre sought to appeal to reason rather than emotion in order to foster understanding of the social forces that shape our lives; he strongly believed that alienation was crucial to any kind of understanding, providing the distance necessary for critical thinking. In 1947, he established the Berliner Ensemble, an organisation dedicated to realising the goals of his Epic Theatre: to show human behaviour 'as alterable; man himself as dependent on certain political and economic factors and at the same time as capable of altering them'.[1]

Brecht's primary contribution to twentieth-century theatre began with his rebellion against the forms of drama that dominated the European, British and American theatre during the early and mid-nineteenth century: the melodrama and the well-made play. Both were very artificial styles that presented well-defined, stereotypical characters (the villain, the hero, the innocent young girl or 'ingenue'). Melodrama primarily consisted of very sentimental, emotional plots with closed, decisive endings. The well-made play, similarly, consisted of very unnatural, declamatory acting and a predictable structure – a clear beginning of the action, a series of climaxes and surprises, and the winding down, or 'denouement', which draws the action together and produces closure, or a well-defined ending.

By the late nineteenth century, writers such as Émile Zola in France, Henrik Ibsen in Norway, and August Strindberg in Sweden resisted these dominant forms of drama that offered mindless entertainment in favour of a drama that offered humanity's 'Truth'. Realism as a dramatic form seeks to provide audiences with *factual* descriptions of events that they could recognise in their own, everyday, middle-class world. It tries to faithfully reproduce life and social relations as they seem to the common audience member, and therefore improbabilities and stylistic effects are rejected, and the audience is rarely, if ever, directly addressed. Stylistically, the setting in a realistic play is 'authentic', using as many genuine props as possible and locating the action in a specific place and time. Language is presented as the common, everyday speech of its audience, and characters aim to represent complex human beings with a consistent and stable personality and psychology. Actor and character are seen as one and the same, and truth is usually presented as something fixed and knowable, something that can be directly and clearly expressed in language. Artificiality is rejected in favour of representing people fully as they 'really are' without censorship: the good, the bad, the grotesque, the beautiful, the boring and the exciting. Politically, realism in the theatre seeks to investigate social and material conditions, mores and values. It deals with potentially disturbing issues such as marital problems, the oppression of women, the class system, madness, venereal disease and political corruption, for audiences who are not used to seeing these issues dramatised on the stage. Overall, however, dramatic realism seeks to naturalise the relationship between stage representation and the outside world, suggesting that the representation is the real. Therefore, while it claims to expose and examine social reality, realism ultimately winds up creating and reinforcing it through the repetition that is representation (see the Introduction).

The rise of realism in drama generally began in Europe during the late nineteenth century with the plays of Ibsen and Strindberg, and is closely related to Zola's theories of naturalism, which he outlined in his 1881 treatise, *Naturalism in the Theatre*. Zola called for a rejection of conventional 'theatre language', a language he saw as simply a stylised version of the author's own, and sought 'to create living people' with 'their individual ways of thinking and expressing themselves'.[2] Naturalism was essentially a product of post-Darwinian biology of the nineteenth century, emerging after the publication of Darwin's *On the Origin of Species* (1859) with its emphasis on evolution, heredity and the survival of the fittest. Following Darwin, the theory of naturalism in the theatre proposes that character and behaviour are determined essentially by the forces of heredity and environment. Naturalism has often been viewed as an extension of realism in its desire to achieve an even more 'scientific' and therefore accurate representation of life and human beings existing in the order of nature. It not only attempts to reproduce the middle-class social world faithfully as realism does, but more specifically seeks to scientifically portray the nature of reality outside human control. Since naturalism is ultimately a deterministic philosophy that aims to reproduce a specific view of reality, Brecht would reject it too as thwarting the possibilities of social change.

Brecht therefore saw both conventional nineteenth-century drama (melodrama and the well-made play) and the new forms of realism and naturalism as limited politically, as these philosophies presented a static world view and reinforced the status quo, albeit through different methods. In contrast to the artificial constructions of melodrama and the well-made play, the 'artificiality' of Brecht's drama does not aim simply to entertain (although it should, he insists, be pleasurable), but rather to distance the audience from emotional involvement and thereby instruct and inspire thought. Instead of ending with defined closure – solving all the play's dilemmas and offering a return to social order (the way things were before the play began) – Brecht's plays end with open-ended questions that seek to stimulate intellectual engagement with the play's moral and social issues and, hopefully, with these issues in the outside world. Rather than reinforcing a vision of the world as it is, Brechtian drama offers possibilities for how the world could be. He championed what he called the 'learning-play' (*Lehrstücke* in German), insisting that 'the aristotelian play is essentially static; its task is to show the world as it is. The learning-play is essentially dynamic; its task is to show the world as it changes (and also how it may be changed).'[3]

As I discussed in the Introduction, a reliance on (re)presentation – the 'presenting again' or reinforcement of often oppressive societal norms and a return to the dominant social order that was Aristotle's legacy to the realistic theatre – discouraged and even denied the notion of social change, and presented the human condition of the moment as natural and permanent. By contrast, Brecht sought the development of an anti-Aristotelian theatre that revealed the subtle and hidden social forces that shape and change our lives, allowing us to see that 'the way things are' is not the way they always have been and, consequently, not the way they always will be. Brecht's recognition that human beings are determined by their material and political circumstances relies heavily on Marxist/socialist ideologies, and resists the notion of a fixed 'human nature' typically embraced by realistic theatre. And since we are under the influence of social forces that can and do change, becoming aware of these forces allows human beings to control them and determine their own destinies. Therefore, rather than representing the condition of human beings in society as fixed and natural, Brecht's Epic Theatre aimed to reveal the human condition as determined by social and political forces such as poverty and material necessity, and thereby capable of change.

While Epic Theatre is highly didactic, aiming to teach, instruct and inspire thought, this is not to say that Brechtian theatre should be tedious or boring. At their best, Brecht's plays and productions of plays that employ his theories should excite, surprise and enlighten. The pleasure in Brechtian theatre comes from a thought-provoking recognition of social forces that have affected and continue to affect the human condition, and the empowerment for change that comes from that recognition. Rather than purging the spectator of revolutionary impulses, it awakens the audience to action and inspires them to carry the lessons of the play back into the social world, rejecting the 'catharsis' that Aristotelian realism demanded.

In order to achieve his theoretical and political goals for the theatre, Brecht employed several anti-realistic conventions that were designed to promote an intellectual distance from the action and maintain a deliberate consciousness of the performance. He desired to produce in the audience what he called Alienation Effect (also known as A-effect), a term that comes from the German word *Verfremdungseffekt*, variously translated as 'alienation effect', 'estrangement effect', or 'defamiliarisation effect'. He insisted that alienation was 'necessary to all understanding', and that 'When something seems "the most obvious thing in the world" it means that any attempt to understand the world has been given up.'[4] In order to inspire Alienation Effect and produce the intellectual distance necessary for critical thinking, Brecht's productions break the fourth-wall barrier between performance and audience that realism relies upon to help foster the illusion necessary for character identification and catharsis. His plays were made up of episodic scenes that were connected but not seamless, as they were interrupted by placards, cards or projections that announced a title for each scene (or episode), serving to highlight and explain the main point or focus of that scene. Blackouts between scenes should be avoided, as they serve only to promote the illusion of seamlessness in the action. Instead of elaborate realistic settings that faithfully reproduce a specific time and place, Brecht called for sets to minimally suggest these markers. Similarly, costume should be minimal, and preferably the actors should perform in their street clothes. The illusion of actor and character as one, coming together on the stage as a 'real person', is to be avoided in Brechtian staging, and so there must be a constant awareness that the actor is not the character. To further resist this illusion and prevent emotional identification with the characters, actors sometimes play more than one part, and minimal costume changes take place right on the stage in full view of the audience. In fact, often the actors remain on the stage throughout the play, moving to the sides when not involved in the action. The language should be inorganic and the acting, Brecht insists, should be 'bad' – that is, there should be no attempt to create the illusion of natural speech or, once again, the illusion that the actor/character is 'real'. In 1926 he complained:

> Nowadays the play's meaning is usually blurred by the fact that the actor plays to the audience's hearts. The figures portrayed are foisted on the audience and are falsified in the process. Contrary to the present custom they ought to be presented quite coldly, classically and objectively. For they are not a matter of empathy; they are there to be understood. Feelings are private and limited. Against that the reason is fairly comprehensive and to be relied on.[5]

In order to continue to disrupt fourth-wall illusionism, characters in Brecht's plays often address the audience and frequently break out into song so as to interrupt the narrative action and, once again, remind the audience that they are watching a performance that requires intellectual engagement. This disruption of realistic illusion is a device he used frequently in plays such as *The Threepenny Opera* (1928), *Mother Courage and Her Children* (1939), *The Good Woman of Setzuan* (1943), and *The Caucasian Chalk Circle* (1948). In all of these plays, social norms and moral conundrums are presented,

Figure 1.1 *The Good Woman of Setzuan* by Bertolt Brecht (English version by Eric Bentley), 1976 production La MaMa's Great Jones Repertory Company. Directed by Andrei Serban, music composed by Elizabeth Swados. (Source: Amnon Ben Normis.)

complicated and questioned, demanding thoughtful consideration and decisions from the spectator. Brecht's anti-realistic Epic Theatre helped liberate the theatre from the constraints of the nineteenth-century well-made play, as well as from the superficialities and political limitations of dramatic realism.

Although Brechtian theatre is certainly anti-realistic, not all anti-realistic theatre is Brechtian. While Brecht's Epic Theatre espoused Marxist principles and focused on social change through intellectual political action, Antonin Artaud's 'theater of cruelty' posed another challenge to realistic representation during the 1930s and 1940s in France, but espoused ideologically different goals. Artaud aimed to destroy the veneer of civilisation and force the spectator to confront a more primitive state, undermining the rational discourse of the audience. For Artaud, 'culture' was synonymous with repression

Figure 1.2 *The Good Woman of Setzuan* by Bertolt Brecht (English version by Eric Bentley), 1976 production La MaMa's Great Jones Repertory Company. Directed by Andrei Serban, music composed by Elizabeth Swados. (Source: Amnon Ben Normis.)

and artificiality, and imposed unhealthy boundaries which 'have never been coincident with life, which in fact has been devised to tyrannize over life'.[6] As Elin Diamond writes in 'The shudder of catharsis', Artaud sought 'an immediate and physical language' for the theatre (Artaud's words), which

> would penetrate the spectators, 'act . . . upon [them] like a spiritual therapeutics.' Artaudian cruelty is a theater of 'total spectacle' intended to destroy barrier between 'analytic theater and plastic world, mind and body' – a theater composed of and addressed to the 'entire organism.'[7]

In his 1938 treatise, *The Theater and Its Double*, which was translated into English in 1958, Artaud proposed a 'theater of cruelty' that did not involve 'the cruelty we can exercise upon each other by hacking at each other's bodies, carving up our personal anatomies . . . but the much more terrible and necessary cruelty which things can exercise against us. We are not free. And the sky can fall on our heads. And the theater has been created to teach us that first of all' (p. 79). His cryptic description of his theater of cruelty has been applied to authors as diverse as Jean Genet in France, August Strindberg in Sweden (particularly his later experimental plays), and, also in terms of his later plays, Tennessee Williams in the United States. Artaud insisted upon a theatre that was 'not psychological but plastic and physical', one that highlighted the inadequacy of language to represent human experience.[8] For Artaud, this 'plastic' theatre (the same term Tennessee Williams used in 1944 in his production notes to *The Glass Menagerie* to describe the anti-realistic type of theatre he espoused) should express a 'metaphysical fear' beyond language, and explore what cannot be expressed in words.[9] This theatre concerns itself with the chaos and violence beyond rational constructs – a sort of 'primal scream'. Artaud is not directly interested in violence per se but rather in the impulse beyond violent acts, the primitive, pre-logical human instincts and desires in their purest states before they become repressed by culture and its social taboos and consequently emerge in what he sees as distorted, sublimated forms. Honouring, capturing and presenting these impulses in their purest possible forms through ritualistic spectacle are key to the theater of cruelty.

Artaud's vision sought to liberate the spectator from an over-reliance on plot and narrative language, creating through gesture, sounds and spectacle the cruelty of the real which remains linguistically 'untranslatable'.[10] One key element of Artaud's work is a revelation of the metaphysical cruelty that lies beyond logical representation, marginalising language and instead taking advantage of the physicality of the theatre. In *Postmodernist Culture*, Steven Connor writes:

In the influential work of Antonin Artuad the theatre is seen as a colonized or dispossessed cultural form, dominated as it is by written language. Artaud argues that the theatre should abandon its fealty to the authority of Text and learn to speak its own intrinsically theatrical language of light, colour, movement, gesture, and space. This is not to say that language should be banished from the theatre . . . but language is to be made physical too, communicating as pure sound and sensation rather than through abstract correspondence.[11]

Artaud sought a chaotic liberation from the rational, and a return to a primal theatre experienced directly by the mind and body apart from language's distortions.

'In the true theater', Artaud believed, 'a play disturbs the senses' repose, frees the repressed unconscious, incites a kind of virtual revolt (which moreover can have its full effect only if it remains virtual), and imposes on the assembled collectivity an attitude that is both heroic and difficult.'[12] Artistic rebellion was therefore effective for Artaud precisely because it was not reality but a true image laden with symbolic status that begged to be read as spectacle, not a mere random event. Representations and, therefore, mimetic repetition have no place in the theater of cruelty, as the theatre exists to create something new and explore a terror beyond rational expression. For Artaud, 'cruelty' is manifested in the theatre's disruption of all the audience's prior conceptions, and it is that disruption which leads to social awakening, forcing us to experience in the theatre what civilisation does not allow. Theatre then becomes the transformative and the real, not simply the representation.

This move away from realism's concern with the exploration of psychological problems of individuals and society, and towards a theatre connected to the unconscious mind (favouring intuition, feeling and experience over reason and celebrating these sensory impulses through ritualistic presentation), along with Brecht's anti-mimetic, politically charged emphasis on social transformation through the motivations of intellect, laid the foundation for a rejection of realism and the emergence of the anti-realistic dramatic styles that would characterise European experimental theatre after the Second World War and well into the 1950s and 1960s. After the American director Herbert Blau returned from Europe in 1959, impressed by the new directions in theatre that he had witnessed, his innovative staging of these European plays in the United States helped introduce the theories of Brecht and Artaud that European playwrights had embraced, moving them into the American experimental theatre scene during the 1960s and 1970s. As different as their theories for the theatre are, both Brecht and Artaud reject the conventions of realism and seek to remove the artificial barriers between actor and spectator, stage and social world, maintained by a realistic theatre.

Artaud's theories can best be seen in practice in the plays of the French playwright Jean Genet who, although he had read little of Artaud's work, shared his goals for a primarily ritualistic theatre that focused on accessing pre-logical consciousness and primitive existence through the symbolic realm, where action is separated from function. Both writers sought to invert the conventional moral code of good and evil, and, therefore, what was deemed 'good' in traditional society (culture, repression, self-control, obedience to the law) became universally evil, and what was considered 'evil' (nature, sexuality, violence, power) was encouraged as good. Like Friedrich Nietzsche, both Artaud and Genet want characters to be judged outside of good and evil, and Artaud's 'theater of cruelty' forces the spectator to confront the harsh facts of a cruel world and his or her own isolation. These writers explore the contradictions and hypocrisies of bourgeois society and often champion the 'primitive' impulses of the socially marginalised.

Genet was born in Paris in 1910, and primarily lived the life of an outcast. He was abandoned by his mother, became a thief by age ten, was repeatedly imprisoned, and lived on the streets surrounded by beggars, pimps, thieves and prostitutes. He lived throughout Europe between 1930 and 1940, and began writing prose and poetry about what he knew best, the underworld of social outsiders and prisons, before moving on to writing plays. His social status as an outcast, an 'outlaw' of sorts, set the tone for his plays, which offer ritualistic struggles between outcasts and their oppressors. His work blurs the line between illusion and reality, creating a game of mirrors in such plays as *The Maids* (1946), *Deathwatch* (1949), *The Balcony* (1958), *The Blacks* (1959), and *The Screens* (1966), where each reflection is distorted and any sense of reality proves to be illusory, ultimately collapsing into uncertainty. Martin Esslin argues that Genet's plays are

> concerned with expressing his own feeling of helplessness and solitude when confronted with the despair and loneliness of

man caught in the hall of mirrors of the human condition, inexorably trapped by an endless progression of images that are merely his own distorted reflection – lies covering lies, fantasies battening upon fantasies, nightmares nourished by nightmares within nightmares.[13]

Ultimately, Christopher Innes writes, Genet 'presents social reality as illusory, and the human need for illusion as being so strong that no social order can be based on reality', as he blurs the boundaries between acting and being:

If 'being' . . . is defined as 'doing', but all action on the social level is self-deception, then only the achievement of a state of 'non-being', the negation of the self, can be authentic. Hence Genet's plots always centre on death, while his characters are roles, not personalities defined by a coherent set of internal qualities, but masks giving shape to a void or reflected images in a receding perspective of mirrors . . . The artificial appearance is the essence.[14]

Like Luigi Pirandello's deconstruction of character/actor in *Six Characters in Search of an Author* (1921), where six 'characters', separate from the actors who play them, appear on the stage during a rehearsal and demand a voice, Genet challenges the boundaries between the representation and the real, appearance and essence, role-playing and authenticity. The idea that, in Genet's plays, '[t]he artificial appearance is the essence' – seeming is being – plays with the very idea of a core reality or essence, and clearly relates to postmodern thought, which denies the discovery of a single, 'true' self and sees identity as fluid, a series of masks.

The philosophy behind Genet's plays was part of a revolution in the theatre that was taking place in Europe and Britain, primarily in response to the social and political changes brought about by the Second World War. In 1961, Martin Esslin's landmark study, *The Theatre of the Absurd*,[15] described what he saw as a new movement in European and British drama that had emerged during the 1940s and 1950s, one that reflected the representative attitude after the Second World War 'that the certitudes and unshakable basic assumptions of former ages have been swept away, that they have been tested and found wanting, that they have been discredited as cheap and somewhat childish illusions'.[16] Although Esslin was careful to point out that these plays he brought together under the term Theatre of the Absurd were not part of any conscious, organised movement, what they had in common was an attempt to unite, in form and content, the sense of 'metaphysical anguish at the absurdity of the human condition'.[17] Esslin primarily explored the work of Jean Genet, Eugène Ionesco, Samuel Beckett and Arthur Adamov in France, along with Harold Pinter in Britain and Edward Albee in the United States. While he also included playwrights working in Eastern Europe, the Theatre of the Absurd was primarily centred in Paris, where both French and expatriate writers of various national origins could go to experiment freely. Although this is not the place to thoroughly cover all of these authors in any detail, my point in discussing their work here is to establish their general contribution to innovations in form and content that would influence the contemporary American theatre of the second half of the twentieth century.

Stylistically, their plays challenged traditional dramaturgy in their rejection of the realistic conventions of narrative plot, the developed characterisations that explore motive, a well-defined structure, an accurate reflection of social reality, and a language that rationally expresses meaning. Instead, these plays had 'no story or plot to speak of', were 'often without recognizable characters and present the audience with almost mechanical puppets', had 'neither a beginning nor an end', were frequently 'reflections of dreams and nightmares', and presented language that could be described as 'incoherent babblings'.[18] These anti-realistic experiments deliberately defied Aristotle's famous three unities, his rules for dramatic structure in terms of time, place and action. According to Aristotle, tragedy must have a single plot (unity of action), the action must take place in twenty-four hours (unity of time), and it must be carried out in one place (unity of place).[19] The plays that fall under the heading of Theatre of the Absurd resist such conventions, distorting the surfaces of social reality in favor of a freer expression of human experience, one that suggests rather than delineates.

In the aftermath of the Second World War, Eugène Ionesco's work challenged both the totalitarian ideologies that had persecuted him as he moved between Romania and France during the war, as well as what he saw as the overly simple and didactic Marxist political views championed by Brecht. The confusion of the modern world, a severe sense of alienation, and the futility of existence are key themes in Ionesco's plays, presented in forms that challenge the primacy of surface reality and rational logic. His first play, *The Bald Soprano* (translated in Britain as *The Bald Prima Donna*), premiered in Paris in 1950, and, like many plays of the Absurd that resisted realistic convention and were effectively 'anti-plays' (Ioneseco's description), received a cold reception. *The Bald Soprano* is an indictment of middle-class banality and conformity, depicting the tedious Smith couple and their guests, the Martins. The dialogue begins with empty and clichéd exchanges, and culminates in nonsensical phrases that engage in wordplay, highlighting the materiality of language rather than its signifying powers. The meaning of the title is unclear throughout the play, until finally there seems to be a moment towards the end when its sense, along with the meaning of the play, will be revealed. But Ionesco teases the audience with promises of elucidation, and deliberately resists such understanding. Instead of a revelation of truth or the closure that is central to realism, the audience is pulled further into a web of linguistic play in an exchange that only reveals the ironies of the misleading and contradictory title:

> Fire Chief [moving towards the door, then stopping]: Speaking of that – the bald soprano?
> [General silence, embarrassment.]
> Mrs Smith: She always wears her hair in the same style.
> Fire Chief: Ah! Then goodbye, ladies and gentlemen.[20]

The empty performance of understanding, echoed in the Fire Chief's 'Ah!', serves only to further confuse the audience, as the play ends in an increasingly animated collapse into gibberish.

Ionesco's next plays, *The Lesson* (1951) and *The Chairs* (1952), similarly play with the expectations of realism, and deal with trying to making sense of a world that resists coherency. It was with *Rhinoceros* (1959), however, that Ionesco achieved international fame, especially in Britain and the United States. The play can be seen as a political indictment of both the fascism that swept Romania and the Nazi occupation in France, as well as the communist domination of Eastern Europe. A nightmarish fantasy that criticises mindless social conformity and the fickleness of political allegiance, *Rhinoceros* employs the figure of the rhinoceros as a symbol of conformity and the mob mentality that absorbed Europe during the war. One by one, and increasingly en masse, citizens of a small provincial town turn into rhinoceroses while the main character, Berenger, struggles to resist. The play fuses fantasy and reality, using the outrageous convention of turning characters into rhinoceroses in order to make a strong political point and comment on the nature of social oppression. *Rhinoceros* even goes so far as to play with the line between fiction and reality by having one of the characters ask Berenger if he's read any of Ionesco's plays, blurring any distinction between the representation and the real.

In the plays that fall under the heading of the Absurd, language is separated from its discursive assumptions, meaning is not located or pinned down, and fragmented dialogue often focuses on the paradox of the inexpressibility of human expression. The inability to directly express human experience or represent Truth is often presented in the form of repetitive, minimalistic dialogue, pauses and silences rather than directly expressed in language. In other words, instead of (ironically) *saying* that we cannot communicate, these plays *illustrate* a lack of communication. Following the model of Swiss linguist Ferdinand de Saussure and, later, poststructuralist theory, the Theatre of the Absurd and the contemporary American drama that it influenced maintain an awareness that since the notion of absolute Truth is based on a lack of difference, a 'oneness', then we cannot express it through language, which *relies* on a system of difference. The language we use to express reality is based on a system of signs that have no intrinsic meaning, but depend on relational difference. For example, we only know what the letter 'a' signifies in relation to 'b' and 'c'; and the word 'cat' has no meaning in and of itself, but takes on an agreed-upon meaning we assign to it in relation to 'dog'. Absolute Truth, however, implies one unified, stable reality for all, regardless of history, cultural differences, social circumstances, individual perception, etc. Therefore, if Truth exists, it cannot be directly expressed in language. Anti-realistic contemporary drama accepts that we cannot express Truth through language, a system of difference; we can only approximate it. And so the dialogue reflects this philosophical position. Moreover, the inherent limitations of language in describing abstract sensations and ideas always produce a gap between the abstraction and its material expression; the complexity of the abstraction is reduced by its translation into language. Articulating the silent layers of meaning that 'the gap' contains – expressing the inexpressible – is the challenge of anti-realistic theatre.

In 1949, Samuel Beckett – an Irishman living in Paris and writing in French – challenged the assumption of realistic representation that the artist has a particular point or vision to express, and succeeds in expressing it in his work. He describes this sense of obligation as frustrated by incapacity, and speaks of a new art, one which preferences '[t]he expression that there is nothing to express, nothing with which to express, nothing from which to express, no power to express, no desire to express, together with the obligation to express'.[21] The dialogue in his plays focuses on the subtleties of linguistic play, highlighting the gaps in any attempt to communicate meaning while, simultaneously, the gaps become the meaning. The language focuses on illustrating the incompleteness of communication rather than articulating any attempt at direct expression.

In Beckett's plays, dialogue functions as diversion, and communication often occurs through means other than language. In probably his most famous work, *Waiting for Godot* (1953), the dialogue, rather than being a vehicle for communication, is consciously used to occupy the central characters, Gogo and Didi, while they wait and divert their attention from the alternative – the silent void that signifies death. They often opt for language over action, telling stories that go nowhere in order to pass the time. When Herbert Blau directed *Waiting for Godot* at San Quentin penitentiary in 1957, he asked the audience to think of the plays as 'a piece of jazz music "to which one must listen for whatever one may find in it" '.[22] In Beckett's next play, *Endgame* (1957), Nagg and Nell communicate with each other by knocking on the trash bins in which they are enclosed and rattling the cans. It is linguistic play, rather than any attempt to communicate meaning through language, which drives the action in Beckett's work. When Clov, frustrated with Hamm's

Figure 1.3 The set for the American Conservatory Theater's 2003 production of Samuel Beckett's *Waiting for Godot*, designed by J. B. Wilson. (Source: American Conservatory Theater.)

abusive treatment, asks him, 'What is there to keep me here?' Hamm replies, 'The dialogue.'[23] Clov ultimately expresses his dissatisfaction with the signifying power of language, telling Hamm, 'I use the words you taught me. If they don't mean anything any more, teach me others. Or let me be silent' (p. 44). Language is almost useless as far as the expression of Truth is concerned, but the silence is worse, an unbearable void. Even though there is 'nothing to say' (p. 81), Hamm pleads with Clov to 'say something' (p. 79) before he goes.

In his subsequent plays, such as *Krapp's Last Tape* (1958) – a one-character exploration of time, memory and identity where the main character, Krapp, engages with recordings of himself that he has kept over the last forty-five years – and *Happy Days* (1962) – where Winnie becomes increasingly buried in a pile of dirt as she performs a series of daily routines, reminisces about the past, and talks incessantly to her virtually silent husband, Willie, who serves as her 'audience', the reassurance that she exists – Beckett continued to explore the complexities of language, silence, time and memory, and their place in the drama of existence. *Waiting for*

Godot, *Endgame*, *Krapp's Last Tape* and *Happy Days*, along with the several works of fiction and other stage, television and radio plays in Beckett's extensive oeuvre, often comment on the unreliability of language and memory and their power to shape reality – a theme Sam Shepard would later explore intensely in plays such as *Buried Child* (1978), *Fool for Love* (1983) and *A Lie of the Mind* (1985).

The mystery and unreliability of memory is a primary theme in the work of Harold Pinter, another playwright of the Absurdist tradition, who emerged on the British theatre scene in 1957 with his one-acts *The Room* and *The Dumb Waiter*. These one-acts were followed by his full-length play, *The Birthday Party*, in 1958, which was staged for a one-week run in London and baffled critics and audiences with its experimental style. In 1960, however, Pinter finally came into prominence with his second full-length play, *The Caretaker*, which similarly baffled audiences during its run of 444 performances, but managed to earn critical success. *The Caretaker* was followed by *The Lover* (1963) and *The Homecoming* (1965), which centred on another of Pinter's major themes, the complications of sexual desire. His next plays, *Landscape* (1968) and *Silence* (1969), also dealt with sexuality and marriage, but the situations are less sinister and more poignant. *Landscape* focuses on the emotional separation between Beth and Duff, who each engage in separate monologues about their fragmented and unreliable memories of betrayal. Both *Old Times* (1971) and *No Man's Land* (1974) also deal with memory and the relationship of past to present, suggesting that memory is untrustworthy because the past can be deliberately or inadvertently reinvented.[24]

Beckett's influence on Pinter has been clearly established, and *The Dumb Waiter* in particular echoes *Waiting for Godot* in its depiction of two characters, Gus and Ben, who are two murderers for hire waiting in a basement for a message that will come down to them in the room's serving hatch, the dumbwaiter. The pun of the title signifies both the characters' precarious means of communicating with the outside world, as well as their status as ignorant servants, waiting for word from the mysterious Wilson to come down from 'above' (both literally as it descends from the dumbwaiter and figuratively in terms of an official order) as to whom their next victim will be. Like Godot, however, Wilson 'might not come. He might just send a message. He doesn't always come',[25] so they must simply continue to wait. The dialogue of *The Dumb Waiter*, like that of *Waiting for Godot*, is terse and often meaningless in terms of narrative development; it 'whiles away the time' (p. 90) as they wait for Wilson. The long exchange between Gus and Ben over whether the correct expression is to 'light the kettle' or 'light the gas' (pp. 97–8) provides no narrative purpose other than resolving the battle of wills that takes place through the linguistic struggle, establishing Ben as the 'senior partner' (p. 98). Any attempt at narrative development, such as the mystery of who sent them matches (pp. 95–6), goes nowhere, and mysteries are accepted blindly as not having any particular purpose we can definitively know.

In Pinter's plays, action is kept to a minimum and words conceal rather than reveal meaning. Like Beckett, Pinter eschews the communicative function of language and instead focuses on the silences, pauses and gaps in language, highlighting what is *not* being said, exploring the frustrations of linguistic existence and the paradoxes of incommunicability. Unlike Beckett, however, Pinter's dialogue often signifies an act of aggression and a struggle of wills, as he presents situations that tend to be more menacing and sinister than those of other playwrights of the Absurd. Esslin explains the incommunicability in Pinter's plays as an *unwillingness* rather than a more existential *inability* to communicate, which marks a distinct and important difference from playwrights such as Beckett or Albee, who also employ minimalistic dialogue and explore the instability, unreliability and inadequacy of language as communication. All three authors, however, deconstruct the contradictions and inconsistencies inherent in our constructed realities by prioritising linguistic play over direct communication and exploring how the mind reinvents the past and translates experience into meaning, a focus which would become a marked feature of the contemporary American postmodern theatre.

While it seems logical, even inevitable, that the disillusionment brought on by the Second World War throughout Europe and Britain would give birth to a theatre that questioned the very meaning of individual and social existence, Esslin lamented the scarcity of Absurdist dramatists writing in the United States. He posited that the despair characteristic of nations such as France and

Britain during the years following the war was not matched by America's relative detachment from its atrocities. On the contrary, America seemed to emerge from the war with a continued belief in progress and a renewed sense of the possibilities of the American dream. This sense of security was eventually shattered, however, by the social upheavals of the 1960s and, as Esslin points out, the political disillusionment brought on by the Watergate scandal and the Vietnam War.

In 1958, American playwright Edward Albee attacked the very foundations of American idealism with his first play, *The Zoo Story*, followed by his critique of the shallow fantasies of domestic perfection, *The American Dream* (1959–60), which attacked the hypocrisies of America's national identity embedded in the notions of progress and optimism. Esslin places Albee in the category of the Absurd 'precisely because his work attacks the very foundations of American optimism'.[26] The severe sense of alienation portrayed by the outcast Jerry in *The Zoo Story* is marked by his inability to connect with other human beings or to find any sense of identity in community. He is contrasted with Peter, an apparently well-adjusted bourgeois conformist whom he encounters in Central Park. After a series of taunting and uncomfortable exchanges worthy of Pinter's menacing characters, Jerry impales himself on the knife Peter has been provoked to draw, as he thanks him for that one bizarre and ironic moment of human connection. With *The Zoo Story*, Albee aligned himself with the Absurdists in his illustration of the frustrations of human connection and communication, but this theme is presented primarily through the play's absurd and extreme situations rather than through the truncated and minimalistic dialogue found, for example, in Beckett's work.

In *The American Dream*, the American worship of the superficial, empty of any genuine content, is explored through the presentation of a family who, after having lost the the adopted child they mutilated for failing to live up to expectations, are confronted with a Young Man at the end of the play. This character is apparently the twin of the lost child, but he no longer has the capacity to feel anything, making him a perfect addition to the emotionally dead and sanitised American family. *The American Dream* proposes that the goal, rather than the unfortunate product, of American identity is deliberate emptiness and superficiality. For Albee, the achievement of the American dream requires a denial of the messy complexities of being human, and therefore the 'successful' characters in his plays deliberately seek out inanity. As Gerald M. Berkowitz explains, in Albee's plays the characters' 'comical abuse of language is not the result of linguistic incompetence, but a concerted effort to free themselves from the human obligations implied by communication'.[27] A critique of the American middle class and its definition of success reappears in *Who's Afraid of Virginia Woolf* (1962), Albee's first full-length play that would establish his reputation as a premier American dramatist. George and Martha (with echoes of America's 'founders', George and Martha Washington) are a married couple whose sadomasochistic relationship is held together by, once again, an imaginary child who completes the fantasy of the ideal family in an American dream that has gone perversely wrong.

Although the playwrights of the Absurdist tradition are often read as promoting the notion that communication is impossible and futile, their work points to greater subtlety regarding the nature of communicating the artist's vision in the theatre. For these writers, it is the artist's subjective vision – a multiplicity of truth(s) – rather than one supposedly objective Truth that can and should be communicated. Genet sought freedom from the restrictive logic and superficial conventions of a realistic theatre, believing that while reality's truth(s) could be communicated, they are to be found beyond the conceptual prisons of rational discourse and social codes. Ionesco maintained that communication of the artist's vision was difficult, but certainly not impossible, as that would run contrary to the very idea of art and playwrighting. Despite Beckett's focus on the ironies and inconsistencies inherent in communication, he was still driven by the 'obligation to express', and Pinter's characters engage in complex and sinister linguistic power plays through a deliberate choice, an unwillingness rather than an inability to communicate. For Albee, humanity's truth is layered and complex, not to be found in society's platitudes or the promises of social conformity. He critiqued the sense of alienation and lack of genuine communion embraced by a superficial capitalist society, implicitly suggesting alternative possibilities. Much like the non-representational abstractions that shattered conventions in the visual arts during the modernist period, the plays in this chapter make use of non-rational language and images that distort the delineated surfaces of reality in order to access a glimpse of truth(s) beyond the superficial, as these dramatists sought to free themselves from the representational limitations of the past.

NOTES

1. Bertolt Brecht, *Brecht on Theatre*, trans. John Willett (New York: Hill and Wang, 1964), p. 86.
2. Émile Zola, 'Naturalism in the theatre', in *The Theory of the Modern Stage*, ed. Eric Bentley (Baltimore: Penguin Books, 1968), p. 371.
3. Brecht, *Brecht on Theatre*, p. 79.
4. Ibid. p. 71.
5. Ibid. p. 15.
6. Antonin Artaud, *The Theater and Its Double*, trans. Mary Caroline Richards (New York: Grove Press, 1958), p. 7.
7. Elin Diamond, 'The shudder of catharsis in twentieth century performance', in *Performance and Performativity*, ed. Andrew Parker and Eve Kosofsky Sedgewick (New York: Routledge, 1995), p. 165.
8. Artaud, *The Theater and Its Double*, p. 71.
9. Ibid. p. 44.
10. Ibid. p. 71.
11. Steven Connor, *Postmodernist Culture: An Introduction to Theories of the Contemporary* (Oxford: Blackwell Publishers, 1997), pp. 143–4.
12. Artaud, *The Theater and Its Double*, p. 28.
13. Martin Esslin, *The Theatre of the Absurd* (New York: Penguin Books, 1961), pp. 200–1.
14. Christopher Innes, *Avant-Garde Theatre (1892–1992)* (London: Routledge, 1993), p. 108.
15. *The Theatre of the Absurd* was revised and expanded, along with a new Preface, for a 1968 edition, and so included some of the playwrights, such as Harold Pinter, who were just emerging when the first edition was published.

16. Esslin, *The Theatre of the Absurd*, p. 23.
17. Ibid. pp. 23–4.
18. Ibid. pp. 21–2.
19. While the 'three unities' are attributed to Aristotle, in the *Poetics* he actually only insists on unity of action, mentions unity of time (saying that tragedy tries as far as possible to confine itself to twenty-four hours or thereabouts), and says nothing of unity of place.
20. Eugène Ionesco, *The Bald Soprano and Other Plays* (New York: Grove Press, 1958), p. 37.
21. Samuel Beckett, *transition* (1949), p. 98.
22. Esslin, *The Theatre of the Absurd*, p. 19 (quoting Blau).
23. Samuel Beckett, *Endgame* (New York: Grove Press, 1958), p. 58. Subsequent references appear parenthetically in the text.
24. Harold Pinter's work remains central to contemporary theatre. In 2005, he won the Nobel Prize for Literature.
25. Harold Pinter, *The Caretaker and The Dumb Waiter* (New York: Grove Press, 1961), p. 100. Subsequent references appear parenthetically in the text.
26. Esslin, *The Theatre of the Absurd*, p. 312.
27. Gerald M. Berkowitz, *American Drama of the Twentieth Century* (New York: Longman Publishing, 1992), p. 128.

CHAPTER 2

Revisiting the American Dream

> Biff: He had all the wrong dreams . . . He never knew who
> he was.
>
> Arthur Miller, *Death of a Salesman* (1949)

During the years immediately following the Second World War, two major playwrights, Tennessee Williams and Arthur Miller, dominated the American stage. These playwrights were often interested in exploring social issues, specifically the human costs of postwar industrial capitalism and the contradictory nature of the American dream. Both essentially followed the conventions of domestic realism, yet freely utilised anti-realistic devices in order to most effectively convey their visions for the stage. Williams especially was interested in anti-realistic forms, and employed them more and more after the 1950s. While this volume is primarily concerned with contemporary American drama after 1960 and its relation to an anti-realistic postmodern theatre, it is important to provide a brief analysis of the work of American playwrights who responded to the social and political climate during and shortly after the Second World War as background for the contemporary drama that was to emerge later, just as I provided a synopsis of the European and British theatrical innovations of that time. Although this is not by any means a comprehensive account of the theatrical offerings in the United States during those years, the work of these two classically American playwrights who were writing after the war, Williams and Miller, can serve as examples of early responses by American dramatists to the events that shaped the second half of the twentieth century, as they began to question the viability of the American dream, examine the tension between the individual and the collective in that context, and explore issues of identity in terms of role playing and authenticity in American culture.

Williams's first major success was the production of *The Glass Menagerie* on Broadway in 1945. *The Glass Menagerie* was followed by *A Streetcar Named Desire* (1947), *Summer and Smoke* (1948), *The Rose Tattoo* (1951), *Camino Real* (1953), *Cat on a Hot Tin Roof* (1955), *Orpheus Descending* (1957), *Suddenly Last Summer* (1958), and *Sweet Bird of Youth* (1959). Williams' plays of the 1940s and 1950s often involved a critique of the superficiality of American capitalism, which winds up rewarding appearance over substance. His plays illustrated how capitalism's ruthless obsession with competition and materialistic success at the expense of deeper emotional and artistic values destroyed the sensitive and the weak, discarding human complexity and creating social outsiders who struggled to survive. Yet his work also maintained an awareness of the contradictions of capitalism's role in both making possible and perverting the struggle for the American dream, with its focus on autonomy and unlimited possibility. Along these lines, Williams explored the hypocrisies involved in the promise of individual freedom and the celebration of difference, as the American culture of 'success' simultaneously insisted upon allegiance and conformity.

Many of Williams's plays address the question of American identity and the individual's place in a commodity culture. Both *The Glass Menagerie* and *A Streetcar Named Desire* deal with the transformation from an agrarian to an industrial society brought on by the war and its impact on those left behind, as they struggle to adapt and survive. In *The Glass Menagerie* the stage directions set the social background for the play, which takes place just before the start of the Second World War. Williams makes a point of describing the Wingfield's apartment building as

one of those vast hive-like conglomerations of cellular living-units that flower as warty growths in overcrowded urban

centers of lower middle-class population and are sympto-
matic of the impulse of this largest and fundamentally
enslaved section of American society to avoid fluidity and
differentiation and to exist and function as one interfused mass
of automatism.[1]

He continues this social commentary with the narrator Tom
Wingfield's opening monologue:

> To begin with, I turn back time. I reverse it to that quaint
> period, the thirties, when the huge middle class of America
> was matriculating in a school for the blind . . . In Spain there
> was revolution. Here there was only shouting and confusion.
> In Spain there was Guernica. Here there were disturbances of
> labor, sometimes pretty violent, in otherwise peaceful cities
> such as Chicago, Cleveland, Saint Louis . . . This is the social
> background of the play. (1: 145)

Essentially realistic in its depiction of character, setting and
action, *The Glass Menagerie* is nonetheless a 'memory play' that
manipulates anti-realistic conventions, such as the use of a narrator
and Brechtian titles that were intended to 'give accent to certain
values in each scene' (1: 132).[2] Tom's mother, Amanda, a woman
raised in the old agrarian South to cultivate the feminine charm and
grace that would ensure her survival through an economically
successful marriage, now finds herself and her children deserted by
her husband and making do in a walk-up tenement. Although she
struggles nobly to survive, using her 'charm' to sell magazine
subscriptions by phone and to try and win a husband for her awk-
wardly shy and sensitive daughter Laura, Amanda is out of her
element in the rapidly changing industrial capitalist society. Her
lament for the financially successful 'old admirers' she had rejected
for her now absent husband, who has left her destitute, focuses on
the pioneer spirit and overnight success advertised by the American
dream: 'That Fitzhugh boy went North and made a fortune – came
to be known as the Wolf of Wall Street! He had the Midas touch,
whatever he touched turned to gold!' (1: 149).

Similarly, Jim O'Connor, Laura's 'gentleman caller' in *Menagerie*, reflects the superficial values of American culture, emphasising an attractive and tidy appearance (he is constantly checking himself in the mirror), the 'right connections', and the meaningless performance of 'self-confidence' in his search for '*Knowledge* – Zzzzzp! *Money* – Zzzzzzp! – *Power!*' since that is the 'cycle democracy is built on' (1: 222). Yet while he claims to value Laura's 'difference', insisting that 'being different is nothing to be ashamed of' (1: 227) and highlighting her individuality, he still rejects her in the end. Tom and Laura are both pushed into careers that may have allowed their economic survival but were completely at odds with their temperaments. While Tom does escape at the end, joining the merchant marines in search of adventure, he is still trapped emotionally by guilt, as the fates of Laura and Amanda remain uncertain. The personal merges with the social in this play as all the characters are engulfed by the alienating powers of the American capitalist system in which they are expected not only to survive, but to thrive and find happiness. Instead of becoming empowered and functioning as subjects in control of their lives, the protagonists find themselves subjected to the overwhelming powers of a ruthless, changing society.

In *A Streetcar Named Desire*, the dramatic tension rests between Blanche Dubois, another faded belle of the Old South whose aristocratic principles will no longer assure her survival in an increasingly pragmatic urbanised world, and Stanley Kowalski, a working-class labourer of Polish descent who insists that he is 'one-hundred-per-cent American' (1: 374), emphasising his entitlement as an American male. He will not tolerate any threats to his dominance – he is 'the king around here' (1: 371) – and maintains power over his domain through intimidation and violence. Blanche arrives in New Orleans to stay with her sister Stella and Stella's husband Stanley essentially because she is destitute. Like Amanda Wingfield in *The Glass Menagerie*, Blanche's aristocratic background is useless in the rapidly changing capitalist system restructuring American society during the years just before the Second World War and beyond. Her family's plantation, Belle Reve, had been taken by creditors and, fired from her job as a high-school teacher after her search for intimacy had led her to an affair with a seventeen-year-old student, Blanche is left with no independent wealth and no marketable skill. Beauty and youth are presented as commodities that she once had but are now fading. Her one attempt to enter the world of capitalism rests on her hopes that Shep Huntleigh (a real or imaginary college 'beau' who is now married) will set her and Stella in a 'shop of some kind' (1: 137). But her plans are vague, and Blanche is not exactly an entrepreneur: 'Y'know how indifferent I am to money. I think of money in terms of what it does for you' (1: 316). While she needs money and sees it as 'the way out' (1: 315) of her situation, her idea of an 'investment' is taking a trip to Miami, hoping she would 'meet someone with a million dollars' (1: 316). Blanche is not self-sufficient enough in a capitalistic society to be able to survive. Williams has called Blanche a 'sacrificial victim . . . of society', explaining that she 'was not adaptable to the circumstances as they were, that the world had imposed upon her'.[3]

Cat on a Hot Tin Roof explores issues of identity, desire and deception, all held together by the pursuit of wealth and security. While the play is foremost one that 'deals with human extremities of emotion' (3: 15), Maggie, the protagonist, is determined to defeat her husband's brother and his wife for the family inheritance, since she grew up poor and has now become accustomed to a more comfortable life. Her alcoholic and emotionally tormented husband, Brick, is too weak and indifferent to fight, so Maggie takes on the struggle for herself, insisting that 'You can be young without money, but you can't be old without it' (3: 54). *Suddenly Last Summer* and *Sweet Bird of Youth* also ultimately deal with the power attached to money in a capitalistic society, going a step further in exploring the role of financial power in determining what will count as 'truth'. Both plays are also concerned with racial issues, the complexities of role-playing, and revealing the consequences of prostituting the individual and treating sexuality as a commodity.[4] *Summer and Smoke*, *The Rose Tattoo* and *Orpheus Descending*, plays very different from each other in tone and purpose, focus on issues involving the power of sexuality and its relationship to life and death. Yet *The Rose Tattoo* and *Orpheus Descending* are also concerned with constructions of racial identity in America, with *Orpheus Descending* illustrating the often tragic consequences of transgressing the carefully defined boundaries established by American culture.

In one of his earliest interviews in 1940, Williams spoke about a work-in-progress, *Stairs to the Roof*,[5] emphasising his 'interest in social problems', and claiming that all his plays 'carried some social message along with the story'.[6] Like *The Glass Menagerie*, *Stairs* is set in St Louis during the years just before the Second World War, and deals with the imprisoned state of the human soul in an age of increasing spiritual emptiness and impersonal relations under American capitalism, which seeks to overwhelmingly control the course of human development. The play, however, does not necessarily argue for social reform in America (or even on earth) per se, as it breaks off into fantasy at the end. The solution to the industrial mechanisation of the individual and the entrapment of the human soul, the play suggests, lies not in social change but ultimately in the escape to another planet, where the protagonists, Ben and 'The Girl', will found a new race. As one of Williams's earliest and least explored full-length plays to deal with American identity under capitalism, *Stairs to the Roof* is worthy of serious consideration in this context.

Stairs embraces the post-First World War philosophy of 'make it new' that I discussed in the Introduction to this book, and prefigures its application in a post-Second World War environment, where the 'new' would signal a postmodern embracing of contradictions and differences that are able to coexist in the same sphere in order to create something innovative – new solutions, new identities – with what already exists. Though I am not necessarily arguing that *Stairs* is a postmodern work, I am proposing that its presentation in 1941 of the transformative possibility inherent in uncertainty, contradiction, experimentation and play gestures toward a postmodern American identity that would mark the United States during the second half of the twentieth century. While there had been a vague hope evident in the American theatre between the wars, this hope was fading during the late 1930s and early 1940s as the Great Depression reflected a devastated economy and the Second World War was well under way in Europe. As the United States became involved in the war, the country was entering a more pessimistic age or, more positively put, an age that began to abandon faith in absolutes in favor of an acknowledgement of the concepts of reality and truth as complex, often relative, and open for negotiation.

Stairs combines a superficial critique of American capitalism with an espousal of the mythology that goes hand-in-hand with industrial capitalism. It exalts individualism and personal destiny, while embracing the Anglo-patriarchal American values of freedom, adventure and the conquest of new frontiers. As Ben comes closer to threatening the social order at the office where he works, his supervisors Messrs P and Q offer him a position on 'The road, the road' in Arizona, the open West where there would be 'Nothing but Indians' (88). At the end of the play, the imperialist mentality behind the colonisation of another planet – the ultimate frontier – participates fully in a capitalist ideology. The female protagonist is simply called 'The Girl' and dismissed/silenced throughout the play. This objectification of women as objects of conquest (fulfilling the functions of pleasure and procreation with no complex desire or identity in their own right) is typical of a patriarchal capitalist ethic, even as the play rallies against the commodification of *men's* souls in the workplace. Therefore, while the play certainly does criticise the dehumanisation of the individual (specifically male individual) under capitalism, it simultaneously embraces many of its values, making its protest somewhat contradictory.

What seems, at first, an awkward juxtaposition – the play's simultaneous critique and embrace of capitalism – acquires fresh import when considered as a herald of the postmodern mentality. Seen in this light, *Stairs* illustrates the complexities of social systems and reveals the misleading simplicity of social protest plays, specifically much of the agitprop theatre of the 1930s.[7] *Stairs* gestures toward a postmodern complexity in both content and form during the crucial years of the Second World War, a time of experimentation when the illusive modernist search for absolutes was being transformed to a postmodern realisation of uncertainty where contradictions coexist and identity is seen as fluid.

If, on one level, *Stairs to the Roof* is a social play that criticises the mechanisation of the individual under industrial capitalism and culminates in an escapist fantasy, on another level it can be seen as planting the seeds of a postmodernism that acknowledges the complexity of issues dealing with the individual versus the collective and the need to find entirely new ways of thinking about that binary. We must 'make it new', but new in the sense of taking what already exists and fusing contradictions in postmodern fashion. The open-endedness of *Stairs* (an open-endedness very different from Brecht's)[8] is not existential, as it does not completely deny spirituality, nor is it quite postmodern in the nihilistic sense that some theorists have interpreted postmodernism.[9] Instead, the play's 'solution' lies in postmodern possibility, play and the reimagining of old forms and identities. This prefiguring of a new postmodern American identity under capitalism is one of the factors that makes *Stairs to the Roof* a pivotal work for 1941.

While *Stairs to the Roof* was formerly dismissed as one of Williams's 'apprentice plays' until New Directions published it in 2000 with Allean Hale's insightful introduction, *Camino Real* was his first mature full-length experiment that not only critiqued the contradictions of American commodity capitalism after the Second World War and its negative impact on individuality, but also departed completely from his essentially realistic plays, making full use of the 'freedom' of anti-realistic conventions.[10] This play was an indirect but undeniable indictment of McCarthyism – a term coined for the infamous crusade against communism in American politics led by the Republican junior senator from Wisconsin, Joseph McCarthy, from 1950 to 1954. By the time *Camino Real* premiered in 1953, McCarthy had accused hundreds of Americans, over 300 in the film and theatre industry alone, of communist ties or sympathies without credible evidence, leading to the 'blacklisting' that denied them employment in the United States and ruined careers, reputations and productive lives.

The seeds for the so-called McCarthy era began shortly after the war in response to the Cold War, the ideological and economic struggle between capitalism and communism represented by the superpowers of the United States and the Soviet Union. In 1947, President Harry S. Truman issued Executive Order 9835, creating a loyalty and security programme for internal use in the federal government. The Order created an Attorney General's List, a checklist of organisations with ties to any activities defined as subversive, such as communism or fascism, and any applicant

Figure 2.1 Scene from the original 1953 Broadway production of Tennessee Williams's *Camino Real* with Jo Van Fleet (centre). (Source: Alfredo Valente, used courtesy of New Directions Publishing Corp.)

connected to these organisations would require close scrutiny before being employed in a government position. After Truman allowed the list to be published, however, it was used unscrupulously by blacklisters not only to investigate federal employees, as was the intention, but to deny individuals employment in any responsible position in the public or private sector without evidence or direct charge of illegal activity. The activities of Executive Order 9835 were ultimately seized by the House Un-American Activities Committee (HUAC), an until then relatively insignificant committee of the House of Representatives created in 1938, eventually becoming a permanent committee in 1946, which investigated threats of subversion to American democracy.

It was in 1950, however, that Senator McCarthy saw an opportunity to exploit American fears of communist subversion, making a claim in his famous speech to the Ohio County Women's Club in

Wheeling, West Virginia that he was in possession of a list of 205 known members of the Communist Party working within the American federal government. With this, McCarthy launched the period of 'hysteria' that would later be characterised as the communist 'witch-hunts', seeking out and persecuting the perceived enemies of democracy. In 1954, McCarthy lost power after he went too far and accused army officials of communist sympathies. After an investigation, the Senate voted to condemn McCarthy's methods as unscrupulous, lacking credible evidence and thwarting free speech. Although the communist hunt was to continue for almost two more years, the period of intense hysteria was essentially over in 1954, and HUAC was eventually abolished in 1975.

The period of McCarthyism had a tremendous impact on those working in the theatre, as several actors, directors and playwrights had been intellectually interested in the egalitarian ideas espoused by communism, especially during the 1930s, a time of economic struggle during the Great Depression. While most of these artists were eventually disillusioned by communist rhetoric, their investigation of its principles or any brief association with those who embraced communism as a viable form of government served as a red flag and was enough to lead to a formal investigation of their political activities. In 1947, Bertolt Brecht, living in California, was one of the first in the theatre industry to be called in front of HUAC in order to account for his communist allegiances. Brecht gave evidence testifying that he had never actually held membership in the Communist Party, yet he was still blacklisted by American film studios. The day after his testimony Brecht left for Switzerland and shortly thereafter settled in East Germany.

In 1952, director Elia Kazan, who collaborated closely with Williams and directed several of his plays and films, among them *A Streetcar Named Desire* and, later, *Cat on a Hot Tin Roof* and *Camino Real*, was called in front of HUAC. While he refused to 'name names' and implicate others during his first appearance in front of the committee, in a second appearance months later he identified eight people who had been members of the Communist Party with him in the mid-1930s, damaging the lives and careers of several of his colleagues. Williams did not publicly comment on Kazan's decision, and did not allow it to affect their friendship or professional collaboration. Arthur Miller, on the other hand, publicly condemned Kazan's decision to give names to HUAC, and the two had a bitter falling out. By the time of Kazan's testimony in 1952, he had directed two of Miller's plays, *All My Sons* (1947) and *Death of a Salesman* (1949). Miller and Kazan did not speak to each other for ten years, and never regained the closeness they once shared. Eventually, Miller himself was called in front of HUAC in 1956, and while he willingly answered all questions regarding himself and his own activities, he refused to give the names of alleged communist writers with whom he attended a few meetings in New York in 1947. He was cited for contempt for refusing to testify and was blacklisted by Hollywood. In 1958, however, he was officially cleared of contempt after a two-year legal battle.

This was the social and political climate in which Williams wrote *Camino Real*, a work that was ahead of its time in struggling with questions of personal freedom, authenticity and role-playing in the midst of public surveillance during the height of the McCarthy years. In the foreword to *Camino Real*, which he dedicated to Elia Kazan, Williams drew on the inspiration of musical improvisation in his attempt to realise the 'unusual degree of freedom' one can experience in the theatre. He described 'a new sensation of release',[11] and wrote that his desire was to give audiences a sense of

> something wild and unrestricted that ran like water in the mountains, or clouds changing shape in a gale, or the continually dissolving and transforming images of a dream. This sort of freedom is . . . the result of painstaking design, and in this work I have given more conscious attention to form and construction than in any work before. (p. vii)

This was a 'freedom' of form that Williams had sought as early as *The Glass Menagerie* in his description of a 'new, plastic theatre' that would replace the 'exhausted theatre of realistic conventions' (1: 131), or in the one-act play 'The Purification', written in 1945 and published in 1953, which he describes as 'A play in verse to be performed with a musical accompaniment on the guitar' (6: 40). Williams was working on both 'The Purification' and *Camino Real* as early as the mid-1940s, and he had completed a one-act version, 'Ten Blocks on the Camino Real', in 1946, publishing it in *American Blues* in 1948.

Despite the critical establishment's tendency to see Williams as a traditional 'poetic realist' or Southern Gothicist throughout his career, he always saw himself as a radical playwright, experimenting with form and content in his quest to represent the inconsistencies and contradictions of the human situation.[12] He maintained that the distinctly experimental *Camino Real* was 'one of his five best plays',[13] despite its initial unsuccessful run. The characters in *Camino Real* are lifted from the discourses of literature and myth – Jacques Cassanova, Baron De Carlus, Lord Byron, Marguerite Gautier, Don Quixote – romantic pioneers of personal freedom in the face of social oppression. They have all been brought together outside of time or place on the Camino Real, a totalitarian state of limbo that both imprisons and protects them from the unknown – the 'Terra Incognita' – and their situation is a far cry from the elusive time 'when the street was royal' (p. 145). The main character, Kilroy, especially exists outside of time or place, a 'Traveler' of 'unknown' origins (p. 111), who ultimately refuses to be a 'patsy' for the totalitarian state.

In 'Reflections on a revival of a controversial fantasy,' an essay that first appeared in the *New York Times* on 15 May 1960 before the off-Broadway revival of *Camino Real*, Williams presented what he called a 'TV commercial' for the play, emphasising the ubiquitous commodifications of postmodern culture, asking: 'Has your public smile come to resemble the grimace of a lion-tamer in a cage with a suddenly untamed lion . . . And do you have to continue your performance betraying no sign of anxiety in your heart? Then here is the right place for you, the Camino Real.'[14] *Camino Real* is Williams's statement of his 'own philosophy . . . that romanticism is absolutely essential',[15] as he insists on the need for tenderness and sincerity, associated with a triumph of the human spirit. Yet hope in this play ultimately rests in movement and process, a belief in the possibility that 'the violets in the mountains can break the rocks if you believe in them and allow them to grow' (p. 97).

In his 1947 essay 'On a streetcar named success,' Williams laments how success traps the artist in image. He called his 'public self' an 'artifice of mirrors',[16] a 'fiction created with mirrors', and insists that 'the only somebody worth being is the solitary and unseen you that existed from your first breath and is the sum of your actions and so is constantly in a state of becoming under your own volition'.[17] This 'somebody worth being', the 'solitary and unseen you that existed from your first breath', implies an original, authentic self that is separate from public image. But for Williams this self is still defined by 'the sum of your actions' and is in flux, 'constantly in a state of becoming'. The self is in process, unstable, but we have the freedom to shape it according to our 'own volition'. Williams sees the world too as 'an unfinished poem',[18] and '[h]umanity is just a work in progress' (*Camino*, p. 113). Hope therefore lies not in a return to origins or Truth, an unattainable stable centre, but in the process of living, uncertainty, moving forward into the 'Terra Incognita', where all we can do is *'Make voyages! – Attempt them! –* there's nothing else' (*Camino*, p. 78). Williams's personal banner throughout his career was the ultimate call to going on: 'En Avant!' or, as Quixote says in *Camino Real*, 'Forward!' (p. 5). This insistence on movement and growth in the play reveals both a realisation that the cultural moment's political tyranny can be fought and overcome, and a postmodern sense that the power of identity lies in instability and a lack of fixed boundaries.

Almost all the characters in the play, excepting, of course, the oppressive representatives of the State, are 'fugitives' on the Camino Real, but Kilroy, the main character who wanders onto the scene, is the ultimate fugitive. The identification of Kilroy as the fictitious American soldier, created by troops who left the inscription 'Kilroy was here' around the world during the Second World War, is related in the play to the more general use of the term to describe an extensive traveler, someone who wanders around the world, and indeed the characters on the Camino Real are all wanderers, displaced from their original literary texts. They exist in a limbo which is 'a port of entry and departure, there are no permanent guests' (p. 96), steeped in slogans that signify their spiritual dislocation:

Gypsy's Loudspeaker: Do you feel yourself to be spiritually unprepared for the age of exploding atoms? Do you distrust the newspapers? Are you suspicious of governments? [. . .]

Does further progress appear impossible to you? Are you afraid of anything at all? Afraid of your heartbeat? Or the eyes of strangers! Afraid of breathing? Afraid of not breathing? Do you wish that things could be straight and simple again as they were in your childhood? Would you like to go back to Kindy Garten? (p. 28)

The hysterical tone and paradox of existence that marks this passage ('Afraid of breathing? Afraid of not breathing?') echo both the political anxiety inspired by McCarthyism and the existential dilemma of Beckett's characters, who can't go on yet still go on and simultaneously crave silence and speech. It expresses a desire to return to the comfort of origins, to 'childhood', in search of an essence or purity – the 'unseen you that existed from your first breath'– that is characterised by an infantile breakdown of language ('Kindy Garten'). Historical progress is presented in this play as not only 'impossible' but undesirable. The gypsy's speech suggests that it is in looking backwards, not forwards, that real or essential identity – something 'straight and simple' – is to be found, and with it the peace and stability that Kilroy craves in the post-war age of 'exploding atoms.' The play reveals, however, that this seductive return to origins is fantasy, and the nostalgic desire for it is what keeps us oppressed.

In the timelessness of the Camino Real, there is no going back and no origin to which to return. This is clear from the beginning of the play, as Quixote and Sancho arrive on the scene:

Sancho [urgently]: Let's go back to La Mancha!
Quixote: Forward!
Sancho: The time has come for retreat!
Quixote: The time for retreat never comes! (p. 5)

For the moment, they cannot go forward, but they cannot go back either. The future is unknown, the Terra Incognita, and the past or history is unattainable and irrelevant, as the Baron asserts, 'Used to be is past tense, meaning useless' (p. 37). His desire to '[m]ake a departure' from his 'present self' to himself as he 'used to be' (p. 73) is answered by Gutman, 'a lordly fat man' (p. 3) who presides over the Camino Real: '*That's* the *furthest* departure a man can make!' (p. 74). For Byron, however, 'There is a time for departure even when there's no certain place to go!' (p. 78). Kilroy too is caught in limbo on the Camino Real, with no locatable origins. In response to the Gypsy's interrogation of the 'date and place' of his coming into the world, he replies: 'Both unknown' (p. 111). He identifies himself as a 'Traveler' in response to her request for an address (p. 111), and his parents are 'Anonymous' (p. 112). He insists that he is 'a free *agent*' (p. 49, emphasis added), in possession of the individual *agency* that allows him to control the construction of self. His identity is unstable and slippery, as he claims to 'like situations [he] can get out of' (p. 112). Kilroy does possess a history of images, however, and performs a 'triumphant, eccentric dance' in which he pantomimes 'his history as fighter, traveler, and lover' (p. 106), the series of past roles that make up his present self. History is a malleable fiction, a performance that can be manipulated, just as the virginity of the Gypsy's daughter Esmeralda is regularly restored with the new full moon for the 'fertility rites' that follow. Esmeralda is trapped in her role, and her attempted escape occurs simultaneously with Kilroy's attempted escape from the Officers who want to make him a 'patsy'. Their identities merge in empathy as Esmeralda cries out, 'They've got you! They've got me!' (p. 53). When the Gypsy later proposes that Kilroy 'sign something' (p. 112) and get 'some kind of shot' (p. 113) – arbitrary gestures divorced from original meaning that are a rehearsed part of the process – to fulfil his destiny as her daughter's 'chosen hero', Kilroy tells her that doesn't know what's going on. The Gypsy can only answer 'Who does? The Camino Real is a funny paper read backward!' (p. 114), a series of distorted images. Nothing here is known or certain, and we are '[n]ot even [sure] of our existence . . . [T]he perch we hold is unstable!' (p. 96).

On the Camino Real, authenticity merges with image, and it is a place of contradictions.[19] The play's search for authenticity can be seen in Kilroy's desire for 'sincerity' from Esmeralda, in contrast to surrounding images of Hollywood myth – the romantic images of 'television' and the 'Screen Secrets' fan magazine she reads (pp. 108, 121, 136). When Esmeralda is excited over her ability to express human emotion and shed a tear, the Gypsy answers her with the reprimand that she has been watching too much television (p. 136), warning her not to confuse image with reality. Esmeralda is satisfied to believe that Kilroy is sincere '[f]or a while' (p. 131), and he too seems comfortable with the temporary arrangement, this lack of stability, responding, 'Everything's for a while' (p. 132). Yet he disdains Esmeralda's malleable performance of virginity, complaining that it lacks sincerity, and wants her to 'talk' to him honestly. His desire for conversation, however, rests in performance, roles that are familiar, a script for romance: 'That's the way we do things in the States. A little vino, some records on the Victrola, some quiet conversation – and then if both parties are in the mood for romance . . .' (p. 122). When Esmeralda starts talking, her incredible knowledge and interest in socio-political matters is daunting for Kilroy, and he rejects her discourse, prompting her to revert to performance once again: 'What sort of talk do you want?' (p. 123). He is fixated on the loss of his one 'real–true woman', the wife he left behind, but even she is an image inspired by Hollywood myth, 'a platinum blond the same as Jean Harlow' (p. 121).

At the end of the play, Kilroy collapses while attempting to fight off the 'Streetcleaners', the harbingers of death on the Camino Real. As an 'unidentified vagrant' with 'no legal claimants' (pp. 148–9) – no fixed identity – his dead body is given over to the State for scientific dissection. But once the Medical Instructor opens up his chest and extracts a heart 'of pure gold and as big as the head of a baby' (p. 150), La Madrecita de los Perditos commands him to 'Rise, ghost! Go! Go bird!' (p. 150), and Kilroy is resurrected. Williams says in the opening directions that 'a phoenix painted on silk' should be softly lighted now and then in the play, 'since resurrections are so much a part of its meaning' (p. 1). Kilroy must be resurrected, as hope, once again, depends on malleability and movement:

Kilroy: Hopeful?
Jacques: Always!
Officer: Keep moving! (p. 45)

Kilroy the phoenix then 'snatches the golden sphere from the Medical Instructor', refusing to give up his heart of gold, his essence, to the oppressive State (p. 152), and even though he realises that he 'had one true woman, which [he] can't go back to ', he has now 'found another', Esmeralda, and can go forward (p. 155).

Esmeralda, however, is unaware of his ghostly presence, and Kilroy retreats in despair. Yet the fountain that has been dried up from the beginning of the play suddenly 'begins to flow' (p. 158), begins to show signs of movement and flux. Kilroy too decides 'uncertainly' that he 'was thinking of – going *on*' from the Camino Real (p. 159), and Quixote too is going on, but is not sure as to where (p. 159) . The inscription on the wall that had changed from 'Kilroy is Coming' to 'Kilroy is here' (p. 24), continues to mark movement and the passage of time as Kilroy replaces 'is' with 'was' (p. 160). Gutman, finally, reveals the play as a performance, 'a pageant' (p. 160), and takes a bow as the 'Curtain Line' is spoken by Quixote: 'The violets in the mountains have broken the rocks!' (p. 161). Endurance and forward motion have triumphed, and Kilroy's resurrection confirms his status as a 'free agent' who is able to control his own destiny, consistent with 'true' American values.

In the same year that *Camino Real* premiered, Arthur Miller's *The Crucible* was also produced on Broadway. Both *Camino Real* and *The Crucible* were clear denunciations of what Donald Spoto calls 'the fascist demagoguery then spreading over the country in the voice, especially loud, of Senator Joseph McCarthy', and both failed commercially on Broadway.[20] *The Crucible* ran for only 197 performances, but was eventually to become one of Miller's most popular plays, transcending its immediate relevance to McCarthyism and receiving productions around the world. Miller had already won a Tony Award in 1947 with *All My Sons*, which deals with a factory owner who knowingly sells defective parts to the government during the Second World War, exposing the complex moral and legal responsibilities involved in American business and the pursuit of the American dream. Miller's next major success, *Death of a Salesman* in 1949, ran for 742 performances, receiving the Pulitzer Prize for Drama, the Tony Award for Best Play, and the New York Drama Critics Circle Award.

Death of a Salesman, Miller's best-known play, is concerned with the character Willy Loman, an ageing salesman whose dreams of excessive wealth and respect within the American capitalist system are shattered by its reality. Willy believes in the American dream, which he interprets as instant material success through minimal work, getting ahead through a system of connections, appearance and charm – the quality of being 'well-liked'. He is seduced by the American fantasy that '[o]ther men . . . do it easier',[21] and has passed his values onto his sons, Biff and Happy, who are both in their thirties and dissatisfied with their empty lives. To the dismay of his father, Biff, like Laura and Tom in *The Glass Menagerie*, 'never fit in business' (p. 60). Not sure of what he's 'supposed to want' (p. 22), Biff dreams of going 'out West' with his brother to 'buy a ranch. Raise cattle', and live the frontier myth 'out in the open' (p. 23). Although Happy, who has his 'own apartment, a car, and plenty of women' but is still lonely and doesn't 'know what the hell [he's] workin' for' (p. 23), considers this proposition, he still has to prove his success within the capitalist system before thinking of abandoning it. He envies his manager, since 'when he walks into the store the waves part in front of him', and convinces himself that he needs to 'walk into the store the way he walks in' (p. 24) before going out West with Biff. Happy and Biff used to believe in their father, but are now losing respect for him and his values. Biff, especially, was disillusioned after high school when he caught Willy cheating with another woman while traveling on the road, and this event haunts Willy's memory throughout the play as well. Willy's wife Linda respects and loves her husband and is essentially satisfied with him, but he cannot release his ambition and accept their life together. Willy longs for solid values and truth, a core of stability on which to rely and set 'roots', symbolised by his obsessive desire to work in the garden planting (p. 125). Ultimately, however, his value system embraces facile American promises that prove to be illusory for him, and he is left behind by a changing technological world that ruthlessly emphasises profit. Although he *has* worked hard all his life, he is now reduced to begging his former boss' son Howard, who has taken over the business, for a meagre salary that would sustain his family. Proud of the 'streak of self-reliance' (p. 81) in his family that corresponds to an individualistic American value system, Willy's reliance on Howard highlights his humiliation as he defensively demands, but does not command, respect throughout the play. Howard rejects Willy's request, simply explaining that 'business is business' (p. 80), and condescendingly calling him 'kid' (pp. 81, 84).

Completely self-absorbed and insensitive to Willy's plight, Howard represents the impersonality of a changing industrial technological world. As Willy tries to secure a small salary for his survival, Howard insists on demonstrating his new device, a tape recording machine on which he has taped the disembodied voices of his ideal American family – a wife and two children, a boy and girl – with pride. The indulgence of the expensive new technology and the inane taped voices that function as a representation of domestic American life – interrupted at one point where 'the maid kicked the plug out' (p. 77) – are interspersed with Willy's humiliated pleas. Howard is simply too self-involved to either understand or care about Willy's situation, interrupting him with a list of all the old 'toys' – a camera, a bandsaw and 'all his hobbies' – that he is going to carelessly discard (as he discards Willy) in favour of his new tape recorder, the 'most fascinating relaxation' he ever found (p. 78).

In contrast to Howard, Willy seems afraid of the new technology at one point, as he 'leap[s] away with fright, shouting' when Howard accidentally switches the recorder back on (p. 83). In order to build a relationship with Howard on equal footing, however, Willy feels he needs to participate in his enthusiasm for technology, and claims that he is 'definitely going to get one' himself. Insensitive to Willy's financial situation, Howard encourages his feigned interest without thinking of the cost: 'Sure, they're only a hundred and a half. You can't do without it' (p. 78), as Willy is reduced to begging for sixty-five, then fifty, and finally forty dollars a week. What Willy actually 'can't do without' is some respect and a place in society after thirty-four years of struggling.

Like *The Glass Menagerie*, *Death of a Salesman* is essentially realistic in structure, but makes use of anti-realistic devices. The fluid, changing setting, for example, represents the increasingly industrial world that emerged after the Second World War and a nostalgia for an era when Willy thought he knew the rules for success, as the urban environment disappears and is replaced with a rural landscape whenever Willy journeys into the past (pp. 27, 40). The characters' names are also highly symbolic, as

Willy 'Loman' can be read as Willy 'Low man', reflective of his social status. His son, 'Happy', may be superficially happy, the 'All American' guy in appearance, but ironically he is lost and unhappy even though he's 'making money' (p. 23). Willy's brother Ben appears on stage as an apparition from Willy's memory at key points in the play, and symbolises the life of risk, adventure and apparently effortless material success that Willy had passed up. Ben, who has just died in Africa, 'The Gold Coast!' (p. 48), appears and tells Willy that '[o]pportunity is tremendous in Alaska' (p. 45), the ultimate American frontier.

The legend of how Ben 'walked into the jungle' of Africa at seventeen and walked out a rich man at twenty-one (p. 48) torments Willy throughout the play, making him feel that he missed an opportunity and has not accomplished enough. He feels 'temporary about [himself]' (p. 51) – fragmented, unfinished. Willy is constantly seeking 'the answer' (p. 84) from Ben, convinced that there must be some secret to success that can be revealed. He is haunted by the success of his brother and father, who Ben claims 'made more in a week than a man like [Willy] could make in a lifetime' (p. 49). But Willy's mind is failing and he contradicts himself repeatedly throughout the play, so we are never sure if his stories of his brother's success, or even his own past success years ago, have any truth behind it.

Willy sees success in America as a performance, a show of wealth and status, complete with the appropriate costumes and an adoring public. He wants to be 'known' (p. 126), to command a social identity that counts. Sadly, however, he measures his life's worth by imagining his 'massive funeral' (p. 126), a big show with a large audience attending from all over the country. Willy claims that he chose his career after meeting an eighty-four-year-old salesman who made his living in his hotel room, wearing his 'green velvet slippers' and calling buyers who 'remembered and loved and helped' him. What really sells Willy on this life is that this man died 'the death of a salesman', with 'hundreds of salesmen and buyers' at his funeral (p. 81). But when Willy's end finally arrives, no one but his family and his neighbour Charley attends his funeral (p. 137).

The empty performance of success without any solid accomplishments to back it up is contrasted with the hard work and perseverance of Bernard, Charley's son who grew up with Biff. While Bernard studied and planned for his future, Biff, a high school football star, was convinced that he should be exempt from the pettiness of studying and following rules because of his athletic prowess, an impression that Willy constantly reinforced. While Willy dismissed Bernard's success in school and placed more value on the 'well liked' man 'who creates personal interest' as a measure for a solid future (p. 33), Bernard ultimately winds up having the security and power denied Biff. As a lawyer, Bernard goes off to 'argue a case in front of the Supreme Court', but is too modest to mention it to Willy. When Willy is amazed that Bernard 'didn't even mention it', Charley responds, 'He don't have to – he's gonna do it' (p. 95). Talk is a performative action that only serves to compensate for a lack of substance. Since Bernard has substance in the form of achievement, he can afford to forgo the empty appearance of success.

In *Death of a Salesman* the risks of a capitalist system that offers the possibility of becoming a millionaire with minimal effort,[22] an opportunity theoretically open to all Americans, are juxtaposed with more conservative American values that offer security, embracing hard work and the establishment of a solid, but perhaps less glamorous, place in society. Both elude Willy, however, and failing to find any financial security as he ages, he desperately turns to suicide, deliberately crashing his car so that his family can collect the insurance money, which they most likely will not even receive.

Miller's next play, *The Crucible*, continued to expose the hypocrisies inherent in American promises of freedom and individualism, focusing on the infamous seventeenth-century witch trials that took place in Salem, Massachusetts. In 1692 nineteen men and women were hanged, and one man crushed to death with stones, on accusations of witchcraft. Based on this actual historical event, Miller's representation of the Salem witch trials reflects the anti-communist hysteria fuelled by McCarthy's 'witch-hunts', a term which has come to indicate a political agenda carried out under the pretext of investigating activities that are considered subversive to the State. While Miller explains in his 'Note on the Historical Accuracy' that he took dramatic liberties with the characters and situations in the play, he insists that this does not compromise its exploration of 'the essential nature of one of the strangest and most awful chapters in human history'.[23]

Both the Salem witch-hunts and McCarthyism were essentially about power, control and the nature of authority, and the accusations were essentially fuelled by jealousy, ambition, pride or personal disputes. Like all trials, the Salem witch trials and the McCarthy hearings were about the *performance* of guilt or innocence. During both historical moments, the fears were certainly felt strongly, but the eventual 'hysteria' generated was based on exaggeration and false accusation, encouraged by a repressive totalitarian movement. The reductive mentality of the court in the play, which declared 'that a person is either with this court or he must be accounted against it, there be no road in between' (p. 87), echoes McCarthy's extremism during the hearings.[24] Just as in the 1950s, the justification for the totalitarian nature of 'justice' in Salem was that 'these are new times' (p. 69). Like witches, communists were considered an insidious menace dwelling among law-abiding American citizens, as 'the Devil is a wily one' (p. 61). Whether the Devil is the actual dark force of Satan or a symbol of evil in the ideology of communism, what must be eradicated is the threat to the current social order. The Puritans in Salem had set up a theocratic government, and Miller writes, 'The witch-hunt was a perverse manifestation of the panic which set in among all classes when the balance began to turn toward greater individual freedom' (p. 6). Just as the United States during the 1950s was experiencing social changes and moving into a phase of increasing industrialisation, Puritan society in the seventeenth century was in the process of rapidly transforming from a communal society to a more commercial individualistic one, leading some citizens to respond with guilt, fear and the search for a scapegoat.

In her book, *The Devil in Massachusetts*, which Christopher Bigsby tells us Miller came across in 1949, Marion Starkey posits that 'the medieval idea of malefac witchcraft' has been replaced in modern society 'by a pseudo-scientific concept like "race," "nationality" and by substituting for theological dissension a whole complex of warring ideologies'.[25] In the Introduction to *The Crucible*, Bigsby writes, 'The question is not the reality of witches but the power of authority to define the nature of the real, and the desire, on the part of individuals and the state, to identify those whose purging will relieve a sense of anxiety and guilt' (p. xi). Miller explains that he saw that

> the hearings in Washington were profoundly and even avowedly ritualistic . . . The main point of the hearings, precisely as in seventeenth-century Salem, was that the accused make public confession, damn his confederates as well as his Devil master, and guarantee his sterling new allegiance by breaking disgusting old vows – whereupon he was let loose to rejoin the society of extremely decent people. (p. x)

Initially, the accused in Salem – reflected as characters in *The Crucible* – were those with little power in the community, such as slaves, beggars or widows. Others were outsiders who had in some way transgressed social taboos, such as women who engaged in premarital sexual affairs, gave birth to illegitimate children, did not attend church, or otherwise flaunted their irreverence and independence, thereby threatening the social order. By the end of the play, however, Reverend Hale warns Deputy Governor Danforth that solid moral citizens have been accused, and therefore rebellion is being threatened. But Danforth remains firm, bent on punishing all transgression in order to retain power: 'If retaliation is your fear, know this – I should hang ten thousand that dared to rise against the law, and an ocean of salt tears could not melt the resolution of the statutes' (pp. 119–20). Just as in the case of Joseph McCarthy, however, who lost power after he accused a more powerful American institution, the US Army, of communist infiltration, so too did the magistrates of Salem Village lose power after those in high social positions began to suffer accusation, leading the Governor of Boston to become involved. The Governor formed a new court, acquitted the prisoners who had been awaiting trial, and put an end to further accusations.

The Crucible begins with the Reverend Parris, who is highly distressed that his daughter Betty has fainted and now lies unconscious after he found her and his niece Abigail 'dancing in the forest like heathens' (p. 9) with Tituba, his slave from Barbados. From the beginning of the play, however, we see that Parris is primarily concerned for his reputation, since if it turns out that the girls 'conjured spirits in the forest' his enemies will use this information to undermine his position in the community and take away his power (p. 10). Before long, 'the rumor of witchcraft is all about' (p. 9), and the girls begin accusing each other and several other members of the community of cavorting with the Devil. Their accusations come first out of fear of punishment, and later out of wanting to hold onto the new power that they have acquired in the community. Hysteria ensues and confessions abound during the subsequent trials, as the accused attempt to save themselves and their loved ones from execution. Only John Proctor has the courage to stand up to his accusers, expose the hypocrisy and challenge the court, but this attitude only succeeds in further condemning him. And while he eventually does agree to confess in order to save his life, he refuses to condemn his fellow citizens, just as Miller later refused to answer questions regarding anyone's activities but his own in front of HUAC. Proctor insists that he 'speak[s] his own sins' and 'cannot judge another' (p. 131). He reluctantly agrees to a signed confession, but emphatically refuses to let it be hung outside the church and be made public. He will not allow his name to be 'used' in such a way for posterity so that others might assume that he 'sold [his] friends' (p. 132) – an obvious reference to Elia Kazan's testimony in front of HUAC. Proctor refuses to cooperate with the magistrates any further, tears up the confession, and is sent to his execution with a clear conscience (pp. 132–4).

During the 1950s and 1960s, Miller continued to secure his place in the American theatre with plays such as *A View from the Bridge* (1955), *After the Fall* (1963), *Incident at Vichy* (1964) and *The Price* (1968), exploring human relationships and the tension between individualism and community, self-interest and responsibility to others. His career flourished well into the 1990s, and he remained prolific until his death in 2004. Williams and Miller were representative of American playwrights after the Second World War who were beginning to view the American dream as precarious, a problematic mythology that relied on superficial appearance and exclusion rather than the freedom, diversity and opportunity it advertised. Their explorations of both form and content paved the way for anti-realistic postmodern presentations that embraced the freedom inherent in the characterisation of American identity as a performance that could be manipulated and transformed, rather than as an essential and stable entity that functioned consistently. Playwrights such as Sam Shepard and David Mamet, for example (see Chapter 5), were part of a generation that began their careers during the 1960s and 1970s and were therefore, consciously or not, steeped in the uncertainties and instabilities of postmodern identity. While Williams was part of the previous generation of writers who had earned their reputations during the 1940s and 1950s, he was still eager to respond to the changing times with his art. During Williams's later period, generally considered to begin after *The Night of the Iguana* in 1961, his plays were increasingly experimental and dealt with the sort of postmodern fragmentation that was being explored by playwrights during the 1960s, 1970s and 1980s. Williams was very interested in moving away from presenting his work in large commercial Broadway theatres and offering more and more of his plays off-Broadway, especially after his double-bill of *Suddenly Last Summer* and *Something Unspoken* was staged off-Broadway at the York Playhouse in 1958 under the title *Garden District*. His one-acts were among the plays that were produced at the off-Broadway institution Café Cino during its early days, and Ellen Stewart, founder and artistic director of La MaMa E.T.C. (Experimental Theatre Club), produced a dramatic adaptation of his short story 'One Arm'.[26] While Williams essentially saw himself as a Broadway playwright, he began to expand his horizons as productions of his plays in the 1960s, 1970s and 1980s were increasingly staged off- and off-off-Broadway at venues such as the Eastside Playhouse, Truck and Warehouse Theatre, Hudson Guild, and the Jean Cocteau Repertory. In 1975 he told Charles Ruas that his 'great happiness in the theatre' was now 'off-Broadway and off-off-Broadway'.[27]

Williams's interest in the slippery and ephemeral distinctions of identity was at his height during the 1960s and 1970s with experimental plays such as *The Gnädiges Fräulein* (1966), *In the Bar of a Tokyo Hotel* (1969), and his several versions of *The Two-Character Play / Out Cry* (1967, 1973, 1976),[28] especially in terms of the image of the artist and the breakdown of distinctions between the individual and his work that could lead to madness. His late plays often address the issue of psychic fragmentation and the collapse of stable identity. The setting of *The Two-Character Play*, for example, suggests the 'disordered images of a mind approaching collapse'[29] and presents a brother and sister, performers who 'have the same thought at the same time' (5: 366) and are not sure of the boundaries that separate themselves from each other or from the play they perform. *In the Bar of a Tokyo Hotel* uses truncated dialogue to echo the emotional, existential breakdown of Mark, an artist who no longer sees any separation between himself and his work (7: 21). The Fräulein in *The Gnädiges Fräulein* was once a great performer who now offers only grotesque re-enactments of her past glory, documented as a fixed image in the graveyard of her scrapbook. She is fragmented both psychically and physically, as she is prone to '[t]emporary amnesia resulting from shock' (7: 247) and her body is progressively ripped apart by the cocaloony birds throughout the play, 'streaked and dabbled with blood', with '[p]atches of her fuzzy light orange hair . . . torn away' (7: 260). She does, however, survive and go on; the play's last image is of the Fräulein bravely starting 'a wild, blind dash for the fish-docks' (7: 262), going off to meet the cocaloonies that will, more than likely, tear her apart once again as she fights them for the fish that allows her to earn her keep.

While the plays that Williams was writing during the 1970s and 1980s retained many of his earlier concerns with the ravages of time, the predatory nature of human beings (often acted out in the sexual arena and the site of the body), and the inevitable struggle to survive and endure in a changing capitalist society, the late works express these concerns in a much more brutal and direct manner than the early work. The subtlety of symbolism and metaphor in the early plays is replaced with an irreverent representation of the human 'tragicomedy' (to use Samuel Beckett's term), as a new social permissiveness allowed Williams to turn to a sense of the outrageous, the 'camp', and the extreme in dealing with intersections of the personal and the political. The outrageous and perverse comic elements in several of the late plays, such as *THIS IS (An Entertainment)* (unpublished; 1976), *Kirche, Küche, und Kinder* (unpublished; 1979) or *The Remarkable Rooming House of Mme LeMonde* (1984),[30] for example, are countered with a sense of the brutality of human nature stripped of cultural artifice, reminiscent of the work that was being done in France by Antonin Artaud and Jean Genet from the 1930s to the 1960s.

While I have found no evidence that Williams was directly familiar with Artaud's work, it is likely that he encountered Artaud's theories during his studies at the New School in New York City during the 1940s, and he was certainly familiar with Genet's work. In fact, in an essay which appeared in the *New York Times Magazine* in 1960, Williams cited Camus, Genet, Brecht, Beckett, Anouilh, Ionesco, Durrenmatt and Albee as his 'fellow defendants' in writing honestly about life.[31] *THIS IS (An Entertainment)* and *Kirche, Küche, und Kinder* especially contain moments of remarkable similarity to Artaud and Genet's work. A scene in *Kirche, Küche, und Kinder*, for example, where a minister throws a paper bag over the character Hotsy's head and 'plops a huge Bible under [her] derriere and mounts her [as] members of THE PRESS' burst in is reminiscent of the same dismissal of good taste in Count Cenci's violent pursuit of his daughter as he seeks to rape her in Artaud's *The Cenci* (1935), an adaptation of the texts by Percy Bysshe Shelley and Stendhal. There are similar scenes of brutal rape and incest in *The Remarkable Rooming House of Mme LeMonde*, where 'a delicate little man with a childlike face' named Mint, whose 'legs are mysteriously paralyzed', is repeatedly raped by his landlady's son, a 'muscular' boy 'hung like a dray horse' who is 'kept on the place for . . . incestuous relations with the lady'. In *THIS IS*, the role-playing of the Count and Countess that opens the play is strikingly similar to Genet's *The Maids* (1947), and the invasion of the hotel by the revolution outside, with the Countess's lover, General Eros, leading the way echoes the ending of Genet's *The Balcony* (1956). Furthermore, Michael Paller points out in his book *Gentlemen Callers* that *THIS IS* 'seems to have been inspired by . . . Genet's *Splendid's*'.[32]

These later plays often present a world view that is simultaneously comic and bleak, illustrating a postmodern sense of irony that can be seen not only in a lack of romanticism, but also in the blurring of high/low culture (such as the numerous nods to popular culture and current events alongside self-conscious references to classic works like *Medea*, *The Sea Gull* or 'Dover Beach' in *Kirche, Küche, und Kinder*), as Williams rejected the bourgeois and the conventional, and indulged the taboo and the unacceptable in order to write more honestly about life through a new lens. The new freedoms that American society increasingly embraced also led Williams to finally feel comfortable coming out publicly as a gay man in 1970, as political movements such as Gay Liberation made it safer, both personally and professionally, to claim membership in American society on the basis of one's 'true' identity.

NOTES

1. Tennessee Williams, *The Theatre of Tennessee Williams*, 8 vols (New York: New Directions, 1971–92), 1: 143. Subsequent references to this collection will be cited parenthetically by volume and page number in the text.
2. The titles, however, were not used in the original production. See Annette J. Saddik, *The Politics of Reputation: The Critical Reception of Tennessee Williams' Later Plays* (London: Associated University Presses, 1999) for a discussion of realism and anti-realism in *The Glass Menagerie*.
3. Albert J. Devlin (ed.), *Conversations with Tennessee Williams* (Jackson: University Press of Mississippi, 1986), p. 277.
4. For a detailed discussion of sexuality in *Suddenly Last Summer*, see Annette J. Saddik, 'The (un)represented fragmentation of the body in Tennessee Williams' 'Desire and the Black Masseur' and *Suddenly Last Summer* ', *Modern Drama*, 41 (Fall 1998), 347–54.
5. *Stairs to the Roof* was written in 1941, produced in 1945, and finally published by New York publisher New Directions in 2000, edited and introduced by Allean Hale. Subsequent references appear parenthetically in the text.
6. Devlin, *Conversations with Tennessee Williams*, p. 5.
7. During the 1920s, 1930s and 1940s, 'social plays' that clearly espoused a Marxist ideology and a call to political action were characterised most notably by the work of Bertolt Brecht and, in a different manner, by the genre of Workers' Theatre or 'agitprop' theatre, a label that stood for 'agitation propaganda'. These agitprop plays were performed in public

spaces, usually by amateurs, for the purpose of sending a direct political message and inspiring practical action. *Stairs to the Roof*, while maintaining a social message regarding the commodification of human beings in the workplace, does not fall comfortably into the category of agitprop political theatre in the tradition of Clifford Odets's *Waiting for Lefty* (1935), for example, which ends with a call to 'STRIKE, STRIKE, STRIKE!!!'

8. The clear espousal of Marxist ideology and a call to political action, presented most notably in the plays of Bertolt Brecht and 'agitprop' theatre, is absent from *Stairs to the Roof*. Brecht's solutions were much more direct, even as he offered the audience open-ended conclusions to ponder. Agitprop or Workers' Theatre dealt more superficially with the aspects of living under industrial capitalism, but its aims were more immediate, hoping to reach a wide audience and incite protest. Much of Brecht's brilliance, in fact, lies in his complex anti-Aristotelian presentations that, for all their didacticism, avoid coercing the spectator or reducing the issues. Brecht, however, saw political reform on earth as a possibility, a duty even, whereas *Stairs to the Roof* is less assured of its political ideology and seems to abandon concrete political solutions.

9. The debates surrounding postmodernism are complex and varied. Critics with Marxist leanings especially tend to criticise postmodernism's scepticism of social progress and unified perspectives as undermining a progressive cultural politics. They therefore see postmodernism not as a theory of excess that is limitless in its inclusion of multiple meanings, but as a theory of lack, nihilistic in its emptiness of meaning, and therefore highly problematic. See, for example, the work of Fredric Jameson, Terry Eagleton and David Harvey. While I acknowledge the validity of these varied readings of postmodern culture, this book takes the position that the influence of postmodernism in contemporary drama opened up opportunities for diversity and marginalised voices in American culture (see the Introduction).

10. While Williams's successes of the 1940s and 1950s such as *The Glass Menagerie*, *A Streetcar Named Desire* and *Cat on a Hot Tin Roof* certainly made use of anti-realistic stylistic

conventions, they remained realistic in purpose through narrative consistency and the stable representation of character.

11. Tennessee Williams, *Camino Real* (New York: New Directions, 1953), p. vi. Subsequent references appear parenthetically in the text. It is significant to note here that while the play's action 'takes place in an unspecified Latin-American country' (p. xii), the setting is more universal than that, as Williams describes the central plaza where it takes places as belonging to 'a tropical seaport that bears a confusing, but somehow harmonious, resemblance to such widely scattered ports as Tangiers, Havana, Vera Cruz, Casablanca, Shanghai, New Orleans'. At the same time, however, the play is also expressly 'American', a fact emphasised by Williams's insistence that the anglicised pronunciation of 'Cá-mino Réal' should be used.

12. For a discussion of Williams's experimental work, especially the late plays, see *The Undiscovered Country: The Later Plays of Tennessee Williams*, ed. Philip C. Kolin (New York: Peter Lang, 2002) and *The Politics of Reputation: The Critical Reception of Tennessee Williams' Later Plays* (London: Associated University Presses, 1999). Also see Ruby Cohn, 'Tennessee Williams: the last two decades', in *The Cambridge Companion to Tennessee Williams*, ed. Matthew C. Roudané (Cambridge: Cambridge University Press, 1997).

13. Devlin, *Conversations with Tennessee Williams*, p. 298.

14. Christine R. Day and Bob Woods (eds), *Where I Live: Selected Essays by Tennessee Williams* (New York: New Directions, 1978), p. 111.

15. Devlin, *Conversations with Tennessee Williams*, p. 142.

16. Ibid. p. 19.

17. Ibid. p. 21.

18. Ibid. p. 92.

19. We see this from the beginning of the play, as the 'Survivor' dies early on in the action (pp. 23–4).

20. Donald Spoto, *The Kindness of Strangers: The Life of Tennessee Williams* (New York: Ballantine Books, 1985), p. 208.

21. Arthur Miller, *Death of a Salesman* (New York: Viking Penguin, 1949), p. 37. Subsequent references appear parenthetically in the text.

22. The allure of the possibility of extreme wealth with minimal work is still very much alive in the American psyche, as evidenced by the ubiquitousness of advertisements for 'get-rich-quick' seminars that emphasise the importance of confidence and positive thinking (characteristic of Jim O'Connor in *The Glass Menagerie*), and books such as Donald Trump's *Think Like a Billionaire: Everything You Need to Know About Success, Real Estate, and Life* (New York: Random House, 2004).

23. Arthur Miller, *The Crucible* (New York: Penguin, 1953), p. 2. Subsequent references appear parenthetically in the text.

24. Critics of the US government's 9/11 proclamation that nations were either 'with us or against us' have been quick to point out similarities to the era of McCarthyism.

25. Marion L. Starkey, *The Devil in Massachusetts* (New York: Alfred A. Knopf, 1949), p. ix.

26. Michael Smith, 'The good scene: off-off Broadway', *Tulane Drama Review*, 10:4 (Summer 1966), 164.

27. Devlin, *Conversations with Tennessee Williams*, p. 291.

28. For a discussion of the various versions of *The Two-Character Play/Out Cry*, see Felicia Hardison Londré, 'The Two-Character Out Cry and Break Out', in *The Undiscovered Country: The Later Plays of Tennessee Williams* ed. Philip C. Kolin (New York: Peter Lang Publishing, 2002).

29. Williams, *The Theatre of Tennessee Williams*, 5: 308. Subsequent references appear parenthetically in the text by volume and page number.

30. These plays will be available shortly, as I am currently editing a collection of Williams's previously unpublished later plays, forthcoming from New Directions Publishing in Spring 2008 under the title *The Travelling Companion and Other Plays*.

31. Tennessee Williams, 'Tennessee Williams Presents his POV', in *Where I Live: Selected Essays*, ed. Christine R. Day and Bob Woods (New York: New Directions Publishing, 1978), p. 115.

32. Michael Paller, *Gentlemen Callers: Tennessee Williams, Homosexuality, and Mid-Twentieth Century Drama* (New York: Palgrave Macmillan, 2005), p. 211. *Splendid's* was one of

Genet's earliest plays, and written while he was in prison. The manuscript was rediscovered only in 1993 and produced in London in 1995, so it is unclear whether Williams would have known it, but the similarities are there.

CHAPTER 3

African–American Theatre: Voices from the Margins

Sarah: I want not to be.

> Adrienne Kennedy, *Funnyhouse of a Negro* (1964)

To be American is to flaunt what you got . . . and to try to have a little more than the next man.

> Ice Cube, in an interview with Charlie Rose, 1998

During the 1960s and 1970s, the notion of American identity as performative was becoming increasingly evident in the work of African-American playwrights, who were often presenting race as a series of roles based on cultural expectations rather than as an essential and stable core of being. Playwrights such as LeRoi Jones (a.k.a. Amiri Baraka), Ed Bullins and Ron Milner were central to organising the Black Arts Movement (BAM), a social, political and artistic movement that took shape in 1965 after the assassination of Malcolm X and lasted ten years, providing a forum for many new African-American writers. Adrienne Kennedy and Ntozake Shange were also instrumental in opening up new avenues for African-American voices with their plays that pushed boundaries and challenged traditional dramatic form. Their highly symbolic language and fragmented structures reflected the cultural experience of being a black woman in America, and were followed more recently by Suzan-Lori Parks, who uses fragmented repetitive language to comment on established historical narrative.

In his seminal 1968 essay, 'The Black Arts Movement', Larry Neal aligned Black Arts with Black Power, the 1960s movement that broke with the passive tactics of Civil Rights and demanded political and artistic freedom by 'any means necessary', embracing black leader Malcolm X and advocating armed resistance and racial separatism. An overtly political and militant artistic movement, the Black Arts Movement coalesced in 1965 with writer and activist LeRoi Jones's move from Manhattan's Lower East Side uptown to Harlem after the assassination of Malcolm X. Jones, who had already established a successful career as a poet, publisher and playwright – winning the Obie Award for his play *Dutchman* in 1964 – founded the Black Arts Repertory Theatre/School (BARTS) in Harlem. Unlike the writers of the Harlem Renaissance, BAM artists sought a black-oriented voice distinct from the prevailing white literary establishment. An overtly political movement, BAM grew out of the social upheavals of the turbulent 1960s, reflecting the revolutionary frustration that was fermenting in US cities around the country. Riots in New York – mainly in Harlem and Rochester – began in 1964, setting off the expressions of frustration and anger around racial issues that exploded in the infamous riots of 1968, as cities such as Los Angeles, Detroit, Newark and Cleveland went up in flames following the assassination of Martin Luther King, Jr.

Led primarily by Jones, who changed his name to Amiri Baraka in 1967, BAM became instrumental in the development of black theatre groups, poetry performances and the publication of journals. An impressive array of black writers – Ed Bullins, Larry Neal, Ben Caldwell, Jimmy Garrett, John O'Neal, Ron Milner, Woodie King, Jr, Bill Gunn, Adam David Miller, Sonia Sanchez and Marvin X – were featured in the Summer 1968 special issue of *The Drama Review* dedicated to black theatre. While the movement was often legitimately criticised – both by black writers and the white mainstream critical establishment – for being sexist, homophobic and racially exclusive, BAM opened important doors for black writers to be heard on their own terms. By 1974, however, the influence of BAM began to decline along with the disruption of the Black Power movement by government organisations. By 1976, BAM had broken up as an organised movement, but its indelible influence continues to be felt.

In 1966, Baraka (as Jones) published his manifesto on 'The Revolutionary Theatre', which presented an aggressive and, both intellectually and socially, violent proposition for an emerging African-American theatre, a 'theatre of assault'.[1] He declared: 'The Revolutionary Theatre should force change; it should be change . . . The Revolutionary Theatre must EXPOSE! Show up the insides of these humans, look into black skulls. White men will cower before this theatre because it hates them.'[2] Baraka wanted a theatre that would be honest about African-American anger and frustration, one that would 'Accuse and Attack anything that can be accused and attacked. It must Accuse and Attack because it is a theatre of Victims. It looks at the sky with the victims' eyes, and moves the victims to look at the strength in their minds and their bodies.'[3] This theatre was to be 'a social theatre' that would attack anglo-patriarchal standards and translate art into social change, a 'political theatre, a weapon to help in the slaughter of these dimwitted fatbellied white guys who somehow believe that the rest of the world is here for them to slobber on'.[4] Ultimately, Baraka anticipated that 'Americans will hate the Revolutionary Theatre because it will be out to destroy them and whatever they believe is real'.[5]

Baraka's plays were no less subtle in their indictment of Anglo-American patriarchal values, and were applauded for their honesty, exposing African-American identity as a mask, a performance that covered up hatred and anger. These plays, however, were also criticised for embracing violence and for their reductive character portrayals and simplification of complex issues.

In 1964, Baraka (also under his former name LeRoi Jones) had four of his plays produced: *The Baptism*, *The Toilet*, *The Slave* and *Dutchman*, which Edward Albee helped produce at the Cherry Lane Theatre in New York's Greenwich Village. In plays such as *Great Goodness of Life (A Coon Show)* (1967), *Madheart* (1967) and *Police* (1968), he continued to produce anti-realistic work that rejected traditional Western realism, spoke to and from African-American experience, and aimed to spur political action. His two best-known plays, *The Slave* and *Dutchman*, both force the audience to confront its own prejudices through violent dramatic presentations that challenge society's assumptions about race. The title of *Dutchman* recalls the legend of *The Flying Dutchman* ship, reportedly started in 1641 when a Dutch ship sank off the coast of Africa, and later the subject of an opera by Richard Wagner. The legend goes that one Captain van der Decken was sailing around Africa's Cape of Good Hope when a storm threatened to sink the ship. As the ship began to sink, Captain van der Decken, resisting defeat, screamed out: 'I WILL round this Cape even if I have to keep sailing until doomsday!' Legend now has it that the ghost ship appears whenever a storm brews off the Cape of Good Hope, and anyone who sees the ship will die a horrible death. Baraka makes use of *The Flying Dutchman* as a metaphor for a cycle that is repeated endlessly throughout history, and *Dutchman* is an allegory of race relations in America. It signifies the cycle of history to which we are all, in some sense, doomed. The play's title can also refer to the Dutch traders who brought African slaves to America during the seventeenth century. In any case, the play is highly symbolic and the characters are meant to be taken as representative of particular attitudes, social positions or points of view, rather than as complex human beings in the tradition of realism.

The setting too is symbolic, as the play takes place underground in a New York City subway car that references the unconscious depths of the mind, the place where prejudice, cruelty and anger lie dormant. The play's two characters are Lula, a beautiful thirty-year-old white woman with 'long red hair'[6] who represents the sadistic temptress, and Clay, a twenty-year-old black man who believes he can live as an individual in American society and avoid the trappings of history and the politics of race relations. The two meet underground as Lulu smiles at Clay through the subway window and begins to flirt with him, alternately baiting him sexually and refusing the implications of her behaviour. Characteristic of her biblical counterpart Eve, she eats apples as she rides the subway and even offers one to Clay, which he accepts.

In terms of identity, Clay, as a black man, is not allowed to be an individual. Lulu constantly refers to him as a 'type', claiming that she 'knows' him. At first, Clay playfully participates in her game, as when Lulu asks him what his surname is and he responds with: 'Take your pick. Jackson, Johnson, or Williams' (p. 1001). Clay's response, however, not only highlights an awareness of his lack of individuality as a black man in America, it dismisses the 'slave names' imposed on African-Americans who were forced to take on the surname of their owners, names that have been stamped on them throughout history, as insignificant. Clay wants to fit in and be accepted as a part of American culture, but Lulu, representing society's relentless persecution and the forces of history, does not allow that. She baits Clay both sexually and intellectually, pointing out that his identity as an American is 'wrong', that he has no right 'to be wearing a three-button suit and striped tie' since his 'grandfather was a slave, he didn't go to Harvard' (p. 1002). While Clay keeps his cool, not understanding at first the cruelty of Lulu's intentions, he is eventually provoked to violence, slapping Lulu hard across the mouth (p. 1005) and exploding into an angry rant about the 'truth' of black life in America and the rage brewing below the surface of civilised social performance. When he is finished, he attempts to leave, but Lulu casually stabs him dead and orders the other passengers to throw his body off the train. As another young black man gets on at the next stop, Lulu readies herself for her next performance, giving him 'a long slow look' (p. 1007) as the cycle is doomed to repeat itself.

From a feminist point of view, Lulu as a character symbolising the white seductress, apple and all, who baits and then coldly destroys the innocent Clay, is obviously problematic. Moreover, in the opening stage directions, Lulu is reduced to a face staring through the subway car window, leading her to be described in the opening stage directions as 'it' (presumably referring to the face, which 'very premeditatedly' smiles) rather than 'she'. While this usage is grammatically sound and is in keeping with the style of the play as an allegory that eschews conventional realism and resists any psychologically complex depiction of character, it still uncomfortably serves to objectify Lulu in ways that a feminist reading might, with good reason, find troubling. The play, however, is primarily ritualistic, not realistic, and neither Lulu nor Clay is presented as an individual, but rather as a representative of historically determined racial categories. *Dutchman* is Baraka's vision of the fate of African-Americans in white America, and was intended to provoke a collective response and consequent political action within the black community.

In *The Slave*, Walker is a black militant who was once married to Grace, a 'blonde woman'[7] who has now married a white English professor, Bradford Easley, and lives with him and her two daughters by Walker. He bursts into their home with a gun, 'dressed as an old field slave' (p. 43) – an image which creates a connection between oppressive history and violent present – and drags the couple into a race war that he is fighting. While Grace and Easley are held hostage, debates and discussions regarding issues of identity, language, the politics of personal relationships, and the line between truth and lies take place among the three characters. The historical notion of blackness as a pollutant or disease that 'infects' identity, an issue that also comes up in Adrienne Kennedy's *Funnyhouse of a Negro* in her depiction of a yellow, jaundiced Jesus, is clearly expressed by Walker, as he tells Grace that their daughters 'are niggers. You know, circa 1800, one drop makes you whole?' (p. 55). Finally, *The Slave* ends with Walker leaving the house after an explosion that kills their two daughters, destroying a part of them both.

The Slave deals interestingly with the complexities of identity and the connection between identity and language. Walker tells Grace that he 'did come into the world pointed in the right direction. Oh, shit, I learned so many words for what I wanted to say. They all come down on me at once. But almost none of them are mine' (p. 53). Walker sees identity not as essential, but as a role or performance coded in the mythologies by which we live. As an English professor, Easley represents the Western tradition that dictates Anglo-American systems of identification, ways of seeing ourselves, that have excluded African-American experience. Walker, using the mythology of literature to play with shifting identities, identifies himself as 'a second-rate Othello', Grace as Desdemona, and Easley as Iago, 'at least between classes' (p. 57). Black identity in America is portrayed as an identity of doubleness, confusing the mask with the truth, and finally not being able to distinguish the difference between the two. Grace tells Walker:

You're split in so many ways . . . your feelings are cut up into skinny horrible strips . . . like umbrella struts . . . holding up whatever bizarre black cloth you're using this performance as your self's image. I don't even think you know who you are any more. No, I don't think you *ever* knew [. . .] It must be a sick task keeping so many lying separate uglinesses together . . . and pretending they're something you've made and understand. (p. 61)

With *The Slave*, Baraka continued exploring the theme he presented in *Dutchman*, the 'false' identity of blacks in America and the confrontation of a black poet/revolutionary with the white society that seeks to destroy him.

Like Amiri Baraka, Ed Bullins believed that art must be revolutionary in order to be successful. Yet even though Bullins addressed powerful social themes in his plays, they were typically not as confrontational as Baraka's and were essentially traditional in form, using sustained narrative and realistic dramatic conventions. Bullins began his career with *Clara's Ole Man* in 1965, and while 1968 was a prolific year for him, staging several of his plays such as *Goin' a Buffalo* (first staged reading 1968; New York production 1969), *In the Wine Time* (1968), *A Son, Come Home* (1968) and *The Electronic Nigger* (1968), his more famous works include *The Fabulous Miss Marie* (1971), *Daddy!* (1977) and *The Taking of Miss Janie* (1975), for which he won both an Obie and the New York Drama Critics Circle Award.

Bullins calls *Clara's Ole Man* 'A Play of Lost Innocence', as it deals with the revelation of a young man, Jack, who discovers that 'Big Girl', the roommate of the girl Clara whom he is courting, is actually her domineering lover. Jack and Clara spend the afternoon together in her apartment with Big Girl, who has called in sick from work, and other characters who wander in and out of the apartment. Since Clara had told Jack to come by 'when her ole man would be at work', he is eager to leave before 'Clara's ole man gets home'.[8] When Big Girl realises that Clara had not told Jack about their situation, Clara pleads that she was simply lonely and just wanted some company, 'to talk to somebody' (p. 281), but Big Girl must assert her power and sends Jack outside to get beaten by her friends.

The title of the play highlights its focus on manipulating expectations in terms of identity, as the term 'ole man' could signify either a father, a husband or a lover. The fluidity of identity is therefore layered; not only is gender identity challenged, but so is the nature of intimate relationships. Whether father, husband or lover (male or female), Clara's 'ole man' represents both protection and a sense of ownership, an imposing figure whose power must be feared.

Questions of power in a society where one inhabits a powerless identity are central to *Clara's Ole Man*. For Big Girl, power lies in transgressing not only gender expectations but all social propriety and convention. She is proud that she has taught Baby Girl, her mentally retarded teenage sister, to use curse words because she felt that the use of improper language would 'give her freedom' (p. 256) and 'spirit' (p. 257). Big Girl speaks her mind, and as an employee in a mental institution she understands the difference between actual control and the performance of control, telling Jack that when the patients are given shots to quiet them, 'the docs think they're getting better, but really they ain't. They're just learn'n like before to hold it in . . . just like before, that's one reason most of them come back or are always on the verge afterwards of goin' psycho again' (p. 257). Just as those who are 'quieted down' will build up their frustrations and explode again, African-Americans performing social adjustment and inclusion need real outlets, healing solutions, not simply a 'ritual action of purging and catharsis' (p. 257).

In *Goin' a Buffalo*, Bullins plays with realistic form, using fantasy sequences and shifts in time in which the lights change, and stating that in Act II: 'the effect should be directed toward the illusions of time, place, and matter. Reality is questionable here.'[9] But the context of the play is undeniably realistic: the disjunction between the promises of the American dream for all Americans and the reality of African-American life in the 1960s. Former convict Curt, his wife Pandora, who works as a stripper, and Curt's new friend Art, a guy he met in jail, dream of getting out of their dead-end situation in Los Angeles, starting over in Buffalo. But just as in David Mamet's play, *American Buffalo* (where the 'Buffalo' in this case signifies a buffalo nickel coin, not the town in New York State),[10] the characters in *Goin' a Buffalo* see their only access to the American dream through crime, as Curt chooses Buffalo because it's 'a good hustlin' town' and he's 'a good thief', making money by his 'wits' (p. 31). Curt emphatically believes that, as African-Americans, 'this ain't a world we built so why should we try to fit in?' (p. 69).

The men in the play make their living illegally – by selling drugs, theft or 'pimping' – and the women sell sexual services, either through stripping or prostitution. Even the characters who try to make a living legally with their talent – the musicians in the strip club – are cheated out of their pay by the owner. And while Curt is making plans for the future with Art, whom he trusts and respects, Art and Pandora are betraying him by having an affair behind his back. After a series of violent episodes where Pandora gets punched by the bouncer at the strip club and Curt beats the owner unconscious, Curt eventually gets caught with drugs and arrested. Even though Pandora wants to stay and help Curt, she has no choice but to leave town with Art, who insists they leave and 'slaps her viciously' (p. 97), reminding her to bring her 'box' – both the drugs they have stashed and a euphemism for her sexual usefulness – making it clear that the cycle of crime, violence and betrayal will continue in Buffalo.

Another pivotal figure in the Black Arts Movement, Ron Milner, a Detroit-born playwright and essayist, was introduced to New York in 1966 with a play *Who's Got His Own*, which deals with the issue of black male identity in American culture. He achieved commercial success with *What the Winesellers Buy*, the first play by an African-American to be produced by Joseph Papp and the Shakespeare Festival at Lincoln Center in 1974. His comedy-drama *Checkmates* (1988), which explores the lives of two black couples of different generations struggling with new definitions of the roles of women and men and the shifting expectations of marriage in a world of expanding opportunities, ran on Broadway for 172 performances.

The complexity of the black experience in America, particularly the black female experience, is probably best explored by playwright Adrienne Kennedy, who was the first woman playwright to have her work performed at the Yale Repertory Theatre in 1973 with *An Evening with Dead Essex* and was a founding member of the Women's Theatre Council in 1971. Kennedy has won Obie awards for *Funnyhouse of a Negro* (1964) – her debut off-Broadway at the East End Theatre with Edward Albee as one of its producers – *June*

Figure 3.1 *A Rat's Mass* by Adrienne Kennedy, 1969 production La MaMa E.T.C. Directed by Seth Allen. Photo of Mary Alice as 'Sister Rat', Tony Award winner for *The Delany Sisters* on Broadway. (Source: Conard Ward.)

Figure 3.2 *A Rat's Mass* by Adrienne Kennedy, 1969 production La MaMa E.T.C. Directed by Seth Allen. (Source: Conard Ward.)

and Jean in Concert (1995) and *Sleep Deprivation Chamber* (1996). During the 1960s and 1970s, plays such as *The Owl Answers* (1965), *A Rat's Mass* (1966), *A Lesson in Dead Language* (1970) and *A Movie Star Has to Star in Black and White* (1976) addressed the performance of the self as an outsider, the doubleness of seeing oneself through the eyes of a hostile and alien world. Her work departed from the social protest plays of writers such as Baraka or Bullins, and while she was sometimes criticised during the 1960s and 1970s for not dealing with the social issues of race in a more aggressive manner that directly championed black pride, her work addresses racial issues, cultural identity and self-worth in a biased society in a completely different style than revolutionaries such as Baraka or Bullins, using the breakdown of conventional narrative and fragmented structures reminiscent of nightmares that reflect the chaotic workings of the mind. Philip Kolin calls her work 'unsettlingly postmodern – surrealistic, dreamlike, without traditional narrative plots comprising a beginning, middle, and end'. Kennedy's plays, he writes, are 'disturbing, complex, hypnotic'.[11] He argues that, like Edward Albee, Kennedy 'bolted from the conventions of realistic/naturalistic theatre. But she went far beyond the influence of a European theatre of the absurd, which inspired Albee's early plays, to combine surrealistic techniques with the rituals and rhythms of the African culture she had witnessed firsthand in 1961 in Ghana.'[12]

Funnyhouse of a Negro is brilliant in its depiction of the struggles of identity and identifications that haunt the African-American psyche. The main character, Negro-Sarah, is a young African-American girl who is split into four other characters that represent her various identifications, her 'selves': The Duchess of Hapsburg, Queen Victoria Regina, Jesus and Patrice Lumumba. The title of the play refers to the ways in which identity is represented and distorted in the reflections of society's mirrors, Sarah's 'funnyhouse'. Other characters are the 'Funnyhouse Lady', who is her landlady, and her Jewish poet boyfriend Raymond, who is cold, cynical and tormenting, identified as the 'Funnyhouse Man'. Sarah's mother appears as an apparition with wild, straight, black hair that falls to her waist, carrying a bald head and crossing the stage. Sarah lives in her room in New York City, which contains a bed, a writing table, a mirror, photographs, books, and a white plaster statue of Queen Victoria that looms as a symbol of the Anglo-imperialism Sarah idolises throughout the play. Her father is imagined throughout the play as an African living in the jungle, a 'wild black beast'[13] who killed himself when Patrice Lumumba was murdered, but in the end Raymond reveals that her father is actually a doctor married to a white woman and living in New York 'in rooms with European antiques, photographs of Roman ruins, walls of books, and oriental carpets' (p. 23).

Sarah's first appearance in the play is as 'the Negro'; she emerges 'faceless, dark [. . .], with a hangman's rope about her neck and red blood on the part that would be her face' (p. 4), foreshadowing her suicide by hanging at the end of the play. She has 'wild kinky hair' and a 'ragged head with a patch of hair missing from the crown' that she carries in her hand as she begins her opening monologue (pp. 4–5). Her various 'selves' are characters taken from history: The Duchess of Hapsburg was the wife of Austrian Archduke Maximillian, who was appointed Emperor of Mexico, having been duped into thinking the Mexican people wanted a monarchy. When Napoleon II withdrew his troops from Mexico, the Hapsburgs were left at the mercy of the revolutionaries, penniless and desperate. The Duchess sailed for Europe to ask Napoleon III for aid, and when he refused her, she went to Rome to ask the Pope. In the Vatican, she collapsed and went insane. Back in Mexico, Maximillian is shot as a traitor. The lives of the Hapsburgs were made into a 1939 film, *Juarez*, starring Bette Davis, significant because of Kennedy's great interest in black and white films. Queen Victoria, of course, was Queen of England (1832–1901) during an age of aggressive colonisation of the East. Patrice Lumumba was an African nationalist leader and the first prime minister of the Democratic Republic of the Congo (subsequently Zaire). He was assassinated shortly after being forced out of office, and appears in the play with a shattered head. Jesus appears as a dwarf in the play, and is 'yellow', metaphorically infected perhaps by jaundice or 'blackness'. He is therefore characterised as physically, and perhaps even spiritually, impotent.

In an article for *Theatre Journal*, Rosemary Curb suggests that *Funnyhouse*, 'set in the central character's mind, portray[s] the elusive, almost timeless moment just before death, when horrifying images and past events replete with monotonous conversations kaleidoscopically flash throughout the memory and imagination of the protagonist'.[14] She argues that Kennedy's characters are 'mentally and emotionally torn between their real external Black selves and the glorious white selves which they imagine and desire'.[15] Claudia Barnett writes in *Modern Drama*, 'Sarah transforms her world into a house of mirrors where she watches herself in the glass; she becomes an outsider observing her life.'[16]

Funnyhouse of a Negro is a very visual play – the colours of the play are primarily white, black and red (appearing usually as blood), and hair figures strongly as a racial marker and a site of anxiety, often ripped out of the characters' heads in patches. In the opening scene of the play, The Duchess and Queen Victoria appear looking exactly alike, dressed in a cheap white satin with white headpieces with 'a headful of wild kinky hair' (p. 3) and nets that fall over their faces. They are covered in masks of an alabaster whitish yellow with high cheekbones, eyes that seem gouged out of their heads, a full red mouth, and a head of frizzy hair. They are obviously not characters in the realistic sense but nightmarish symbols, conflations of racial identity in Sarah's mind, condensed and displaced.

Sarah's sense of her own identity is so conflicted, torn between images of whiteness as good and blackness as 'evil' (p. 5), that it leads to her self-destruction, culminating in suicide. Her psychic experience of annihilation is completed in the physical act of death. For Sarah, the ideal American image of blackness is two-dimensional, 'pallid like Negroes on the covers of American Negro magazines; soulless, educated and irreligious' (p. 5). Her identity as a black woman becomes a non-identity, as she seeks to 'possess no moral value, particularly value as to [her] being' (p. 5). Already erased and invisible, Sarah repeatedly declares that she 'want[s] not to be' (p. 5). The syntax of this recurrent phrase is interesting in its emphasis on the affirmation of desire; Sarah does not say 'I don't want to be', but rather 'I want not to be', a very different declaration. She wants, she desires, but what she wants is negation, the physical negation that would correspond to the social, psychic and emotional negation of blackness in America and offer her a sense of wholeness or completeness, however empty.

In *A Movie Star Has to Star in Black and White*, Kennedy similarly uses highly poetic, symbolic language and images to examine the complexities of identity as unstable. The central character, Clara, is refracted in various 'selves', movie stars who are both themselves and the characters they play in particular black and white films of the 1940s and 1950s, and 'All the colors [in the play] are shades of black and white'.[17] As Kennedy notes in the stage directions, Clara's 'movie stars speak for her', she 'lets her movie stars star in her life' (p. 87). The lines between reality and Hollywood films, autobiography and fiction, are self-consciously blurred in this play. Jean Peters, speaking for Clara, also speaks for Kennedy when she describes images and lines from her plays *The Owl Answers* and *A Lesson in Dead Language*. Moreover, *Movie Star* directly includes autobiographical elements of Kennedy's family life, such as the play's immediate context, her visit home in 1963 to see her brother in the hospital after a car accident left him paralysed. In Kennedy's plays, the line between acting and being dissolves, and identification becomes multiple and layered. Clara's identification with the white movie icons of black and white films is an ironic one, as the glamour of Hollywood is an American institution that excludes her as a black woman. Kolin cites Suzan-Lori Parks's comment that Kennedy's plays epitomise the great tragedy of 'fall[ing] in love with something that didn't include you'.[18]

Kennedy's focus on the fragmentation of identity/identifications experienced by cultural 'others' had a tremendous influence on the black women playwrights who followed her. In 1975, Ntozake Shange's 'choreopoem', *for colored girls who have considered suicide/when the rainbow is enuf*, was workshopped at Woodie King's New Federal Theatre of the Henry Street Settlement on the Lower East Side, and was later produced by Joseph Papp at the Public Theater, eventually reaching Broadway in 1976. *for colored girls* broke with dramatic convention altogether, fusing a series of poetic vignettes, the 'words of a young black girl's growing up, her triumphs and errors, our struggle to become all that is forbidden by our environment, all that is forfeited by our gender, all that we have forgotten'.[19] This dramatic experiment, a mixture of poetry, dance and music, was a revolution in both form and content, dismantling linguistic structure, eschewing conventional spelling, capitalisation and grammar (especially evident, of course, in the published edition) in order to resist the established power structures in favour of a freer mode of expression. It begins with seven women who 'run onto the stage', each wearing a particular colour, and 'freeze in postures of distress' (p. 3) before beginning their poetic monologues. The black woman's experience of fragmentation in America – 'she's half-notes scattered' (p. 5) – is echoed by her sense of alienation, always on the 'outside' of cities like Chicago, Detroit, Houston, Baltimore, San Francisco, Manhattan, St Louis (p. 6). A performance by and for the African-American woman at a time when she was marginalised by even African-American revolutions in the arts, Shange's choreopoem emphasised empowerment, self-determination and individuality for women who 'have moved to the ends of their own rainbows' (p. 6).

Dealing with the contradictions of love and sex, growing up female and black in a society that not only censors behaviour and action but instils a sense of self-censorship for thought and feeling, Shange's work celebrates the moments when the black woman can '[become] herself' (p. 34) rather than accept the false choices and categories that are offered to her: 'beau gotta shoutin again how he wanted to marry her / & waz she always gonna be a whore / or did she wanna husband' (p. 58). Like Kennedy's *Funnyhouse of a Negro*, Shange's choreopoem deals with the suicidal impulse 'not to be', the pressure to erase the self in a society where one does not seem to count: 'i wanted to jump up outta my bones / & be done wit myself' (p. 63). Unlike Kennedy's play, however, *for colored girls* ends not with suicide, but on a note of self-acceptance and strength: 'the holiness of myself released . . . i found god in myself & i loved her / i loved her fiercely' (p. 63).

The legacy left by Kennedy and Shange and their revolutions in dramatic form strongly influenced the work of the next generation of black women playwrights such as Suzan-Lori Parks. A Pulitzer Prize for Drama winner in 2002 for *Top Dog/Underdog*, a play about family identity and the struggles of African-American life, Parks is also best known for *The Death of the Last Black Man in the Whole Entire World* (1990) and *The America Play* (1994). Her other plays include *Betting on the Dust Commander* (1987), *Venus* (1995) and

Imperceptible Mutabilities in the Third Kingdom (1989), which won Obie awards, *In the Blood* (1999) and *Fucking A* (2000) – both a retelling of Nathaniel Hawthorne's 1850 novel, *The Scarlet Letter* – and in 1996 she wrote the screenplay for Spike Lee's film *Girl 6*.

The America Play and *The Death of the Last Black Man in the Whole Entire World* are both highly anti-realistic in structure, resisting causal plot and relying on language that is playful and overdetermined. In other words, Parks's language is layered, multiple, recalling several meanings at once that are both contradictory and compatible. *The America Play* focuses on history, particularly the founding mythologies of American history and our sense of origins and meaning as 'The Great Hole of History', simultaneously a 'hole' (with its sense of absence and loss) and a 'whole', a coherent image of historical cohesiveness – 'Made-up and historical'.[20] The 'Hole is our inheritance of sorts' (p. 1157). The central character of Act I, 'The Foundling Father as Abraham Lincoln', appears as an African-American man who tells of one who is not the 'Great Man' but a 'Lesser Known' with 'several beards which he carried around in a box. The beards were his although he himself had not grown them on his face' (p. 1149). Like history, identity does not belong to us; it is not fixed and stable, but a series of costumed performances that depend upon 'fakin' (p. 1155). History in *The America Play* is seen as something that is simultaneously excavated and performed, ultimately malleable and incomplete, as the characters work on (re)imagining our founding myths.

The Death of the Last Black Man in the Whole Entire World similarly addresses the complexities of identity in the context of history, along with the erasure of African-American subjectivity. Written in vernacular and highly symbolic, *The Death of the Last Black Man in the Whole Entire World* opens with archetypal characters, 'Black Man with Watermelon' and 'Black Woman with Fried Drumstick', surrounded by figures from literature and mythology: Bigger Thomas from *Native Son*, who appears as 'And Bigger and Bigger and Bigger', as well as 'Ham' (recalling 'Ham Bone'), 'Before Columbus', 'Old Man River Jordan' and 'Queen-then-Pharaoh Hatshepsut'. Other characters include embodiments of food symbolically associated with African-American life, such as

'Lots of Grease and Lots of Pork', and a ubiquitous source of cultural identity within the contemporary American imagination, 'Voice on thuh Tee V'. The 'Black Man' repeatedly dies metaphorical deaths, as he is hanged over and over again, only to be resurrected each time.

The marker of existence in this play is clearly material, rooted in testimony of language: 'You should write it down because if you dont [sic] write it down then they will come along and tell the future that we did not exist.'[21] The character 'Black Man with Watermelon' explains that his 'text was writ in water' (p. 1624), and 'And Bigger and Bigger and Bigger' laments, 'I would like tuh fit in back in thuh storybook from which I camed [. . .] I am grown too big for thuh word thats me' (p. 1624). The malleability of the 'facts' of history emerges as the 'Black Man' reminds us of when 'thuh worl usta be roun' in a time 'Before Columbus' (p. 1618). The history of slavery and the civil rights movement is enacted through archetypal images and dialogue, as the play's black 'Everyman' and 'Everywoman' repeatedly insist on a place in history, asking to be 'remembered'.

Perhaps the most commercially successful of American black playwrights to date has been August Wilson, whose dramatic style has remained essentially realistic in comparison to the fragmented imagery of Baraka, Kennedy, Shange or Parks. Yet while Wilson's plays rely mostly on realistic narrative and plot, their structure is clearly influenced by musical rhythms, particularly the blues, and is rooted in his youthful vocation as a poet, most evident in the dialogue of his very early plays. In 1968, during the height of the Black Power movement, Wilson and his friend Rob Penny co-founded the Black Horizons Theatre in Pittsburgh 'with the idea of using the theatre to politicize the community, or, as we said in those days, to raise the consciousness of the people'.[22] But Wilson's plays are not primarily political: 'I don't write particularly to effect social change,' he said in a 1999 interview:

I believe writing can do that, but that's not why I write. I work as an artist. All art is political in the sense that it serves someone's politics. Here in America whites have a particular view of blacks. I think my plays offer them a different way to look at black Americans.[23]

Wilson's main contribution to the American theatre is his cycle of ten plays about African-American life, each chronicling a different decade of the twentieth century, called *The Pittsburgh Cycle*. Nine of the plays are set in Pittsburgh, with one, *Ma Rainey's Black Bottom*, set in Chicago. They were written over a period of twenty-three years and are here listed in order of the decade which they depict (beginning with 1900): *Gem of the Ocean* (2003), *Joe Turner's Come and Gone* (1986), *Ma Rainey's Black Bottom* (1984), *The Piano Lesson* (1987), *Seven Guitars* (1995), *Fences* (1985), *Two Trains Running* (1990), *Jitney* (1982), *King Hedley II* (1999) and *Radio Golf* (2005). Two of these works, *Fences* and *The Piano Lesson*, won the Pulitzer Prize for Best Play. Wilson is the also the recipient of numerous theatre awards, including several New York Drama Critics Circle Awards, Great Britain's Oliver Award for *Jitney*, and a Tony Award for *Fences*, his most popular play.

Like most of Wilson's plays, *Fences* was directed by Lloyd Richards, who also directed the original 1959 production of Lorraine Hansberry's *A Raisin in the Sun*, the first play by a black woman to reach Broadway. Often compared to Arthur Miller's *Death of a Salesman*, *Fences* chronicles the life of Troy Maxson and his family during the 1950s, exploring an African-American family's search for the American dream. Troy is a former Negro League baseball star who now works as a trash collector and supports his family. His two sons, Cory and Lyons, are growing up in a world very different from Troy's. They don't necessarily share their father's values or his views on life and success, leading to misunderstanding and conflict. Troy's loyal wife Rose is trying to hold on to a sense of stability and keep her family together, and his brother Gabriel, who was injured in the Second World War and collects government assistance, lives with them, giving Troy his welfare cheque to assist with expenses. Gabriel has a metal plate implanted in his head and consequently experiences delusions that sometimes also qualify as insight. He believes that he is the Angel Gabriel, a role that becomes significant at Troy's funeral the end of the play, when Gabriel blows his trumpet to 'tell St. Peter to open the gates' of heaven.[24] This symbolic moment, along with flashback scenes throughout the play, is strikingly anti-realistic in an otherwise essentially realistic play; the opening of the gates does not

Figure 3.3 Caesar (Gregory Wallace, centre) explains to Aunt Ester's maid, Black Mary (Roslyn Ruff), and Solly (Steven Anthony Jones) how he became the man he is, in the American Conservatory Theater's 2006 production of August Wilson's *Gem of the Ocean*. (Source: American Conservatory Theater.)

happen only in Gabriel's 'head', but occurs on the stage, as expressed in the stage directions: 'The gates of heaven stand open as wide as God's closet' (p. 1535).

The title of the play is both literal and metaphoric. Troy wants his son Cory to help him finish building the fence around their house, and as the play opens the fence appears partially built, with timber and other fence-building equipment set off to the side of the stage. But the image of the fence resonates throughout the play, and Troy's need to build fences with his son stands for his desire to build a stronger father–son relationship as well. In addition, the metaphorical 'white picket fence' symbolises the idealism and stability of the American dream, a dream Troy steadfastly pursues in his insistence that the traditional values of land ownership, a steady pay-packet and responsibility are the duty of a man and represent the right 'dream', taking precedence over any dreams his sons may wish to pursue. Rose, who realises that her husband is involved with another woman, wants the fence built to hold her family together, and for her it symbolises protection as she sings the hymns that comfort her: 'Jesus, be a fence around me every day' (p. 1511). Troy, on the other hand, sees the fence in terms of shutting out the outside world and its impending changes that were taking place after the Second World War, even as he continues to feel 'fenced in', limited by the social structures of American industrial capitalism. Rose tells Troy, 'The world's changing around you and you can't even see it' (p. 1518), and Troy's friend Bono explains, 'Some people build fences to keep people out . . . and other people build fences to keep people in' (p. 1524). Troy's extramarital affair allows him to experience another identity, 'a different understanding' about himself so that he can 'be a different man' and 'get away from the pressures and problems' of domestic life (p. 1526). His affair, however, ultimately leads only to more responsibility – pregnancy and the birth of a child whose mother dies while giving birth, so that he and Rose go on to raise the child together as their own.

As a former baseball player who was denied a professional career because he was black, Troy is suspicious of the intangible promises of dreams in a racist America. He sees baseball as a metaphor for life's struggles, and '[d]eath ain't nothing but a fastball on the outside corner' (p. 1508). Bono attests to Troy's talent – 'Ain't but two men ever played baseball as good as you. That's Babe Ruth and Josh Gibson' – but Troy scoffs: 'What it ever get me? Ain't got a pot to piss in or a window to throw it out of' (p. 1507). Even though 'times have changed a lot since then' and '[t]hey got a lot of colored baseball players now' (p. 1507), Troy refuses to accept that sports could offer viable opportunities for African-Americans. When Cory is recruited for a college football scholarship, Troy dismisses the offer and wants his son to keep his steady job at the supermarket. Troy's attitude is similar towards his thirty-four-year-old son by another marriage, Lyons, who works as a musician (when he does work), and often comes to Troy to borrow money. Lyons refuses to pursue a steady job, as he 'don't wanna be punching nobody's time clock' (p. 1510).

Despite the stability and steady income that Troy's job offers, both his sons want bigger dreams, as is the American way, often making Troy feel dismissed and discarded by both American society and his own family, like he 'don't count' (p. 1531). With a limited education – Troy 'can't read' (p. 1528) – and negative experiences with the possibilities offered to African-Americans, Troy doesn't feel entitled to dream, and doesn't want his sons to be similarly disappointed. On the other hand, Troy is not completely passive about his place in society; the play opens with a discussion of his union petition for blacks to be able to drive the rubbish trucks. Dissatisfied with limited opportunities for African-Americans at his company, he can separate which limitations are practical and which are racially motivated. He takes a bold step by approaching his boss to ask: 'Why you got the white mens driving and the colored lifting? [. . .] [W]hat's the matter, don't I count? You think only white fellows got sense enough to drive a truck. That ain't no paper job! Hell, anybody can drive a truck' (p. 1505). Even within the oppressive social structures presented to him, Troy wants recognition of his skills and his humanity; he needs to 'count'.

Wilson died of liver cancer on 3 October 2005 at the age of 60. On 16 October 2005, the Virginia Theatre in New York's Broadway theatre district was renamed the August Wilson Theatre in his honour, the first Broadway theatre to be named after an African-American. Yet despite the success of African-American playwrights since the 1960s, Wilson reminded us in a 1997 interview for *Neworld Renaissance: A Multicultural Magazine of the Arts* that the cultural divide still exists: 'There are literally hundreds of playwrights, let's say there's five hundred Black playwrights. And there's one Black theater [Crossroads Theater] of the 66 [members of the] League of Resident Theaters . . .'[25] With so few opportunities still for 'legitimate', mainstream black drama, African-Americans at the close of the twentieth century began to move beyond the boundaries of strict definitions of what constituted theatre, highlighting other modes of African-American cultural expression, such as hip hop/rap.[26] Hip hop performance can be seen as a postmodern form of drama that draws on a long tradition of African-American performance – incorporating, revising and recreating as it sees fit to serve more current social needs.

In her 1999 *Sourcebook of African-American Performance*, Annemarie Bean asks readers to 'move beyond and between the limited vision with which African-American performance has been considered thus far', and she 'embraces the vision that African-American performance has a history based in continuum, not renaissances'.[27] Hip hop/rap is clearly part of this continuum of African-American performance. Hip hop as style of expression did not arise in a cultural vacuum outside of the tradition of theatre, and it is only one of the more recent performative genres of African-American cultural expression. It has received so much attention over other theatrical art forms because it has managed to achieve mainstream popularity and generate capital as a multi-billion dollar industry. The rise of highly dramatic black art forms such as step shows or 'stepping' in the 1940s and 1950s and the growth of hip hop/rap performance on the streets of New York City during the 1970s developed in direct reaction to the need for social expression that was suppressed in more legitimate and con-servative theatre circles.[28] Both step shows and hip hop draw on African-American folk traditions and the personal and social tensions of black communities to create art forms which express these dramatic tensions and explore the contradictions of identity.

On 14 April 1998, Ice Cube appeared on the Charlie Rose show as a rapper, actor and director of his currently running film, *The Player's Club*. His statement that I quoted at the beginning of this chapter on what it means to be 'American' locates the foundation of American identity not only in what is conventionally seen as natural and healthy competition within the system of commod-ity capitalism, but in the proud display of one's capital – the 'flaunt-ing' or performance of ownership, wealth and material success. Reasserting Chuck D's well-publicised position that the culture of hip hop allows black artists to 'use rap as our CNN' – a medium which fosters social communication in the absence of formal net-works – Ice Cube reminds us that this communication has long included not just young African-Americans but 'even white' kids – any American youth who identifies with the culture of hip hop – and that 'It's done in a storytelling, theatrical way'.[29]

In response to a question as to whether or not rap bears any 'social message', Ice Cube was careful to make a distinction between the occasions when rappers were 'just having fun' and the times when they were performing a more serious 'social message'. His distinction between informal 'play' and more formal 'message', he argued, was apparent to the kids who could 'tell the difference' even when their parents could not. He defended rap music's account-ability for what is often seen as violent lyrics by comparing the violence of rap to the violence of film representation, '[i]n movies like *Terminator* and *Heat*,' for example, 'where the violence is *visually* represented'. Ice Cube's defence implies that, similar to the violence in films, the linguistic violence in rap music should be taken not as reality but as *representation* – performance, play and perhaps even social message all at the same time – a 'theatrical' rather than a supposedly objective or mimetic 'CNN' – and that the performance should not be confused with the performer.

The relationships that Ice Cube posits among hip hop culture, theatrical performance and film focus on the unique subjectivity of rap *as* performance and a keen awareness of 'being seen'. This awareness, evident in the music, films and interviews of rappers such as Ice Cube, Dr Dre, and the late Tupac Shakur and Biggie Smallz (a.k.a. the Notorious BIG) grants these artists, as well as many others, a powerful place in the phenomenon of hip hop culture – in this case, more specifically 'gansta rap' or 'reality rap' – as self-conscious performers of the complexities and commodifi-cations of black male identity in America. Tupac, for example, with revealing album titles such as *All Eyez on Me* (1996) and *Me Against the World* (1995), clearly exhibits this self-consciousness of the theatrical performer as well as an awareness of American culture's capitalist focus on individualism and self-reliance. In his book *Hip Hop America* (1998), Nelson George observes that Tupac 'spoke with an actor's urgency and an actor's sense of drama', and reminds us of the rapper's theatrical training in high school as well as his career in Hollywood film (Ice Cube, of course, has likewise had a very successful acting career in films such as *Boyz in the Hood* and *The Player's Club*). George speaks of Biggie in a similarly theatrical manner, noting the rap star's sense of costumed performance, as he 'covered himself in layers of expensive clothing and the regal air that led him to be dubbed the "King of New York" after the '90s gangsta film'.[30]

In the song 'AmeriKKKa's Most Wanted' from the CD of the same title (1990), Ice Cube raps about how he used to get away with stealing while he was 'robbin [his] own kind' in a world where 'it's all about survival of the fittest,' but 'when he start robbin the white folks,' the police more aggressively hunted him down and now he's 'in the pen wit the soap-on-a-roap'. He describes theft as 'the American way', and brags of his former ability to tauntingly elude the police: 'I'm slick as slippery . . . I'm the nigga that flaunt it.'

Ice Cube's pride in 'flaunting', both on 'AmeriKKKa's Most Wanted' and in his Charlie Rose interview, is characteristic of the tendency in hip hop to boldly display signifiers of masculine power and wealth. Gold jewellery, expensive cars, guns and women as objects of sexual conquest and pleasure have always been central to the patriarchal, capitalist American dream. Mainstream America's hypocrisy resides in masking these signifiers in favour of a more muted puritanical performance which sees display as gaudy. The American dream dictates that one can and should obtain power and wealth, and that others must know that one has acquired these, but the signifiers of power and wealth – Ivy League college degrees, exorbitantly priced couture clothing, and 'luxury' cars, for example – must not be ostentatious, must not be 'flaunted'. One's success must be veiled in earth-tone colours, controlled hair styles and 'simple', 'elegant' jewellery from Tiffany's.

Disenfranchised black men, however, excluded both from the wealth and the knowledge of the signifiers employed by white America's most entitled groups, have no patience for these hypocrisies. These black men perform wealth in hip hop culture in ways that highlight their having 'made it' in mainstream America. Their performances of success 'ostentatiously' oppose the elitist cultural display codes, patently resisting the hegemonic dictates of the mainstream.

The celebration of immediate wealth and pleasure in videos that show copious gold jewellery, bright colours, fast cars and scantily dressed women as objects is a complex comment on the contradictions of the American dream for black men. And, to make matters more interesting, amid the excessive displays there is also often a self-conscious acknowledgement that the urban rappers have not lost their 'roots'. Dr Dre's video *Been There Done That* (1996), for instance, performs several scenes where he exhibits massive wealth (planes, champagne, money, tuxedos), but at the end of the video we find that the whole scene has been a dream. Dre wakes up poor in a house in the 'hood. Similarly, the displays of black masculine power and violence in much of hip hop can be read both as a window into the 'reality' of the pressures of economically disenfranchised urban black Americans and as a conscious unveiling of what these rappers see as the hypocrisies of the capitalist, patriarchal values of the mainstream American dream.

While economically excluded white Americans resist this restrictive discourse of style as well (the 2000 film *Erin Brockovich* and Country & Western music/videos are examples), often these resistances are not as ironic or as obviously aggressive as the challenges enacted by hip hop artists (gold chains, gold teeth, etc.). George reads the hypocrisy of the American dream in terms of hip hop culture, reminding us that 'the values that underpin so much hip hop – materialism, brand consciousness, gun iconography, anti-intellectualism' – and to this I would add misogyny – 'are very much byproducts of the larger American culture'.[31]

Although the category of 'gangsta rap' is a suspect one, this style of the late 1980s and 1990s was especially representative of a new form of subversive postmodern drama, precisely because the reductiveness of this label illustrates that it has been the most misunderstood by the American public at large, the most easily targeted by political conservatives, and yet is arguably the most 'theatrical' style of rap in terms of black masculine performativity within commodity capitalism and dominant power structures. In gangsta rap's deliberately ironic performance of 'the real', there is a postmodern gesture using contradictory constructions of black male identity in American culture in order to undermine them and expose their contradictions. Black America has always seen these contradictions, and gangsta rappers have used the culture of hip hop to comment on the place of black masculinity in the American value system, as well as to imagine alternative spaces where the power structures may be redefined.

Gangsta rap's comfortable contradiction between self-conscious *role-playing* (or 'performance') in its aggressive display of blackness, masculinity, wealth or subjectivity, and the centrality of *authenticity* (or 'keeping it real'), is a point of intersection that makes its subversion keenly postmodern, and therefore difficult to locate and contain. The work of rappers as diverse as NWA, Dr Dre, Snoop

Doggy Dogg, Easy E and Rakim, as well as Tupac, Biggie and Ice Cube has been tagged gangsta rap on one occasion or another, glossing over genuine differences in style, subject matter and artistic sophistication.

George argues that hip hop is a postmodern art 'in that it shamelessly raids older forms of pop culture – kung fu movies, chitlin' circuit comedy, '70s funk, and other equally disparate sources – and reshapes the material to fit the personality of an individual artist and the taste of the times'.[32] The 'sampling' in rap recordings can be seen as simultaneously acknowledging a debt to African-American music, history and culture (MC Hammer's sampling of Rick James's 'Superfreak' in 'U Can't Touch This' (1990) is one of the most notable examples) and incorporating culture(s) which have been closed off to African-Americans. Rap sampling is an appropriation of the past in postmodern terms – rather than a shameless theft or blatant lack of originality, as is often argued.

The self-conscious awareness of the construction of identity as role-playing is also key to understanding hip hop as a form of postmodern drama. Rappers consciously take on roles. They almost never use their birth names in their artistic lives. Instead, they invent theatrical names, simultaneously inhabiting 'characters' (there is even one rapper who calls himself 'Drama') and reinventing their selves in the tradition of African-American renaming as an empowering gesture that overcomes the disability inherent in accepting 'slave names'. Renaming, in the context of hip hop, signifies both the inhabiting of a fictional character and, at the same time, an acknowledgement that historically even 'real' black identity is a fiction. Rappers call for a reappropriation of the self. Ironically, Tupac Shakur, who did not change his name, perfectly exemplifies this theory. Tupac had no need to change his name, as he was already given a non-slave name signifying his African roots by his mother, Afeni Shakur, a notable revolutionary in her own right. By contrast, artists such as Sean Combs (Puff Daddy, Puffy, P-Diddy), Christopher Wallace (Notorious B.I.G. or Biggie), and O'Shea Jackson (Ice Cube) created names for themselves in order to consciously resist the identities imposed on them by white, mainstream culture.

Gangsta rap can ultimately be seen as redefining American identity by revealing identity and the power relations it generates not as something fixed in essentialist concepts such as race and gender, but as a performance which, like all things American, can be commodified and sold as 'truth'. At the same time, however, gangsta rap problematises this paradigm by highlighting – rather than erasing – the power of race in the process of (re)constructing identity, placing on centre stage and making visible what has traditionally been marginalised, hidden and dismissed as 'savage' and 'unruly'.

One of the central reasons that hip hop artists, music and culture as a whole have been criticised as 'dangerous' lies in the power of the performing body to subvert traditional, hence safe, modes of representation in America, even as it embraces the commodity capitalism of the American dream, 'flaunting' wealth and bourgeois definitions of success. In hip hop's postmodern complexity of performance (of race, of gender, of sexuality, and finally of capitalist America) lies the chaotic force that threatens to overthrow conservative power relations while simultaneously working within the system of commodity capitalism. As Ice Cube pointed out, rapping is both 'just having fun' and delivering a 'social message', and hence, like the most effective kind of performance, confuses the boundaries between 'innocent' entertainment and revolutionary impulse.[33] This kind of subversive theatrical performance can be seen as an exposition of the black male rap artist as the disobedient 'other' of white patriarchal control. That is precisely where the social 'danger' of rap lies.

Therefore, rather than merely reporting the 'truth' of black culture as an alternative CNN (and let us keep in mind, of course, that CNN is a kind of performance in and of itself), rap is self-consciously involved in the tricky business of postmodern representation, signaling the emergence of a new, socially relevant yet simultaneously 'playful' American drama.

The theatrical power of rap has not been lost on playwrights, many of whom have incorporated rap's poetic style and themes. As early as 1980 Glenn Wright and Raul Santiago Sebazco's *The Crime* was performed entirely in rap. *The Crime* tells the story of a 'Mugger' and his 'Victim' who, during the course of a violent encounter, realise they are from the same neighbourhood and had been friends in school. It was originally developed with disenfranchised Lower East Side youth at New York's Nuyorican Poets Cafe.

It premiered at Princeton University to an enthusiastic audience, heralding the emergence and growing popularity of hip hop culture. *The Crime* begins with the Mugger rapping about 'aggrivation . . . humiliation . . . being treated like an idiot . . . being looked upon like some fool . . . even though you've been through fourteen years of school' and lamenting the lack of job prospects.[34] The Mugger explains his life of crime as a result of racism and the lack of legitimate opportunities for success – a convincing position at the end of the economically depressed 1970s and the start of the Reagan administration. The short play/rap/performance presents, on one level, an obvious and didactic moral. At the same time, however, it resists simplification by playing with reified stereotypes and shattering the spectator's sense of 'them' and 'us'.

Similarly, Ishmael Reed's *The Preacher and the Rapper*, presented in the mid-1990s (during the heyday of gangsta rap) at the Nuyorican Poets Cafe, is a commentary on the hypocrisy of the institutions that wield power and the misunderstandings surrounding innovative art forms.[35] It jumps back and forth between conventional dialogue and rapping. More recently, Danny Hoch's one-man show, *Jails, Hospitals, and Hip Hop* (1998), uses rap to highlight the pervasive influence and importance of hip hop in both black and white American youth culture.[36] Hoch, a white man who grew up in a multiethnic Brooklyn neighbourhood, performs character sketches that explore the ironies of representation as he experiments with the relationship of language to character.

In his introduction to *Colored Contradictions*, an anthology of contemporary African-American plays, Harry J. Elam, Jr discusses the 'concurrent and decidedly variant social, political, and economic concerns facing black America'. Elam argues that for African-Americans, 'the contemporary social and cultural condition is one of paradox, complexity, despair, and contradiction'.[37] The plays in Elam's collection deal with stereotypes that intersect race, gender, sexuality and history. Plays in this mode include Carlyle Brown's *The Little Tommy Parker Celebrated Colored Minstrel Show* (1991), Keith Antar Mason's *for black boys who have considered homicide when the streets were too much* (1991), Pomo Afro Homos's *Fierce Love* (1991), Robert Alexander's *I Ain't Yo' Uncle: The New Jack Revisionist* Uncle Tom's Cabin

(1992), and Breena Clarke and Glenda Dickerson's *Re/membering Aunt Jemima: A Menstrual Show* (1992). Like the hip hop artists I have mentioned, the plays in *Colored Contradictions* struggle to uncover (recover?) a new space where more inclusive and self-determining African-American/American identities may be imagined and enacted.

In *I Ain't Yo' Uncle*, Alexander uses hip hop to signify youthful rebellion and resistance. Harriet Beecher Stowe is put on trial for creating and perpetuating black stereotypes in *Uncle Tom's Cabin*. One of the novel's central characters, Topsy, is reconfigured as a slave who embraces hip hop/rap culture. She performs the contradictions of her own empowered identity while ironically rapping on command for her new 'owner', Augustine St Clare, who exclaims that he 'couldn't resist buying her. I thought she was a rather funny specimen on the Jim Crow line. (Smothering a laugh).'[38] In the second act, Topsy 'folds her arms like a 20th-century rapper' and does a 'breakdown dance' after she finishes rapping about her superior ability to pick cotton and her efficient usefulness as a slave:

> I can pick as much cotton as any man
> And bag it all up one hand
> I can milk all you cows 'fore the sun comes up
> And fit all my belongings in to a little tin cup
> No job is too big, no job is too small
> I'm Topsy Turvy, I can do it all. Word. (p. 43)

Topsy's next rap in Act II is longer, violently revolutionary, more concerned with race than gender, and louder (it is presented in capital letters):

I'M TOPSY TURVY I'M WICKED AND I'M BLACK.
ALL YOU YELLOW-ASS NIGGERS BETTER WATCH
   YOUR BACK.
I'M WICKED AND I'M SO SO MEAN.
I'M THE BADDEST BLACK NIGGER YOU EVER SEEN.
[. . .]
I AIN'T SPEAKING FOR THE HOUSE NIGGER
I'M TALKING FOR THE BLACK RACE

THE ONE'S OUT SWEATIN' IN THE FIELD AND FOR
  WHAT
SO A KNOW-NOTHIN' PECKERWOOD CAN SIT ON
  HIS BUTT
I DON'T CARE IF ALL THE WHITEYS DIED TODAY
WHITE PEOPLE ALWAYS GOT SOMETHIN' STUPID
  TO SAY
[. . .]
BUT REMEMBER, I'M TOPSY, I'M WICKED AND I'M
  BLACK
I STAND HERE WITH MY EVIL ASS READY TO
  ATTACK
I KEEP YELLING AND 'BELLING LIKE I DO IT
'CAUSE THAT'S THE ONLY WAY I KNOW TO GET
  THROUGH IT. (pp. 49–50)

Proclaiming her empowered sense of self deriving from her 'blackness', Topsy's second rap is aggressively threatening. However, the
contradiction between her traditional personality (as the 'good
colored girl') and the violent rapper is not uncharacteristic of her as
envisioned by Alexander. Topsy's character functions as a 'person'
existing within the tradition of realism, but also as a postmodern
construction, someone capable of revising (his)her story/history.
Topsy is fluid, conflicted and changeable. Even her name, 'Topsy
Turvy', suggests a turning, a contradiction.

By the end of the play, Topsy appears dressed and adopting the
style, dance and lyrics of a rapper. Just as the play is ending, Topsy
confronts the spectators aggressively, addressing them in Brechtian
fashion: 'Any volunteers to take Topsy? Ya'll think she come from
nowhere? Do ya 'spects she just growed?' (pp. 89–90). bell hooks
discusses this historically rebellious aspect of African-American
performance, and points out that '[a]ll performance practice has,
for African-Americans, been central to the process of decoloniza-
tion in white supremacist capitalist patriarchy' and has historically
been important because 'it created a cultural context where one
could transgress the boundaries of accepted speech, both in relationship to the dominant white culture, and to the decorum of
African-American cultural mores'.[39]

In *Race Matters* (1993), Cornel West asserts that 'people, especially degraded and oppressed people, are . . . hungry for identity, meaning, and self-worth'[40] in a culture where 'the implication is that only certain Americans can define what it means to be American – and the rest must simply "fit in" '.[41] It is this resistance to 'fitting into' a definition of American identity and a desire to expand it which the culture of hip hop continues to articulate through its music, videos and live concerts, exposing the contradictions implicit in American capitalist structures while simultaneously working within them.

NOTES

1. Amiri Baraka/LeRoi Jones, 'The Revolutionary Theatre', in *The Harcourt Brace Anthology of Drama*, 3rd edn, ed. W. B. Worthen (Orlando, FL: Harcourt, 2000), p. 1166.
2. Ibid. p. 1164.
3. Ibid. p. 1164.
4. Ibid. p. 1164.
5. Ibid. p. 1166.
6. LeRoi Jones, *Dutchman*, in *The Harcourt Brace Anthology of Drama*, p. 999. Subsequent references appear parenthetically in the text.
7. LeRoi Jones, *The Slave*, in *Dutchman and The Slave: Two Plays by LeRoi Jones* (New York: William Morrow and Company, 1964), p. 41. Subsequent references appear parenthetically in the text.
8. Ed Bullins, *Clara's Ole Man*, in *Five Plays by Ed Bullins* (New York: The Bobbs-Merrill Company, 1968), p. 280. Subsequent references appear parenthetically in the text.
9. Ed Bullins, *Goin' a Buffalo*, in *Five Plays by Ed Bullins*, p. 48. Subsequent references appear parenthetically in the text.
10. I discuss Mamet's *American Buffalo* in detail in Chapter 5.
11. Philip C. Kolin, *Understanding Adrienne Kennedy* (Columbia: University of South Carolina Press, 2005), p. 2.
12. Ibid. pp. 26–7.

13. Adrienne Kennedy, *Funnyhouse of a Negro*, in *Adrienne Kennedy in One Act* (Minneapolis: University of Minnesota Press, 1988), p. 4. Subsequent references appear parenthetically in the text.

14. Rosemary K. Curb, 'Fragmented selves in Adrienne Kennedy's *Funnyhouse of a Negro* and *The Owl Answers*', *Theatre Journal*, 32:2 (1980), 180.

15. Ibid. 180.

16. Claudia Barnett, 'A prison of object relations: Adrienne Kennedy's *Funnyhouse of a Negro*', *Modern Drama*, 40:3 (1997), 382.

17. Adrienne Kennedy, *A Movie Star Has to Star in Black and White*, in *Adrienne Kennedy in One Act*, p. 80. Subsequent references appear parenthetically in the text.

18. Suzan-Lori Parks, quoted in Kolin, *Understanding Adrienne Kennedy*, p. 16.

19. Ntozake Shange, *for colored girls who have considered suicide when the rainbow is enuf* (New York: Macmillan Publishing Company, 1977), p. xv. Subsequent references appear parenthetically in the text.

20. Suzan-Lori Parks, *The America Play*, in *The Harcourt Brace Anthology of Drama*, p. 1156. Subsequent references appear parenthetically in the text.

21. Suzan-Lori Parks, *The Death of the Last Black Man in the Whole Entire World*, in *The Bedford Introduction to Drama*, 4th edn, ed. Lee A. Jacobus (New York: Bedford/St Martin's, 2001), p. 1618. Subsequent references appear parenthetically in the text.

22. August Wilson, interviewed by Bonnie Lyons and George Plimpton, 'The art of theater no. 14', *The Paris Review*, 153 (Winter 1999), 4.

23. Ibid. p. 11.

24. August Wilson, *Fences*, in *The Bedford Introduction to Drama*, 3rd edn, ed. Lee A. Jacobus (Boston: Bedford Books, 1997), p. 1535. Subsequent references appear parenthetically in the text.

25. August Wilson, quoted in Ed Bullins, 'Black theatre 1998: a thirty-year look at black arts theatre,' in *A Sourcebook of*

African-American Performance, ed. Annemarie Bean (London: Routledge, 1999), pp. 11–12.

26. The terms 'hip hop' and 'rap' are often used interchangeably, but there is, in fact, a difference. In an article for *Time* (8 February 1999), rapper Chuck D. of Public Enemy fame distinguishes hip hop as 'the term for urban-based creativity and expression of culture', whereas rap 'is the style of rhythm-spoken words across a musical terrain' (p. 66). In other words, hip hop signifies the culture at large, which included the b-boys and b-girls (the break dancers and graffiti artists who emerged in New York City during the mid-1970s and early 1980s), as well as the fashion, commerce, film, television shows, music videos and the general 'style' that the culture embraces. Rap, on the other hand, is often seen as the more specific style of poetic or musical expression. In *Black Noise: Rap Music and Black Culture in Contemporary America* (Hanover, NH: University Press of New England, 1994), Tricia Rose explains rap music as a 'black cultural expression that prioritizes black voices from the margins of urban America. Rap music is a form of rhymed storytelling accompanied by highly rhythmic, electronically based music. It began in the mid-1970s in the South Bronx in New York City as a part of hip hop, an African-American and Afro-Caribbean youth culture composed of graffiti, breakdancing, and rap music' (p. 2). Bakari Kitwana, in *The Rap on Gangsta Rap: Who Run It? Gangsta Rap and Visions of Black Violence* (Chicago: Third World Press, 1994), makes a similar distinction (pp. 11–12). Still yet another distinction that has emerged defines hip hop music as the more progressive 'art', which has remained true to its cultural heritage, while much of what is labeled as rap is seen as a more commodified and mainstream product (see Kitwana, pp. 19–20, for example).

27. Annemarie Bean, 'Introduction', in *A Sourcebook of African-American Performance*, ed. Annemarie Bean (London: Routledge, 1999), pp. 1–2.

28. See Elizabeth C. Fine, 'Stepping, saluting, cracking, and freaking: the cultural politics of African-American step shows', in Bean, *Sourcebook*, p. 165. In her 1991 article, Fine describes the

lesser-known practice of stepping, or 'blocking', as a popular performance tradition among African-American fraternities and sororities that incorporates ritualised combinations of dancing, singing, chanting and speaking, drawing on African-American folk traditions and communication patterns as well as American popular culture.

29. Of course, hip hop has become a popular phenomenon around the world, especially in Europe and Japan. Since I am dealing specifically with how it creates and reflects African-American identity for Americans, however, redefining what it means to 'be' American in performance, I am only addressing its relevance to youth culture in the United States.

30. Nelson George, *Hip Hop America* (New York: Penguin, 1998), p. 48.

31. Ibid. p. xiii.

32. Ibid. p. viii.

33. In *Spectacular Vernaculars* (Albany: SUNY Press, 1995), Russell Potter similarly insists that '*play* – and not only in obvious forms, such as parody and satire – is potentially a powerful mode of resistance. Play can certainly be an idle distraction, but it can also be the mask for a potent mode of subversion, and indeed I argue in this book that hip-hop culture in particular, and African-American culture in general, is precisely such a form' (p. 2).

34. Glenn Wright and Raul Santiago Sebazco, *The Crime*, in *Action: The Nuyorican Poets Cafe Theater Festival*, ed. Miguel Algarin and Lois Griffith (New York: Touchstone, 1997), p. 284.

35. Ishmael Reed, *The Preacher and the Rapper*, in Algarin and Griffith, *Action*, pp. 258–83.

36. I address Danny Hoch's work in more detail in Chapter 8.

37. Harry J. Elam, Jr, 'Colored contradictions in the postmodern moment', Introduction to *Colored Contradictions: An Anthology of Contemporary African-American Plays*, ed. Harry J. Elam, Jr and Robert Alexander (New York: Plume, 1996), p. 1.

38. Robert Alexander, *I Ain't Yo' Uncle*, in Elam and Alexander, *Colored Contradictions*, p. 43. Subsequent references appear parenthetically in the text.

39. bell hooks, 'Performance practice as a site of opposition', in *Let's Get It On: The Politics of Black Performance*, ed. Catherine Ugwu (Seattle: Bay Press, 1995), p. 212.
40. Cornel West, *Race Matters* (New York: Vintage Books, 1994), p. 20.
41. Ibid. p. 7.

CHAPTER 4

Avant-Garde Theatre Groups: Revolutions in Performance

To express the extreme joy of being alive at a certain moment is practically impossible – and really worth trying.
                    Joseph Chaikin, Director of the Open Theater

Bluebeard: I never cease in my experimenting. My dream is to remake Man.
                    Charles Ludlum, *Bluebeard* (1970)

The cultural revolutions and social upheavals of the 1960s gave rise to an alternative kind of theatre that was more immediate and ephemeral than traditional drama, one that emphasised performance and the present moment rather than the stability of the authoritative text.[1] These performances, which were strongly influenced by the visual arts, were less interested in the language of a play as a means of direct, rational expression, and instead focused on the visual and physical aspect of a play's production. They resisted the economic pressures of Broadway and were more frequently produced in off- and off-off-Broadway venues, even in warehouses, abandoned buildings or in the performers' apartments. Regional theatres, beginning with the founding of the Guthrie Theatre in Minneapolis in 1963, were beginning to emerge throughout cities outside New York, marking a shift from the financial risks of lavish and expensive Broadway openings to the presentation of classical repertoire and touring productions of successful Broadway plays. With the establishment of the National Endowment for the Arts (NEA) in 1965, regional theatres began to receive federal subsidy, the first government support for theatre in the United States since funds for the Federal Theatre Project were discontinued in 1939. Broadway, with its focus on theatre for entertainment and profit, was quickly losing its status as the centre of new American drama, and emerging theatre groups with a social and political emphasis were gaining increasing attention during the 1960s, mainly in New York City.

These new groups were interested in creating theatre that rejected realism's boundaries between spectator and performer, as they typically broke the fourth wall and encouraged spontaneous encounters between audience members and actors. They emphasised defiant, individualistic behaviour, while simultaneously embracing the notion of theatre as community and public space. A primary focus on physical performance rather than on the sanctity of the play's written text, along with a celebration of sexuality and the performing body, was central to these productions. The spirit of collaboration, collective creation and improvisation dominated these groups, and often the entire company conceived a theatre piece, rejecting any distinctions among the work of performer, director, designer or playwright. Productions were presented in real time and place in an attempt to avoid what was seen as the mind-numbing illusions of realism, and instead encouraged the spectators and actors to unite in the present and effect social change. These avant-garde theatre groups used unconventional techniques to move beyond the superficiality of realistic representation in the theatre and access the more subtle and powerful effects of capitalism's social and economic pressures on American identity. Many of the theatrical events of the 1960s and 1970s occurred as 'happenings', performances or gatherings that, since the late 1950s, were presented as artistic events and often employed a variety of forms – music, dance, poetry, recitation and drama – in combination with one another. These events sometimes employed improvisational techniques and sought to include the audience, resisting the formal boundaries between audience and performers in an effort to create a spirit of communion.

In 1947, Judith Malina and Julian Beck founded the Living Theatre, with the idea of resurrecting poetic language in the theatre and dissolving the boundaries between theatre and life, performer and audience. Their productions sought to present experience beyond language, a communication of feelings and ideas beyond the rational. Strongly influenced by Brecht's epic theatre and Artaud's emphasis on theatre as a ritualistic celebration that broke the chains of 'civilised' repression and espoused the freedom of anarchy, the Living Theatre endured poverty, imprisonment, deportation and public scepticism in its mission to bring about spiritual, socio-economic and political revolution, eventually becoming one of the most important experimental theatre groups of the 1960s and 1970s. During the 1950s, the group was among the first in the United States to present works by innovative European playwrights such as Brecht and Jean Cocteau, and helped to originate the off-Broadway movement.

One of the most significant plays of the Living Theatre to blur this line between fiction and reality was their pivotal production in 1959 of Jack Gelber's *The Connection*, one of the first off-Broadway works to receive mainstream critical attention. The structure of *The Connection* is essentially that of a play-within-a-play, blurring the line between actor and character, and aggressively breaking the fourth wall separating audience and performer. As the audience enters the theatre, several 'heroin addicts', who, the producer explains, have agreed to come to the theatre and participate in a documentary film in exchange for a heroin 'fix', are hanging about the stage. The action of the play does not include a conventional or developed plot, but primarily consists of the addicts (and the audience) waiting for 'Cowboy' to arrive with the heroin. During the intermission the addicts solicit the audience for money, and in Act II Cowboy arrives and provides them with their promised fixes. The reaction of the unsuspecting spectators was to take the events of the play for real-life events, satisfying Malina and Beck's goal of eliciting an authentic and raw emotional reaction from the specta-tor, rather than the orchestrated emotion associated with realistic drama.

Among the Living Theatre's most significant works was a production of Brecht's *Man Is Man* (1962) that reflected the group's concerns about the loss of individual identity in an increas-ingly dehumanising society. Other major productions of the 1960s include *The Brig* (1963), *Mysteries and Smaller Pieces* (1964), *Antigone* (1967), *Frankenstein* (1968) and *Paradise Now* (1968). The company went on to win Obie Awards for *The Connection*, *The Brig* and *Frankenstein*. Kenneth H. Brown's *The Brig*, an anarchist view of conditions in a military prison that exposed the authoritarian nature of American society and the consequent master/slave dichotomy, was the Living Theatre's last production in New York before going into voluntary exile in Europe. From 1964 to 1968, the company primarily toured abroad. After returning to New York, the group produced their best-known play, *Paradise Now*, which was essentially a performance piece in the sense that it relied heavily on improvisation, physicality and spectacle. Therefore, like most of the performances discussed in this chapter, it has little impact as a written text, and any examination of the play's particular language would not be faithful to the spirit of the productions, which changed with each performance. The piece focused on non-violent revolutionary action in an anarchist society, and aimed to be a polit-ical and spiritual voyage for both the actors and the spectators that was necessary for political change. It resisted the repressions and restrictions imposed upon the individual by the state, and the actors infamously recited a list of social taboos, including nudity, as the performers simultaneously disrobed, leading to multiple arrests for indecent exposure. In fact, during the group's long history, arrests for nudity, simulation of sexual acts on stage, or other acts of 'indecency' were not uncommon. In *Gentlemen Callers*, Michael Paller reminds us that even in New York State, certainly one of the more progressive venues for theatre, since 1927 it had been illegal to produce plays 'depicting or dealing with the subject of sexual degeneracy, or sex perversion'. The penalties for breaking this law 'included the padlocking of the theatre where the play was produced'.[2]

After *Paradise Now*, the original group broke apart; Beck and Malina left the United States once again to tour with the remaining members in Brazil, eventually returning to New York to form a new version of the Living Theatre. With Julian Beck's death in 1985, Hanon Reznikov joined the Living Theatre as Malina's co-director, and it still survives and thrives today. In 2006 the company signed a ten-year lease on a theatre space in New York City's Lower East

Side, opening in 2007 with a new production of *The Brig*, which the group first presented in 1963 at its 14th Street and Sixth Avenue space. The group's indelible influence on American experimental theatre is ubiquitous, but its direct influence can most strongly be seen in former member Joseph Chaikin's Open Theater.

After working as an actor with the Living Theatre, Joseph Chaikin left in 1963 to help found one of the most influential experimental theatre groups in the United States, the Open Theater, which he went on to direct for its entire ten-year existence. Its early productions include the first plays to deal with the Vietnam War: Jean-Claude van Itallie's *America Hurrah*, a trilogy of short plays which premiered at the experimental downtown theatre La MaMa E.T.C. in New York in 1964 and went on to be produced at the off-Broadway Pocket Theatre in 1966, and Megan Terry's *Viet Rock* (1966), a piece inspired by 1966 newspaper headlines to become the very first rock musical and run for 62 performances. *America Hurrah* ran for 640 performances in New York and was heralded as a watershed play of the 1960s as the first major dramatic expression that dealt with the anti-war movement.

Figure 4.1 *America Hurrah* (motel section) by Jean-Claude van Itallie, 1965 production La MaMa E.T.C. Directed by Michael Kahn, designed by Robert Wilson. The play was later moved off-Broadway under the direction of Joseph Chaikin and Jacques Levy. (Source: The La MaMa Archive.)

The Open Theater began with a group of students who embraced acting teacher Nola Chilton's departures from Method acting, the style of acting which focused on developing the illusion of character as a 'real person' with a psychology and consistent personality. Instead, these students were interested in emphasising the presence of the *actor* and the actor's body, as opposed to the illusion of 'character'. In order to explore the artistic, political and social issues that they felt were central to avant-garde theatre, the group developed and employed various psycho-physical exercises to help the actor move beyond both the style of Method acting that dominated American realistic drama and the European absurdism that typified the avant-garde during the 1940s and 1950s. Under the direction of Chaikin, they used improvisational techniques and theatre exercises, such as Viola Spolin's 'theatre games' – exercises developed to help the actor focus and create freely in the moment as opposed to being blocked by the judgemental limitations of rational thinking.

The Open Theater's most popular exercises, transformations and sound and movement transfers (or exchanges) focused on collective creation and improvisation. Transformation exercises were a development of Spolin's 'games', and sought to liberate the actor from the restrictions of naturalistic consistency, as they changed age, sex, species, relationships, time and place. These exercises also trained actors to remain alert in the present moment, as they had to adjust to the other actors' shifts. Sound and movement transfers similarly worked counter to Method acting, which focuses on development from the inside out and relies on an actor's emotional engagement to create the physical character. Instead, sound and movement exercises worked from the outside in. One actor would perform repetitions of a simple gesture using both voice and body, then would approach another actor, who would attempt to copy the sound and gesture exactly. This second actor would then alter the sound and gesture, transfer them to a third actor, and so on. Variations of these exercises, in addition to many others that the Open Theater and Chaikin helped to develop, were used to discover emotional states that had not previously been part of the actors' experience, and have been widely appropriated as an indispensable part of actor training today.

Some of the Open Theater's most influential productions were *The Serpent* (1969), a non-linear, transformational performance piece which took Bible stories as its point of departure and incorporated contemporary political images from the assassinations of John F. Kennedy and Martin Luther King, *Terminal* (1969), which dealt with the universal human concerns surrounding death, and *The Mutation Show* (1971), which explored the mutability of people and objects in terms of how we negotiate our various potential selves in response to social circumstances until we are transformed into 'freaks'. The group's final piece, *Nightwalk* (1973), addressed the dichotomy of 'presence' versus 'absence' in the theatre, one of Chaikin's main concerns.

An undeniable force in the development of American contemporary theatre, the Open Theater went on to earn an international reputation after their London production of *American Hurrah* and four European tours between 1968 and 1973. Among his many achievements and awards, Chaikin was the recipient of six Obie awards, including the very first Lifetime Achievement Obie Award in 1977. After his work with the Open Theater, Chaikin continued to direct, write and act, and became one of the most important directors of the twentieth century. He was a close collaborator of Sam Shepard, and remained active in the theatre until his death in 2003.

A major influence on the Open Theater was Jerzy Grotowski's Theatre Laboratory in Poland, with its focus on the physical and vocal discipline needed for theatre work and its search for the particular elements of theatre as distinct from other artistic forms. Grotowski referred to his work as 'poor theatre' in order to distinguish it from the 'rich theatre' of the commercial stage, with its emphasis on expensive lighting, lavish costumes and elaborate settings. 'Poor' theatre was interested in the primary relationship between actor and audience above all other aspects of theatre, and explored the presence of the live actor rather than the fictional character, a focus also emphasised in the Living Theatre and one that became the premise of Chaikin's work with the Open Theater. The Theatre Laboratory, which began in 1959, relied on the reconception of existing texts, interpreting them broadly and completely reinventing them for Grotowski's productions. His most famous work, *Akropolis*, was first presented in 1962 and revised frequently from 1963 to 1975. It was an adaptation of a 1904 Polish drama by Stanislaw Wyspiański, reset in modern times with Auschwitz and the mass violence of the Holocaust as its theme.

Another reciprocal influence on the Open Theater was the Bread and Puppet Theater, which Peter Schumann founded in New York City in 1962 and moved to Vermont in 1970 to become Goddard College's theatre-in-residence. In 1974 the company relocated to Glover, Vermont, where it has remained active ever since, preferring to form troupes for a specific touring project rather than operate as a permanent company. Schumann, a German-born dancer, musician and sculptor, was able to blend these arts forms that sought expression beyond language together in his puppet theatre. Like many of the theatre groups discussed in this chapter, the work of the Bread and Puppet Theater protests the dehumanising effects of a capitalist, urban society on individual identity. Bread and Puppet is essentially street theatre, a type of theatre that offers spontaneous performances in outdoor public spaces free of charge, as it aims to bring theatre to the average person as opposed to a specific paying audience.

The Bread and Puppet events are often large outdoor celebrations, sometimes taking place over several days. These festivals feature larger-than-life puppets on stilts wearing oversized, expressive masks, singing, dancing and playing music, in combination with masked performers. The festivals generate a carnival-like atmosphere, sometimes with more than a hundred participants, and recall the spectacle of Punch and Judy shows, medieval morality plays or the circus. A celebration of our common humanity, the Bread and Puppet productions rely on the simplicity of myth and archetype, creating powerful expressions that work on an emotional and visceral level. Its name derives from Schumann's premise that theatre is a basic necessity, just like bread, and from the beginning of the company's inception Schumann passed out pieces of bread among the audience members in a spirit of communion. Heavily influenced by Brecht's theories of dramatic presentation as a tool for social change, some of its noteworthy productions include *The King's Story* (1963), a fable that warns against violence and the futility of the struggle for power, *A Man Says Goodbye to His Mother* (1968), a protest against the inhumanity of the Vietnam War, and *The Cry of the People for Meat* (1969), which, like the Open Theater's *The Serpent*, uses images from the Bible alongside contemporary images to create a historical and mythological parallel and protest the dehumanising effects of materialism and violence.

The Bread and Puppet Theater has become famous throughout the United States and Europe, and is well-known for its recurrent piece, *The Domestic Resurrection Circus*, a weekend-long pageant that deals with the theme of overcoming tyranny and oppression. *The Domestic Resurrection Circus* was first presented in 1970 and recreated each summer since 1974 in a meadow on the Vermont farm. In 1998, however, after the death of a man in one of the campgrounds near the theatre, as well as a series of other complications involving drug overdoses and overcrowding, Schumann announced that the *Circus* would not be held anymore.

While the Bread and Puppet Theater was certainly a force for social and political commentary, it did not see itself as espousing a particular political agenda, but rather as more broadly opposing the forces of dehumanisation and oppression. Other theatre groups of the 1960s and 1970s were more overtly political in their goals. These groups saw their mission first and foremost as promoting social and political change. Outside New York City, West Coast theatre groups such as The San Francisco Mime Troupe and Luis Valdez's El Teatro Campesino ('The Farmworkers' Theatre') combined radical political messages with theatrical experimentation. The San Francisco Mime Troupe was founded in 1959 and reorganised in the late 1960s as a collective with the objective of exposing political oppression in the United States and promoting social change. It employed political satire and, like the Bread and Puppet Theater, took its plays into public spaces: streets, parks, workplaces. In 1962, the San Francisco Mime Troupe began giving free performances in the parks, and the Troupe's founder, R. G. Davis, popularised the term guerrilla theatre, which involved spontaneous and unexpected performances that were done illegally and required that the performers dismantle quickly.

Like many of the theatre troupes of the 1960s and 1970s, the San Francisco Mime Troupe was strongly influenced by Brecht and resisted psychological realism in favour of a more physical style of presentation. It used mime in the tradition of Buster Keaton and

Charlie Chaplin, and focused on movement to convey character and action. Rather than simply expressing character, the actor employed gestures to *comment* on character in a critical and self-conscious manner, a technique central not only to Brechtian theories of presentation, but one that would become central to post-modern drama. The San Francisco Mime Troupe's style of political guerilla theatre won it a special Tony Award for Excellence in Regional Theater in 1987. Although R. G. Davis left in the early 1970s after it reformed as a collective, the San Francisco Mime Troupe is still very active today.

After seeing a performance of the San Francisco Mime Troupe in 1965, Luis Valdez was so impressed that he joined, and began to think about forming a political theatre that would address the concerns of farmworkers and migrant labourers. Also around this time in 1965, the National Farm Workers Association of Cesar Chavez joined the Agricultural Workers Organizing Committee in a strike against grape growers in Delano, California, an event that spurred Valdez's interest. Upon speaking with the union organisers, he joined the strikers and, with a group of workers and students, presented skits on the picket line that marked the beginning of El Teatro Campesino. Since most of the field workers were Mexican-American, or Chicano/Chicana, and some spoke fluent English while others spoke little or none, the Teatro's plays attempted to convey situations without words; the actors wore masks to highlight characteristics of stereotyped characters, and mixed English and Spanish messages in their performances. These plays were presented as actos, short bilingual skits dealing with the lives of the workers in a direct and comic manner. They essentially drew from agitprop or Workers' Theatre pieces in the tradition of the political theatre of the 1930s, as well as from the Italian tradition of improvised situational drama known as *commedia dell'arte*. Agitprop, a contraction of 'agitation' and 'propaganda', is a style of theatre that dealt with the contradictions of industrial capitalism in relation to the individual, clearly espousing a Marxist ideology and a call to political action, aiming to reach a wide audience and incite protest.[3] Yet while El Teatro Campesino began as a farmworkers' theatre, its concerns broadened by the 1970s to include the concerns of urban Chicanos, and its distinction as the first Chicano theatre in the

United States under the leadership of Luis Valdez is one of its main contributions to American contemporary theatre. Valdez's play *Zoot Suit* (1978) was the first Chicano play to be presented on Broadway in 1979. El Teatro Campesino still thrives today as a bilingual theatre company based in San Juan Bautista, California, and aims to address the Chicano experience in America in a context that explores the larger meaning(s) of American identity.

The experimentations with group process, actor training techniques, and the relationship between performer and audience that were taking place in theatre troupes across the country were probably most clearly formalised by Richard Schechner, Professor of Performance Studies at New York University's Tisch School of the Arts and Editor of *The Drama Review: the journal of performance studies*, through his ideas on environmental theatre. Environmental theatre takes place in an real world environment rather than a created one, and seeks to immerse the audience in the performance. In other words, the play uses its actual surroundings, and its events occur in a real place and in real time. There is no separation between real world and created events, in the same way that many performances were delivered before the development of realism in the nineteenth century. Essentially, the main principle of environmental theatre is that both the performers and the spectators are part of the same environmental space.

In 1967, Schechner founded the Performance Group, a collective of theatre artists who were dedicated to presenting new forms of experimental, avant-garde theatre based on the principles of exploring non-traditional performance techniques that demanded physical and psychological vulnerability and aimed to connect the performers to the audience and to their environments. In 1968, Schechner outlined his concept of theatre in an essay published in *Tulane Drama Review* (the original name of *The Drama Review*) and proposed 'Six Axioms for Environmental Theatre', which included a refusal of the traditional distinction between life and art in the theatre; an emphasis on using all the theatre space for both the performance and the audience; an embracing of theatre space that can be either 'transformed' or 'found'; a flexible and variable focus (either single, as in the traditional theatre, local, where only a fraction of the audience can perceive the event, or multiple); a refusal to submerge one element of the performance (such as the performer) for other elements such as audible and visual ones; and a rejection of the importance of the text as a point of departure for the production – there may, as Schechner emphasises, 'be no text at all'. Schechner developed his theories on environmental theatre through practice and experimentation with the Performance Group – particularly with its productions of *Dionysus in 69* (1968), *Makbeth* (1969), and *Commune* (1970). Schechner also directed the original production of Sam Shepard's *The Tooth of Crime* in 1972, a play that I discuss at length in Chapter 5. The last Performance Group production directed by Schechner was Jean Genet's *The Balcony* (1979).

The Performing Garage on Wooster Street in New York's Soho neighborhood became the home of the Performance Group, and its productions usually focused on reinterpretations of classic texts, such as in *Dionysus in 69*, which was based primarily on Euripides' *The Bacchae*, with lines from *Hippolytus* and *Antigone* referenced. Actors simultaneously played characters and themselves, using some of Euripides' speeches and some of their own improvised words, as they eschewed any separation between actor and character. Each production was fluid, with some parts performed differently every night, and focused mainly on the presence of the actor and intimate interactions with the audience. Nudity as a way of focusing on the actors' bodies, increasing psychic vulnerability, and removing social masks was used extensively in the performances. Performers and spectators were encouraged to unite in 'group gropes', where they would intertwine on the floor during the performance, stroking and caressing each other. Constantly evaluated and revised, *Dionysus in 69* ran for over a year, and has come to be known as one of the central texts of the experimental theatre of the 1960s and 1970s.

In 1975, Performance Group members Elizabeth LeCompte and Spalding Gray began a collaboration that resulted in the trilogy, *Three Places in Rhode Island*, consisting of *Sakonnet Point* (1975), *Rumstick Road* (1977), and *Nayatt School* (1978). In these works, directed by LeCompte, Gray presented autobiographical monologues as a solo performer, directly addressing the audience (a style of performance he would continue to develop until his death in 2004). In Gray's monologues, the line between factual documentary and artistic imagination is blurred, as is the line between actor and performer.[4] In 1980, LeCompte and Gray took over the Performing Garage after Schechner withdrew from active participation in order to write and direct other projects, and founded the Wooster Group, along with Willem Dafoe, Libby Howes, Kate Valk, Peyton Smith, Ron Vawter and Jim Clayburgh. Like the Performance Group, the Wooster Group focuses on reconceptions of classic texts and embraces a self-conscious style of acting, seeking to de-naturalise the connection between actor and character in Brechtian fashion: 'Once the idea of total transformation [from actor to character] is abandoned the actor speaks his part not as if he were improvising it himself but like a quotation.'[5] While the Wooster Group does employ segments of realistic acting in its productions, these moments are part of a variety of performance styles that are often thrown together in the same piece, along with a juxtaposition of dissimilar textual elements. Rather than attempting to represent the outside world, the Wooster Group's pieces self-consciously reflect performance itself.

The postmodern practice of deconstructing well-known texts and appropriating them in new forms has been a distinct feature of the Wooster Group's work, and has often raised salient questions concerning the 'ownership' of dramatic texts. In 1983, for example, the Group opened rehearsals of its new work-in-progress, *L.S.D.*, which used sections from Arthur Miller's *The Crucible* prefaced by excerpts from 1960s counterculture hero Timothy Leary's album, *L.S.D.* Despite LeCompte's repeated attempts to petition Miller for permission to use the play, and her assurances that the piece was not a parody or a form of ridicule as he saw it, Miller legally challenged its unauthorised use of his material, ironically imposing the sort of authority and censorship that *The Crucible* rejects. LeCompte closed the production and the piece was reworked with a play by Michael Kirby, *The Hearing*, substituted. Miller's play was reduced to 'Just the High Points'. This new 1984 production of *L.S.D. (. . . Just the High Points . . .)* avoided direct references to Miller's play, but whenever recognisable lines from the *The Crucible* were intelligible, a loud buzzer sounded and silenced the actor, completing the commentary on American censorship.

Problematising their relationship to the text while simultaneously exhibiting a dependence on it, the Wooster Group uses performance to eradicate the differences among various types of textual messages and to collapse distinctions between 'high' and 'low' art. Its reimagining of Chekhov's *Three Sisters*, *Brace Up!*, first performed in 1991 and later reworked for a 2003 production, used technology to project close-ups of the actors onto television screens as they were simultaneously performing on stage, essentially addressing the microphones and video cameras rather than each other. The actors' images were alternated with scenes from Japanese horror movies, and the narrative action of the play broke off into spontaneous dance sequences and moments of blaring music – conventions that, at the very least, served to resist any temptation of realistic illusion in Chekhov's seminal realistic play. Racine's *Phèdre* was the inspiration for *To You, The Birdie!* (2002), which presented a maniacal badminton game on stage. And in 2004, the Wooster Group performed its own version of Grotowski's *Poor Theater*, using film documentation of the Polish Laboratory Theatre's production of *Akropolis* to restage the piece's closing section (in the original Polish). The Wooster Group continues to thrive under the direction of LeCompte, and has most recently produced its interpretation of *Hamlet* (2007).

The appropriation of established literary and cultural texts that was creatively employed by the various theatre groups discussed in this chapter took a turn for the strikingly ironic and the 'queer'[6] in Charles Ludlam's Ridiculous Theatrical Company, which he founded in 1969 after splitting from John Vaccaro's Playhouse of the Ridiculous. Ludlum embraced a playful style that openly resisted conventional, formalised notions of 'art', preferring instead to reference icons of popular culture (especially through film) alongside classical literary texts. His plays dissolve the boundaries between 'high' and 'low' culture, typically characteristic of a postmodern aesthetic, and are especially postmodern in their sense of irony – or making a statement and simultaneously denying it – as if the performer were winking at the audience members as co-conspirators in some cultural joke. In *The Politics of Postmodernism*, Linda Hutcheon defines a key aspect of postmodernism as taking 'the form of self-conscious, self-contradictory, self-undermining statement. It is rather like saying something whilst at the same time putting inverted commas around what is being said.'[7] She emphasises that postmodernism's 'distinctive character lies in this kind of wholesale "nudging" commitment to doubleness, or duplicity', and articulates the paradox that post-modernism

> ultimately manages to instill and reinforce as much as under-mine and subvert the conventions and presuppositions it seems to challenge. Nevertheless, it seems reasonable to say that the postmodern's initial concern is to de-naturalize some of the dominant features of our way of life; to point out that those entities that we unthinkingly experience as 'natural' [. . .] are in fact 'cultural'; made by us, not given to us.[8]

It is in this sense – that of de-naturalising the identities that our culture presents to us as 'natural' (those generated through cate-gories involving gender, sexuality, patriarchy and ethnicity), rather than through any proselytising or dogmatic statement – that Ludlum's work can be seen as political. In this respect, the Ridiculous Theatrical Company was very different from the overtly political Living Theatre productions he saw for the first time in 1959 that strongly influenced his work. In his writings on theatre, Ludlum points out:

> Everybody but a couple of people in my company are gay, but what we do is political in a different way from gay theatre. It's just entertainment, not agit-prop. It isn't preachy and it's for everybody. [. . .] I think that the distinction between gay theatre and what I do, which some people call 'queer theatre,' is that gay theatre is really a political movement to show that gay people can be admirable, responsible members of the commu-nity. It shows their problems. I don't do that. 'Queer theatre' embraces more variation, and the possibility of something being odd or peculiar rather than just simply homosexuality.[9]

Ludlum's year-round repertory theatre was exclusively devoted to his own writings (that he also acted in and directed), and was known for combining parody, pop culture, drag performance and high 'camp' theatricality. He has described 'camp' as a kind of excess, or 'overdoing', in order to make a point, and also recalls Prout's discussion of camp as 'an outsider's view of things other people take for granted', a 'reverse image' that incorporates a sly sense of humour because of its inversions that speak to a particular, usually marginalised, social group.[10]

The fluidity of identity is evident in Ludlum's plays, which all included at least one crossdressing or transgendered role, and played with fixed notions of gender. He sees in his acting 'the ability to slip in and out of characters and make an amalgamation of character out of pieces of other characters and impressions', another postmodern feature of his work.[11] In his first critical success with the Ridiculous Theatrical Company, *Bluebeard* (1970) – based on H. G. Wells's novel, *The Island of Dr Moreau* – Ludlum played a mad scientist focusing on the creation of a 'third gender' through his search for a 'third genital'. In *Camille* (1973), also known as 'A Travesty on *La Dame aux Camélias* by Alexandre Dumas fils', Ludlum took the title role and spoofed Dumas' play as well as the more general conventions of romantic love. He played Maria Callas in *Galas*, 'A Modern Tragedy' (1983), and in 1984 he wrote a 'freely adapted' version of Euripides' *Medea*, which was only staged after his death in 1987. Among his best-known works are *Conquest of the Universe, or When Queens Collide* (1968) and *Big Hotel* (1966), which starred Ludlum as the faded movie star Norma Desmond from the 1950 cult film *Sunset Boulevard*, and contained dozens of other references to popular culture – television ads, songs, comic books – alongside references to canonical literary texts, including Shakespeare. His 1984 play, *The Mystery of Irma Vep*, was his most physically demanding in its requirement that only two actors (originally played by Ludlum and his lover, Everett Quinton) play seven roles through a variety of quick-change techniques. *Irma Vep* was named one of the year's best plays by *Time* magazine and *The New York Times*, has become one of the most-produced plays in the United States. Tragically, Ludlum died of AIDS at the age of 44 during the height of his career, naming Quinton his successor as artistic director of the Ridiculous Theatrical Company.

Ludlum's interest in experimenting with 'the best way to bring about an objective representation of images from an inner world'[12] had become a main concern in the theatre by the late 1960s. In 1968, Richard Foreman's Ontological-Hysteric Theater was founded for the purpose of theatrical exploration, and continues to re-examine the relationship between author and performance today, presenting an annual theatre piece designed, written and directed by Foreman. Foreman's multimedia productions are visual spectacles that attempt to project the unconscious mind onto the stage, championing the unseen as the true reality. His work self-consciously explores the concept of performance as an extension of the author/director, and actors are often directed using a loud buzzer and exhibit repetitive, robotic movements, almost as if in a trance. His sets and costumes resemble circus-like dreams/nightmares and often retain similarities from one production to the next. In 2006, Foreman began incorporating film in his work, presenting 'Film/Performance Project #1', titled *Zomboid!*, which has been followed with *Wake Up Mr Sleepy! Your Unconscious Mind is Dead!*, his most recent 2007 production. These last two pieces explore

> a new kind of theatre in which film and live action trace parallel contrapuntal dream narratives. *Wake Up Mr Sleepy!* postulates the invention of a an airplane (controlled by a horde of baby-doll pilots) as the death knell of the unconscious mind. Foreman is responding to a world in which visionary sages and poets are being replaced by specialists who make platitudes out of the immediately observable and hand-feed them to the public.[13]

Foreman has written over fifty theatre pieces, most of which are immersions in the mysteries of the non-rational, and his

> trademark 'total theater' unites elements of the performative, auditory and visual arts, philosophy, psychoanalysis and literature for a unique result. Foreman's style is not meant to be 'cerebral,' but rather, the density of his compositional theater is an attempt to viscerally reflect and process everything that he has inherited from his explorations in twentieth century thought and art.[14]

Along with the avant-garde theatre companies that emerged in the 1960s, innovations in style and direction continued to explode throughout the 1970s to the 1990s with multimedia productions that transgressed the formal boundaries of genre, fusing the visual arts, music, dance, drama and written text. Director Robert Wilson was at the forefront of these multimedia experiments, and his theatre of images produces spectacles that are highly visual, focusing on colour and geometric shape. One of Wilson's most successful productions was the eight-hour-long *Einstein on the Beach* (1976), written with composer Philip Glass, and in *CIVIL warS* (1983) he continued to experiment with theatre that transcends conventional theatrical boundaries. Wilson also collaborated with musician Tom Waits and writer William S. Burroughs in *The Black Rider* (1990), and with Waits in both *Alice* (1992), based on the life and work of *Alice in Wonderland* author Lewis Carroll, and *Woyzeck* (2000), a reworking of German writer Georg Büchner's 1837 play. This blurring of artistic boundaries, the focus on multimedia presentations, and the

Figure 4.2 Matt McGrath portrays Wilhelm, a clerk who makes a Faustian pact with the Devil, accepting magic bullets in the American Conservatory Theater's 2004 production of *The Black Rider*. (Source: American Conservatory Theater.)

Figure 4.3 (Clockwise) Richard Strange, Matt McGrath and Mary Margaret O'Hara in the American Conservatory Theater's 2004 production of *The Black Rider*. (Source: American Conservatory Theater.)

collapse of any distinction between high and low art/culture that was embraced by innovators such as Wilson, Ludlum and Foreman played a major role in establishing a postmodern aesthetic that would radically redefine the avant-garde American theatre throughout the last quarter of the twentieth century.

NOTES

1. The distinction between 'drama' and 'performance' is one that typically relies on a distinction between a focus on the written text as opposed to a focus on the physical production. The term 'theatre', then, can be seen as a more inclusive term that encompasses both the literary text of a play and its execution in performance, or sometimes either one independently. I attempt to make these distinctions clear when necessary, but when they are not used with such precision it is because the boundaries among them are often fluid. For this chapter, however, there is a distinct focus on the ephemeral physical performance in contrast to any authoritative text.

2. Michael Paller, *Gentleman Callers: Tennessee Williams, Homosexuality, and Mid-Twentieth-Century Drama* (New York: Palgrave Macmillan, 2005), p. 240.

3. A representative example of agitprop theatre in the United States is Clifford Odets's *Waiting for Lefty* (1935), which ends with a call to 'STRIKE, STRIKE, STRIKE!!!'.

4. As a solo performer, Gray's most famous monologue performance is probably *Swimming to Cambodia* (1983), which was made into a 1987 film.

5. Bertolt Brecht, *Brecht on Theatre*, trans. John Willett (New York: Hill and Wang, 1964), p. 138.

6. In the sense of both the 'homosexual' and the 'odd'.

7. Linda Hutcheon, *The Politics of Postmodernism* (London: Routledge, 1989), p. 2.

8. Ibid. p. 2.

9. Charles Ludlum, *Ridiculous Theatre: Scourge of Human Folly*, ed. Steven Samuels (New York: Theatre Communications Group, 1992), p. 230.

10. Ibid. p. 225.
11. Ibid. p. 210.
12. Ibid. p. 3.
13. Promotional material at www.ontological.com [accessed 1 March 2007].
14. Ibid.

CHAPTER 5

Postmodern Presentations: Questioning Boundaries of Representation

Austin: There's nothin' real down here, Lee! Least of all me!

Sam Shepard, *True West* (1980)

Throughout the 1970s towards the end of the millennium, theories of the postmodern situated texts that now fall under the heading of 'contemporary American drama' within a particular aesthetic. Fragmented narrative as opposed to seamless narrative plot, the deconstruction of character, an acknowledgement of popular and mass culture, and a self-consciousness of performance marked a type of drama that had been increasingly influenced by the theories of Brecht and Artaud and by the theatrical innovations of the 1960s. These postmodern experiments with language, form and content tend to differ widely from each other; at times they retain many of the features of traditional realistic representation yet deal with contemporary social and political concerns, only playing tangentially, if at all, with anti-realistic dramatic conventions. More often, however, they rebel more drastically against realist attempts to order and represent the external world; instead they present reality as a subjective construct rather than as an objective truth which is perceived by the artist. Experimentation with theatrical conventions and the subjective representation of the artist's personal vision replace mimesis in their works, as these artists are more interested in redefining what constitutes meaning and experience and testing the limits of drama as performance. What they tend to have in common, however, is a sense of drama as 'play' within a postmodern sensibility that blurs boundaries between role-playing and authenticity, or appearance and being, in order to question the reliability of 'truth' in dealing with salient issues affecting the instabilities of social identity. Two playwrights who gained wide recognition during the 1970s and 1980s, Sam Shepard and David Mamet, were at the forefront of exploring these boundaries in terms of the performance of American identity in their work.

In *Modern American Drama*, C. W. E. Bigsby observes that Sam Shepard has 'found in performance a symbol of lives which are the enactment of stories with their roots in the distant past of ritual and myth as well as in a present in which role and being have become confused'.[1] This 'confusion' of role and being, performance and authenticity, is at the centre of Shepard's characters' search for a stable identity, a fixed reality that both eludes and threatens to trap them as they perform the instabilities of postmodern identity in the late twentieth century. Bigsby addresses this dilemma in terms of a sense of inconsistency and instability in Shepard's work:

> There is no consistency. Moods, dress, identity can switch in a second; characters are fractured, divided, doubled until the same play can contain, as independent beings, what are in effect facets of a single self . . . But if this fluidity contains a threat of anarchy the opposite is equally menacing. As a writer, Shepard has spoken of his desire 'To not be fixed'. This is what keeps his characters on the move. (p. 166)

In several of his experimental plays characterised by truncated and fragmented dialogue, highly symbolic language, and characters lifted from the mythic discourses of Hollywood film, rock 'n' roll or literature, Shepard is concerned with the postmodern question of essence versus appearance and the slipperiness of 'authentic' identity as it relates to image, particularly the image associated with artistic fame. Yet while his characters crave the stability of a fixed core identity and a return to origins, the inevitable contradiction is that they ultimately realise that freedom is possible only through fluidity, instability, movement. They must, therefore, remain fugitives and surge forward, never resting, despite their desperate, romantic need to cling to an unattainable ideal, a core of Truth. Stasis signifies death or confinement (a kind of death), and freedom lies in flexibility and individual agency, the ability to mould image(s) of the self and remain in process.

Shepard's status as an experimental artist – 'the unofficial star of the alternative theatre scene' – is indisputable.[2] From the beginning of his career, he was interested in exploring the experimental dramatic forms that emerged in Europe after the Second World War and took root in the off- and off-off-Broadway American theatre scene during the 1960s and 1970s.[3] Shepard was associated with such downtown experimental theatres as Café Cino, La MaMa E.T.C., and Theatre Genesis, where he got his start in 1964 with *Cowboys* and *The Rock Garden*. The off- and off-off-Broadway theatre scene of the 1960s and 1970s was interested in exploring the period's concern with personal freedom and authenticity apart from political oppression: locating an individual essence or reality outside conformist social roles.

Many of Shepard's plays of this period such as *La Turista* (1967), *Action* (1975), *Angel City* (1976) and *Buried Child* (1979), followed by *True West* (1980) and later *Simpatico* (1994), deal with the fragile boundaries of identity and the impossibility of locating an authentic self outside of the roles, masks, images and performances that mark human action. At the same time, however, this protean lack of stability brings liberation. Shepard's early play *La Turista* is replete with discourses of shape-shifting, instability, transformation and escape, although this fluidity is represented more physically: 'He disappears and becomes the wall. He reappears on the opposite wall. He clings to the floor and slithers along . . . He becomes a mouse and changes into a cobra and then back on the floor.'[4] At the end of the play, Kent escapes being trapped by Salem and Sonny, who 'make a lunge' for him. He 'runs straight toward the upstage wall of the set and leaps right through it, leaving a cut-out silhouette image of his body in the wall' (p. 298). All that is left of him is a representation, an image. As Doc says, 'Just keep yourself movin', son. It's the only way out' (p. 287).

While several of Shepard's plays deal with the question of identity and freedom, I will focus specifically on two works in this chapter, *The Tooth of Crime* (1972), which is often considered

Shepard's first major play, and *True West*, a fully mature full-length play representative of Shepard's concern with authenticity and role-playing in American culture. *The Tooth of Crime*, a drama of confrontation presented through discourses of Hollywood Westerns and rock n' roll, centres around the characters Hoss, who is 'stuck in [his] image' but refuses to be trapped as 'a slave',[5] and Crow, whose 'image is [his] survival kit' (p. 249). Megan Williams reads Shepard's *True West* as an illustration of theories of post-modern identity, and contends that Austin and Lee allegorise 'two ways modern man attempts to solve his feelings of placelessness and alienation'. While Austin initially clings to a lingering nostalgia for a stable sense of identity, relationships and history, Lee 'regis-ters a potentially positive sense of freedom which accompanies man when he loses his nostalgia for history and realizes that identity and the past are only myths to be performed and manipulated'. Lee, she argues, 'challenges the precept behind postmodern theory which assumes that contemporary man's loss of subjectivity and history must necessarily be a negative experience'.[6] Since Lee 'possesses the almost miraculous ability to appear, disappear, and change iden-tities' in contrast to Austin, who 'is "stuck" in his search for a world where identity and history are fixed' (p. 69), Austin 'wishes to . . . relinquish himself to the positive freedom and anonymity of Lee's present' (p. 60). Even though Lee craves 'somethin' authentic. Somethin' to keep me in touch', freedom is ultimately only possi-ble through the fluidity of performance.[7] Both these plays present a triumph of individual agency, but not through locating a stable Truth or an authentic core of identity. Rather, hope is to be found in the acknowledgement of the inevitability of role-playing and the freedom associated with the ability to construct the self, to remain a work-in-progress. Liberation lies in directing our own perfor-mances.

In *The Tooth of Crime*, Hoss is a fugitive who dreams of living 'outside the fucking law altogether' (p. 213); he sees himself as 'a mover' (p. 218) and needs to wander. Yet he craves authenticity, and laments the ubiquitousness of image in 'The Game' of rock 'n' roll performance culture that is his world: a Darwinian staging of com-petition and survival of the fittest where the winners know how to manipulate image. He wants to believe in an individual essence, a style that 'can't be taught or copied or stolen or sold' (p. 249), and the line from Stéphane Mallarmé that gives the play its title ('in your heart of stone there is dwelling / A heart that the tooth of no crime can wound') signifies this yearning for a core of identity and Truth.[8] On the other hand, Crow, a killer 'Gypsy' who does manage to live outside the laws of the game, is free from roots, from essence and stability, precisely because 'There ain't no heart to a Gypsy' (p. 221).

Hoss's search for authenticity, however, people 'just livin' their life' outside the game (p. 219), relies to some extent on image, on myths of the uncontaminated American West: 'What about the country. Ain't there any farmers left, ranchers, cowboys, open space?' (p. 219). The core that he craves cannot be located, and even what he considers his own genuine walk was 'copped from Keith Moon' (p. 228) and later copied from him by Crow. Hoss objects to Crow's appropriation of his style, feeling that his identity and individuality have been stolen, and orders Crow to 'Stop walkin' like that! That's not the way you walk! That's the way I walk!' (p. 232). His assistant Becky, however, is aware of the freedom associated with play, movement and image, and knows that 'the only way to be an individual is inside the game. You're it. You're on top. You're free' (p. 219).

Hoss sees his image in contrast to his essence or authenticity, as he believes that his fame keeps him 'insulated from what's really happening' (p. 207). His experience is framed through the myths of 'John Wayne, Robert Mitchum and Kirk Douglas' (p. 224), and his sense that he is 'pushed and pulled around from one image to another. Nothin' takes a solid form. Nothin's sure and final' (p. 243) disorients him. Crow, on the other hand, has no problem with the image that is 'his survival kit' (p. 249). He is the postmodern quintessence of style for style's sake, or, as Stephen J. Bottoms puts it, he presents 'a style-oriented attitude to the world which functions as an end in itself'.[9] In a sense, Hoss and Crow mirror Austin and Lee in *True West*; while both Hoss and Austin crave a stable authenticity, Crow and Lee know that reality is a malleable fiction, and they are able to use this knowledge to survive in the postmodern world by controlling the multiplicity of contradictory images. Bottoms writes, 'Crow knows what Hoss has not registered; that the past is not a set of concrete facts, but a conceptual history which can be rewritten at will by whomever has the power to do so. In this world of language games, reality itself is a reinventable fiction.'[10]

The language in *Tooth* is highly overdetermined, reflecting the fluidity inherent in identity and history. Becky tells Hoss that he 'ain't *playin*' with a full deck' (p. 219, emphasis added), pointing not only to the metaphor that relates card games to sanity (a *stable* mental state), but also to *Tooth*'s world of 'the game' itself and the playfulness/instability of image. Similarly, Crow's attention to the (possible) origins of the term 'gyped' simultaneously highlights the fluidity of language: ' "Gyped" – coming from "Gypsy" ' (p. 233). References to 'charts' (to signify maps, celebrity ratings or astrological readings) and 'stars' (celebrities or astrological signs) are layered and imprecise, taking on several meanings at once. There is no consensus of language, and the characters speak play-fully in various pop-culture dialects that make it difficult to locate a fixed meaning, highlighting the instability of representation.

The play begins with Hoss singing the lyrics to 'The Way Things Are', a song about the 'confusion' between representation and truth:

> You may think every picture you see is a true history of
> the way things used to be or the way things are
> While you're ridin' in your radio or walkin through the late
> late show ain't it a drag to know you just don't know
> you just don't know
> So here's another illusion to add to your confusion
> Of the way things are.
> [. . .]
> Now everything I do goes down in doubt
> But sometimes in the blackest night I can see a little light
> That's the only thing that keeps me rockin' – keeps me
> rockin'
> So here's another fantasy
> About the way things seem to be to me. (p. 204)

Questioning not only historical narratives of the past, but also 'pictures' of present reality, Hoss's lyrics set the stage for a play that challenges knowledge of the world and of the self, destabilising any certainty regarding both history and identity and privileging doubt. Being and seeming are collapsed, just as in the case of Hoss's Creole friend who 'was black' to the white kids 'even though he looked white' (p. 223). Even Hoss's own narrative is 'a fantasy' based on subjective appearance, the way things 'seem to be' to him. The 'little light' that keeps him 'rockin'', however, could either be his belief in a core of authenticity or, conversely, his hope that he can thrive in this game of image and performance. Either way, the hope is 'little', and both possibilities prove futile for Hoss in the end.

Ultimately, Hoss finds authenticity, stability and a release from image only in death; his suicide is his 'original' gesture that 'can't be copied' (p. 249), as he decides that authenticity can only be found in the reality of the body outside representation. Once he was able to 'shift his personality', but now he is 'stuck' in his image (p. 223). At the end of Act I, just before Crow arrives, Hoss tries to convince himself that 'The road's what counts. Just look at the road. Don't worry about where it's goin'' (p. 225), yet he feels 'so trapped. So fucking unsure' (p. 225). Hoss wants to be a mover, but in order to find the authenticity he craves and escape the game he must stop moving. There is no survival outside the game. His only agency lies in self-destruction, but it is an ironic victory, if a victory at all. For Crow, Hoss was just a 'loser' (p. 250) in the game, too static to keep on playing.

Crow survives and wins because he knows that the only reality lies in performance, and freedom is the ability to invent and reinvent oneself, to manipulate image. 'Crow's Song', in contrast to Hoss's opening lyric, privileges movement and role-playing in a world of uncertainty:

> What he doesn't know – the four winds blow
> Just the same for him as me
> We're clutchin' at the straw and no one knows the law
> That keeps us lost at sea
>
> But I believe in my mask – The man I made up is me
> And I believe in my dance – And my destiny. (p. 232)

Figure 5.1 *The Tooth of Crime* by Sam Shepard, 1983 production La MaMa E.T.C. Directed by George Ferencz. Photo of Ray Wise as Hoss. This production was remounted in October 2006 to celebrate La MaMa's 45th anniversary. (Source: Gerry Vezzuso.)

Crow knows that both he and Hoss are steeped in 'just the same' doubt and uncertainty, but Crow is comfortable with the uncertainty; he revels in it, as it is what frees him and gives him power. He 'believe[s] in [his] mask', and there is no distinction between role and essence, creation and creator: 'The man I made up is me.' The key to Crow's power is the fact that his image bends to his will; he 'made up' his own identity with the fragments of image. It is his 'dance', remaining in motion and constant flux, that enables him to survive while Hoss does not. Crow's destiny is to survive and go on. He is free because he can manipulate his image and '[n]ever show his true face' (p. 235). Control over representation of the self points to freedom, and Crow tried to warn Hoss that he needed to 'get the image in line' (p. 240). While on one level *The Tooth of Crime* can certainly be seen as a critique of the surface reality of a postmodern society steeped in image and lacking substance, on another level the play locates individual freedom in accepting 'Crow's sense that identity is no more than a fragmented composite of surface images' and possessing the power to arrange and rearrange the composite.[11] Identity and history are presented as 'plastic' in this play, artificial yet ultimately malleable.

Matthew Roudané argues that Shepard's characters are caught in a 'terrible binary of hope and hopelessness,'[12] but know they must keep moving, keep changing, to maintain freedom. Playing on the doubleness of the term 'forge' – both moving forward and constructing or shaping – Dodge in *Buried Child* (1979) sums up the notion of the self in process that characterises much of Shepard's work: 'There's nothing to figure out. You just forge ahead.'[13]

By the time he presented *True West* in 1980, Shepard's view of identity as a performance had been extended to the context of the capitalist American dream. *True West* participated in revealing the fiction of any claims to an 'authentic' or intrinsic national being (grounded in cultural origin, race, social class or sexuality, for example), inviting access to the fluid definition(s) of American character that could be presented on the stage and creating possibilities of representation in the blurred boundaries beyond those offered in the character representations of modern realism. Similarly, in the work of contemporary American playwright David Mamet, there is a self-conscious awareness of the performance of identity within social systems, and a focus on capturing the dialogue of American life and making the illusion sound true.[14] Both Shepard and Mamet explore the commodification of cultural myth that is central to the collapse of authenticity. It is only fitting, then, that success in their plays is measured by how well the characters are able to commodify cultural fictions and sell carefully packaged narratives as undeniable truth.

In the work of both Shepard and Mamet, particularly during the 1970s and 1980s, the commodification of myth – the cultural narratives (rules, values and images) by which we live – illustrates a central facet of postmodern American life from, generally, the end of the Second World War to, arguably, the present day. While playwrights such as Arthur Miller began subtly questioning the definitions of American identity associated with our myths of individualism and power in conjunction with the viability of the American dream after the war, during the last quarter or so of the twentieth century the performance of American experience has been continued through more complex examinations of these myths in the work of Shepard and Mamet. These playwrights simultaneously articulate America's central myths of patriarchal capitalism and go on to explore their validity in order to begin to challenge the hegemony of Anglo-patriarchal mythology, illustrating and exposing the power structures surrounding identity and social performance in America. I choose to examine these playwrights in this context because, as heterosexual white men, they do not immediately appear to be writing from the margins – aside from the fact that Mamet is Jewish. Yet their ironic explorations of the construction and performance of identity in America, usually from within the system (even Mamet's Jews are often speaking from assimilated positions), are crucial to opening up a space for marginalised and culturally diverse voices in their exposure of American identity as a performance or 'act' within dominant structures of commodity capitalism.

In the plays of these authors, the American dream is portrayed as a commodity that is bought and sold within an overwhelming capitalist system, and the ability to successfully package the myths of individualism, power, discovery and adventure that sustain this dream is what defines American entrepreneurship. America's *image* – how we see ourselves as a culture – is juxtaposed with the reality of American life in these works, and the defining moment occurs when the characters realise that they, and we, can no longer tell the difference between the myths they strive to perform and the social realities in which they struggle. Both writers are concerned with 'performing America' (or, what it means to 'be American' in performance), and, for both, our myths are simultaneously questioned and embraced as accurate representations of being.

Survival in America – whether in Mamet's urban jungle or Shepard's Western desert – is based on how well one plays the 'game' of making illusion seem like truth. Since the viability of the American dream depends on success within a capitalist system, the central game at stake for these playwrights is 'business'; whether it's the business of real estate, gambling, street crime or Hollywood films, success in the con game of American enterprise rests on the ability to convince others that our cultural fantasies are tangible and available for purchase. The wider social implication of this theme in these works is that human *action* in America is seen as an *act* – a performance or game of representation – that is indistinguishable from the 'real', pointing to a defining aspect of postmodern American identity central to the canon of both Mamet and Shepard, where the boundaries between acting and being are continuously blurred.

These playwrights portray identity, particularly American identity under capitalism, as an empty performance of power and agency, and expose the contradictions of that performance in both limiting and freeing the subject from the chains of being. In 'Capitalism, modernism, and postmodernism' (1985), Terry Eagleton, discussing Jean-François Lyotard's assertion in *The Postmodern Condition* that 'the "performativity principle" is all that counts' in the realm of late capitalism, posits a necessary correlation between the instabilities and displacements of postmodernism and the goals of advanced capitalism. He argues:

It is not surprising that classical modes of truth and cognition are increasingly out of favour in a society where what matters is whether you deliver the commercial or rhetorical goods. Whether among discourse theorists or the Institute of

Directors, the goal is no longer truth but performativity, not reason but power. [15]

Identity under capitalism functions as commodified performance, a product not located in any 'real', original or essentialised self, but rather defined by the slipping in and out of roles and costumes in a struggle for power, a postmodern assertion of its protean nature.

In Mamet's works, Roma, Moss and Williamson from *Glengarry Glen Ross* (1983) and Teach from *American Buffalo* (1976) all seek to gain power by commodifying the cultural illusions that sustain us. Business is clearly a game in both these works, lies are valued, and the American dream is paved with the ability to 'bullshit'. Steven Ryan points out in *Modern Drama* that one of Mamet's most basic themes has to do with 'human beings' never-ending battle to dominate one another', and in Mamet's plays as well as in many of Shepard's works, this fight for domination is characterised by the manipulation of others for survival in America. 'This need to obtain power,' Ryan writes, 'closely linked to our most basic survival instincts, is the sole force that drives such . . . predatory Mamet characters as Bernie Litko from *Sexual Perversity in Chicago* [1974]; Teach from *American Buffalo*; Roma, Moss, and Williamson from *Glengarry Glen Ross* [1983]; the gambler Mike in *House of Games* [1987]; and Charley Fox from *Speed-the-Plow* [1988], all of whom rely, or try to rely, on manipulation and intimidation to accomplish self-serving goals.'[16] The 'manipulation and intimidation' in these works often rests on a talent for language – 'talking shit' – and Mamet's characters in these plays seek to gain *their* piece of the American dream by convincing others that it exists as a reality *beyond* language, thereby winning the game. Steven Connor's reading of cultural critic Fredric Jameson presents this commodification of representation as inherent to the postmodern condition:

Jameson joins with other theorists of the postmodern condition in identifying the new area of commodification for multinational capitalism as pre-eminently *representation itself*. Where an older Marxist social theory saw cultural forms as part of the ideological veil or distorting mirror preventing the real economic relations in a society from being seen, this theory sees the production, exchange, marketing and consumption of cultural forms – considered in their widest sense and therefore including advertising, TV and the mass media generally – as a central focus and expression of economic activity. Here, images, styles and representations are not the promotional accessories to economic products, they are the products themselves.[17]

Connor reads Jean Baudrillard as similarly describing this cultural commodification: 'It is no longer possible to separate the economic or productive realm from the realms of ideology and culture, since cultural artefacts, images, representations, even feelings and psychic structures have become part of the world of the economic.'[18] Mamet's characters know that in the postmodern world, contemporary capitalism is, as John McGowan argues, 'an all-inclusive order from which nothing and no one can escape'.[19]

In *Glengarry Glen Ross*, the real estate business is a portrayed as a competitive game with a tangible prize, a Cadillac which goes to the highest seller, and it is actually language – the salesman's ability to spin convincing fictions – that is the tool of their trade. From the very first scene of the play, Levene tries to discredit Moss's sales ability on the basis that although '[h]e *talks*, he talks a good game',[20] he himself is actually the one with the substantial sales – 'the man to sell' (p. 19), not simply talk. What Levene fails to realise is that in the real estate business 'talking a good game' is the basis of sales – talking is selling – and the ability to back up that 'talk' with substance is not required.

Moss, however, seems to be more aware of the rules of the game, as he tells Aaronow that the 'hard part' of going into business for yourself is 'Just the *act*' – having the courage to stand up and actually do it, 'To say, "I'm going on my own"' (p. 35). Moss's 'act', however, is not just an *action*, but a performance as well – a pose of courage and risk-taking, qualities of masculine bravado long valued in the business world. Roma, the representative of these values and the top salesman whose primary concern is the 'opportunity' of making money, declares that 'the *true* reserve that I have is the strength that I have of *acting each day* without fear' (p. 49). In this play, succeeding in the real estate business requires both *action* and *acting*, to the point where the two become virtually indistinguishable.

In fact, in the world of business in general, acting and being are typically not distinguished; what *Glengarry Glen Ross* implies, of course, is that business is a performance where appearance is generally valued over substance. The key to thriving in post-industrial capitalist America is knowing that what is being sold is *image*, not reality, and the two merge in a postmodern realm which, as Janelle Reinelt and Joseph Roach point out in *Critical Theory and Performance*, 'embraces simulations [and] distrusts claims to authenticity'.[21]

Although the business of *Glengarry Glen Ross* does involve the sale of property from a sanctioned office, offering at least the semblance of legitimacy, what is really being sold is commodified myth. In *American Buffalo*, the illusion of a tangible product plays an even smaller role, and Mamet shows us how myths of the American dream are packaged and sold from nothing on the streets. Dennis Carroll argues, '*American Buffalo* confronts the validity of an entire national mystique, and the premises on which many enterprises and dreams of great moments are founded.'[22] In *Glengarry Glen Ross* Levene tells Williamson that you cannot learn 'to think on your feet' in an office: 'You have to learn it on the streets. You can't *buy* that. You have to *live* it' (p. 97). Similarly, Don in *American Buffalo* proclaims, 'Everything that I or Fletcher know we picked up on the street. That's all business is . . . common sense, experience, and talent.'[23] But business is also, for Don, '[p]eople taking *care* of themselves' (p. 7) – it is a means of survival. For both Levene and Don, business is a talent for survival, a game that is learned on the streets.

Teach too is aware that business is a game of survival in *American Buffalo*, as he questions whether it is 'good business to call Fletch in' (p. 52), since although Fletcher is 'a real good card player' (p. 4) – good at *games* – '[h]e *cheats* at cards' (p. 80). According to Teach, Fletcher's cheating at cards makes him a potential suspect for cheating in business, a reasonable assumption in this play, given the equivalency of business and games. Just as Teach is enraged by Fletcher's cheating at cards, he criticises any transgression of the formal rules he has personally set up regarding business, desiring a strange sort of honour in his transactions. 'Free enterprise', however, is defined by Teach as 'The *freedom* . . . Of the *Individual* . . . To Embark on Any Fucking Course that he sees

Figure 5.2 Damon Seawell (left) as Bobby, Matt DeCaro (middle) as Don, and Marco Barricelli as Teach in the American Conservatory Theater's 2003 production of David Mamet's *American Buffalo*. (Source: American Conservatory Theater.)

fit . . . In order to secure his honest chance to make a profit' (p. 73). 'The country's *founded* on this,' he tells Don. 'Without this we're just savage shitheads in the wilderness' (p. 73). Civilisation in Teach's sense of the frontier myth is defined by the opportunity to make money, and his glorification of 'the *Individual*' as opposed to the collective echoes the individualistic ruthlessness of the American dream, an 'every man for himself' mentality that was obvious in *Glengarry Glen Ross*, most evidently in the character of the successful Roma. Profit equals civilisation for Teach, but he still seeks some sort of stability, some 'truth' or code of ethics as a structure. In *Glengarry Glen Ross* the sales office provided the legitimacy of a structured environment, but out on the streets the illusion of structure is harder to maintain. Mamet has said of *American Buffalo* that it deals with

the predatory aspect of American life. The whole Horatio Alger myth in America is false. It's a play about honour among thieves and the myths this country runs on . . . Calvin Coolidge once said 'The business of America is business.' The ethics of the business community is that you can be as predatory as you want within a structured environment.[24]

With no sense of the business moral code, men like Fletcher are simply 'animals' (p. 75) for Teach – capable of doing anything to survive, to win the game. With Teach's glaring contradiction between a 'civilised' concern for others within a fixed set of social rules and the individualistic pursuit of profit on which this country 'was founded', he ultimately sounds like a perverse rendition of Emily Post when he professes, 'Social customs break down, next thing *everybody's* lying in the gutter' (p. 86).[25]

One way in which Teach tries to bridge the contradiction between moral structure and ruthless achievement is through a separation between business and friendship, as Teach warns Don not to 'confuse business with pleasure' (p. 34). Both business and friendship, however, are defined by Teach rather tautologically. In business, 'The guy's an asshole or he's not, what do you care? It's business' (p. 28), while 'Friendship is friendship, and a wonderful thing' which Teach is 'all for' (p. 15). The important thing, Teach reminds Don, is to keep the two *separate*, 'and maybe we can deal with each other like some human beings' (p. 15). Civilisation, therefore, is defined by Teach not only through individual pursuit of profit, but a distinct separation between business and friendship. Therefore, at the end of the play, when Teach realises that Bobby lied to him, his sense of structure breaks down and he explodes with rage as he 'starts trashing the junkshop' (p. 103). Teach's proclamation that 'My Whole Cocksucking Life. The Whole Entire World. There Is No Law. There Is No Right and Wrong. The World Is Lies. There Is No Friendship' (p. 101) expresses his rage at a strange sense of disillusion. For Teach, the game must have some sort of rules, however loosely defined, in order to preserve civilisation as he sees it.

Don, however, knows that '[t]hings are not always what they seem to be' (p. 8), and while he puts a vague sort of stock in friendship, telling Bobby that 'what you got to do is keep clear who your friends are, and who treated you like what. Or else the rest is garbage' (pp. 7–8), his world does not explode in the end the way Teach's does. Don is mostly just 'tired' and 'need[s] a rest' (p. 104), weary of illusions but not shattered by them. The junk shop will get cleaned up, and life will go on for all three characters, as Teach sums up his violent disillusion which exploded a few moments earlier simply as '[t]his fucking day' (p. 106). Even though '[t]here is nothing out there' (p. 104), he is still going 'out there every day' (p. 103) to brave the frontier and play the game.

In Shepard's *True West*, the commodification of the American frontier myth is most *literally* examined, as America's idealisation of a Western past is often the central theme. Lee and Austin engage in a struggle for money, fame and 'legitimacy' in the Hollywood film industry by writing 'true' screenplays of the American West. The distinction between the representation and the real becomes blurred, and the commodification of myth is a central factor of American life. In this play, 'stability' rests self-consciously on the displacement of *myth* – in this case, very clearly America's cultural narratives – rather than any sort of absolute Truth, which therefore defers the notion of a stable centre, participating in what Connor calls 'the whole centerless universe of the postmodern'.[26]

True West is a play about writing a screenplay. Lee can be seen as a postmodern character who does not need an absolute and stable sense of reality – his 'truth' *is* an illusion, a potential Hollywood script – and he is completely comfortable with that blurred line between reality and representation. Austin, on the other hand, needs to feel 'fixed', even though his rigid version of reality is so frustrating to him that he winds up begging Lee to take him out to the desert to live a life of 'freedom' from the restraints of the modern world. He is both disdainful and envious of Lee's physical and existential mobility, telling Saul that Lee has 'been camped out on the desert for three months. Talking to cactus. What's he know about what people wanna' see on the screen! I drive on the freeway every day. I swallow the smog. I watch the news in color. I shop in the Safeway. I'm the one who's in touch! Not him!' (p. 35). At the same time he cries out that 'There's nothin' real down here, Lee! Least of all me!' (p. 49). Grounded in the material, commodified real, Austin is caught between his nostalgic need for stability and his desire for protean performance.

Ultimately, Megan Williams reads Lee as 'an allegorical representation of a desire to abandon the anxiety of modernism and to embrace the "uncertainty" of a postmodern world' (p. 71). Austin and Lee's divergent ways of constructing the real and evident in their different story-telling techniques. While Austin's writing may be defined as 'Art', he is still aware that it is 'business', and Lee's awareness of the connection between business and the representation of American myth inspires him to cash in on the dream as well. In this play, there is an awareness that business is an art, and vice versa:

Austin: I wish I wasn't – I wish I didn't have to be doing business down here. I'd like to just spend some time with you.
Lee: I thought it was 'Art' you were doin'. (p. 14)

Formal modernist distinctions have broken down, and Lee's entrance into Austin's world through his stories signals this breakdown as he answers Austin's mockery with the proclamation that he is 'legitimate' (p. 37). Whether petty criminal or Hollywood screenwriter, illegitimate or legitimate performance, both 'businesses' require the same talent – constant mobility – the ability to slip in and out of people's houses or in and out of various subjectivities, a multitude of characters. Lee possesses the ability to weave stories, but with the street informality of the orator rather than the formal 'artistry' of Austin's writing: 'I'm not a writer like my brother here. I'm not a man of the pen . . . I mean I can tell ya' a story off the tongue but I can't put it down on paper. That don't make no difference though does it?' (p. 18). It *does not* make a difference, since, just as in *Glengarry Glen Ross*, 'talk' is what matters, and Lee makes up for a lack of literary finesse with a claim of authenticity: 'So ya' think there's room for a *real* Western these days? A true-to-life Western?' (p. 19). His gift for gab is what enabled him to 'convince' (p. 31) Saul to produce his screenplay, a talent which Austin does not respect since it is not 'real'.

Austin also does not value Lee's particular story, since he still believes in a 'truth' that must remain distinct from illusion. When Lee offers Austin 'shared credit' on the screenplay if he will help him write it, Austin cries out: 'I don't want my name on that piece of shit! I want something of value. You got anything of value?'

(p. 40). Lee, of course, has something of value that Austin does not have – the ability to 'convince', to manufacture myth and commodify cultural fantasies, and this is partly what distinguishes him as a postmodern chameleon. In Shepard's plays, 'If a man can tell a story that kills the side of himself that was Austin, if he can learn how to market the death of the past, he will be able to move beyond the "terror" and "chaos" that accompany the twentieth-century loss of identity and history' (Williams, p. 70).

When Austin calls Lee's characters 'illusions of characters' (p. 40), he implies that the characters in his own screenplay are somehow not illusions, but grounded in the real. Lee, however, knows that all characters – even his own self – are illusions of characters, and answers Austin with: 'I don't give a damn what ya' call 'em! You know what I'm talkin' about!' (p. 40). Lee is one step ahead of Austin in his knowledge that all character involves role-playing and representation, and he is able to weave in and out of various characters to suit his needs. 'Character and identity in *True West*', Megan Williams writes, 'can be manipulated, changed, and performed as easily as an actor discards his costume' (p. 61). She goes on to point out, 'Throughout *True West* Lee is the character who knows that any history or narration of the past will only be a fiction' (p. 62). Lee too, however, experiences nostalgic moments where he craves a need for the real ('What I need is somethin' authentic. Somethin' to keep me in touch' (p. 56)), but they pass as they are replaced by the freedom he acquires in his suspicion of representation. Lee's insistence that it is alright for him to break into people's houses and take their televisions since they 'don't need' them – he's actually 'doin' them a service' (p. 22) – signifies the freedom one gets when one loses the connection to nostalgia. He does not watch or sell the TV he stole; throughout the play it sits high on the fridge as a symbol of modern representation watching over them, now dead and obsolete, another useless bit of clutter with no real value in the endless 'sea of junk' (p. 53).

As the brothers struggle with each other amongst the chaos and clutter, 'Mom' returns from Alaska, the last American 'frontier',[27] to the disordered and virtually destroyed house, convinced that '[s]omebody very important has come to town . . . Picasso's in town. Isn't that incredible? Right now' (p. 54). To Austin's news that

Picasso is dead, she stubbornly replies that no, he is not, 'He's visiting the museum. I read it on the bus' (p. 55). Mom confuses the artist with his work, the real with the representation. She thinks that the actual man Picasso is visiting the museum, although he has been dead for several years, and it is only his work that remains in his absence. For Mom, however, there is no distinguishing between the real and the illusion. The return of 'Mom' – the owner of the house and the figure of authority – would have marked a return to order in a realist play. Instead, after her own inability to distinguish reality from illusion for the brothers, she leaves the house in disgust, relinquishing ownership and claiming to not 'recognize it at all' (p. 59).

The definition of 'real life' in this play rests precisely on a lack of the real, on the notion of fluidity and illusion. Rather than being grounded in stable identities, relationships or histories, the reality of *True West* relies on transformation and performance – the manipulation of various roles. As the play progresses and Lee and Austin continue to fight and frantically destroy the contents of the house, this 'sea of junk' lies around in an explosion which, like Teach's 'trashing' of the junk shop in *American Buffalo*, signifies the destruction of an order grounded in material reality – of stable structures that America is supposed to represent – as boundaries are broken down. Unlike *American Buffalo*, however, there is no re-establishment of order in *True West*, as the play ends with the two brothers facing each other in confrontation, struggling among the unrecognisable ruins of certainty.

NOTES

1. C. W. E. Bigsby, *Modern American Drama 1945–1990* (Cambridge: Cambridge University Press, 1992), p. 193.
2. Matthew Roudané, Introduction to *The Cambridge Companion to Sam Shepard*, ed. Matthew Roudané (Cambridge: Cambridge University Press, 2002), p. 3.
3. Both Williams and Shepard have mentioned Samuel Beckett in particular as an influence. In a 1965 interview with John Gruen, Williams said that he admired Beckett, and in 1969 he asserted that Beckett and Albee were his favorite playwrights

(Albert J. Devlin, *Conversations With Tennessee Williams* (Jackson: University Press of Mississippi, 1986), pp. 120, 137). His later plays, especially *The Two-Character Play/Out Cry*, clearly offer a nod in Beckett's direction. Shepard too has repeatedly praised Beckett's work in his interviews, especially during the 1970s, and continued to do so in a 2002 interview with Matthew Roudané (*The Cambridge Companion to Sam Shepard*, p. 73). Beckett's paradox of stasis and movement, going on when you can not go on any longer, is philosophically tied to similar contradictions in Williams and Shepard. Tilden in Shepard's *Buried Child*, for example, knows that 'you gotta talk or you'll die' (*Sam Shepard: Seven Plays* (New York: Bantam, 1981) p. 78), echoing the simultaneous pleas for silence and dialogue in Beckett's *Endgame*.

4. Sam Shepard, *La Turista*, in *Sam Shepard: Seven Plays*, p. 293. Subsequent references appear parenthetically in the text.

5. Sam Shepard, *The Tooth of Crime*, in *Sam Shepard: Seven Plays*, p. 225. Subsequent references appear parenthetically in the text.

6. Megan Williams, 'Nowhere man and the twentieth-century cowboy: images of identity and American history in Sam Shepard's *True West*', *Modern Drama*, 40 (Spring 1997), 58. Subsequent references appear parenthetically in the text.

7. Sam Shepard, *True West*, in *Sam Shepard: Seven Plays*, p. 56. Subsequent references appear parenthetically in the text.

8. This translation by Robert Fry, *Poems* (New York, 1951), is the one quoted in Stephen J. Bottoms, *The Theatre of Sam Shepard: States of Crisis* (Cambridge: Cambridge University Press, 1998), p. 111. Don Shewey quotes a different translation that, as far as I can tell, he doesn't footnote: 'while there exists in your breast of stone / A heart which the tooth of no crime can wound': *Sam Shepard* (New York: Da Capo Press, 1997), p. 84. The different translations imply slightly different meanings, but the differences are not relevant for the purposes of my argument.

9. Bottoms, *The Theatre of Sam Shepard*, p. 103.

10. Ibid. p. 109.

11. Ibid. p. 111.

12. Roudané, *The Cambridge Companion to Sam Shepard*, p. 2.

13. Sam Shepard, *Buried Child*, in *Sam Shepard: Seven Plays*, p. 78.

14. Another instance of the ironies of appearance and reality is revealed in a Tennessee Williams anecdote. Once, when discussing the writing of realistic dialogue with his friend and fellow writer Dotson Rader, Williams advised him, 'Baby, don't write how people talk. Write how we *think* they talk. It's what we think we hear, not what they actually say, that sounds true' (Dotson Rader, *Tennessee: Cry of the Heart* (New York: Doubleday, 1985), pp. 166–7).

15. Terry Eagleton, 'Capitalism, modernism, and postmodernism', in *Against the Grain: Essays 1975–1985* (London: Verso, 1986), p. 134.

16. Steven Ryan, '*Oleanna*: David Mamet's power play,' *Modern Drama*, 39 (Fall 1996), 393.

17. Steven Connor, *Postmodernist Culture: An Introduction to Theories of the Contemporary* (Oxford: Blackwell, 1997).

18. Ibid. p. 51.

19. John McGowan, *Postmodernism and Its Critics* (Ithaca: Cornell University Press, 1991), p. 21.

20. David Mamet, *Glengarry Glen Ross* (New York: Grove Press, 1983), p. 17. Subsequent references appear parenthetically in the text.

21. Janelle G. Reinelt and Joseph R. Roach (eds), Introduction to *Critical Theory and Performance* (Ann Arbor: University of Michigan Press, 1992), p. 1.

22. Dennis Carroll, *David Mamet* (New York: St Martin's Press, 1987), p. 40.

23. David Mamet, *American Buffalo* (New York: Grove Press, 1976), p. 6. Subsequent references appear parenthetically in the text.

24. Mamet, quoted in Carroll, *David Mamet*, p. 32.

25. Emily Post (1873–1966) was an American authority on manners and social etiquette.

26. Connor, *Postmodernist Culture*, p. 8.

27. In Arthur Miller's *Death of a Salesman*, Alaska is similarly the ultimate frontier to be conquered (see Chapter 2). In *True West*, however, the American mythology of Alaska is referenced ironically, typical of a postmodern playfulness.

CHAPTER 6

The Politics of Identity and Exclusion

Song: Miss Chin? Why, in the Peking Opera, are women's roles played by men?
Chin: I don't know. Maybe, a reactionary remnant of male –
Song: No. (Beat.) Because only a man knows how a woman is supposed to act.
David Henry Hwang, *M. Butterfly* (1988)

Prior: We won't die secret deaths anymore.
Tony Kushner, *Angels in America, Part Two: Perestroika* (1992)

The instability and complexity of American identity, particularly in terms of the visibility of marginalised identities in American culture, was a topic that had begun to be increasingly addressed by playwrights after the 1960s. The visibility of 'other' sexual identities was especially brought to the forefront of American politics in 1969, when the Stonewall riots in New York City brought attention to gay rights, marking a watershed moment for social and political recognition that became the national Gay Liberation Movement. In June 1969, police raided the Stonewall Inn, a gay bar in Greenwich Village, which was not uncommon throughout the 1960s. The gay and transgender patrons, however, refused to react passively this time, and violently protested the police harassment in riots that lasted for several days. The political possibilities opened up by 'Stonewall', as history has named the rebellion, led to increased representation of gay characters by gay playwrights, along with examinations of the larger questions of social marginalisation and exclusion. Another factor that was responsible for the increase in the open representation of gay characters in American theatre was the repeal of laws forbidding the depiction of 'sex perversion', including homosexuality as it was classified at the time, in 1968.[1]

Lanford Wilson, an openly gay playwright, began his career in the early 1960s. One of Wilson's earliest plays, his one-act 'The Madness of Lady Bright' (1964), deals with the loneliness of an ageing drag queen, and he continued to depict a variety of gay characters in plays such as *Balm in Gilead* (1965), *Lemon Sky* (1970), *Burn This* (1987) and 'Portrait of the Cosmos' (1987). While his plays therefore do not shy away from homosexuality, his work more often operates within a broader context of marginalised identity. Known for experimental staging and simultaneous dialogue, Wilson's plays give voice to the unseen in American culture, those who 'don't fit'. He brings out the humanity in characters who do not 'count' and are pushed aside by poverty, violence, dreams that have gone wrong, or simply difference from society's mainstream. Wilson first reached Broadway in 1968 with *Gingham Dog*, and won the Pulitzer Prize and the New York Drama Critics' Circle Award in 1980 for *Talley's Folly* (1979). His other plays include *Days Ahead* (1965), *Wandering* (1966), *The Rimers of Eldritch* (1966), *The Hot l Baltimore* (1973) – which won the New York Drama Critics' Circle Award, the Outer Critics' Circle Award and an Obie Award – *Fifth of July* (1978) and *Rain Dance* (2002). In both *Balm in Gilead* and *The Hot l Baltimore* (the 'l' in the neon 'Hotel' sign is dark due to negligence) Wilson gathers society's misfits – prostitutes, pimps, drug dealers, hustlers, the impoverished, the aged and forgotten, wanderers, transvestites, lesbians and runaways who are chasing their dreams and somehow keep making wrong turns – and portrays the drama of their lives in a sympathetic light. His plays often focus on humanising the dehumanised, exploring the problematic cultural attitudes that lead to social alienation.

In *The Rimers of Eldritch*, Wilson explores the hypocritical morality of small-town America, using a Midwestern city as its setting. While *Eldritch* is able to sustain a coherent narrative, the form of the play is fragmented and nonlinear: 'The play takes place during the spring, summer, and fall of the year, skipping at will from summer back to spring or forward to fall.'[2] And, similar to *Balm in Gilead*, the play skips 'from one conversation to another' and key scenes are repeated. Time and place are merely suggested, and Wilson employs the Brechtian technique of having all the characters remain on stage throughout the play (p. 3). The assumptions of identity are called into question in this play, as being and action seem to reliably cohere, then suddenly fall apart.

Eldritch deals with a small town's ethical dilemma during a murder trial after a teenage girl is sexually assaulted, and the town's outcast, a mysterious eighty-year-old man named Skelly who wanders around and watches the townspeople when they are least aware, is killed. The disparity between outward social behaviour and private reality, along with the assumptions of what social identity *means* in terms of predicting future behaviour, is examined and questioned. For the town's initiated, what people are capable of doing is based on who they 'are', and their public performance is confused with their essential identity. What *Eldritch* finally reveals to the audience, however, if not to the characters, is that character is not consistent with image.

In the play, Skelly is condemned for observing, 'creeping through town, looking into things' (p. 22), and is seen as a constant threat. The townspeople automatically assume malicious intent on his part: 'Just looking is doing,' since 'who knows what he might do?' (p. 24). What we 'know' about people is based not on facts or direct observation, but on reputation, what we already believe to be true. Knowledge is dangerously based on assumption within a flawed logic that equates all social transgression. Robert, the young man in the play who appears to perfectly conform to social standards, asserts that 'everybody knows' how Skelly 'spies on people' (p. 61), and therefore it follows that he must be guilty of assault. Shortly before he is killed, Skelly insists that the townspeople are blind, that '[t]hey don't see' the truth (p. 38).

Along with Skelly, Cora, the café owner who took a young lover after her husband left her, openly transgresses the hypocritical codes of behaviour in Eldritch and so is also a sort of outcast. Cora, however, is 'forgiven' by the townspeople, as Wilma tells Martha that since Cora's husband left her she's 'not responsible for her own actions' (p. 5) – her being and her actions are suddenly disjointed. Skelly and Cora see and know the truth about character in Eldritch that removes the polite social mask, but because of their marginal social status their testimony is invalid, their words already deemed false. In contrast to Skelly and Cora, Robert is hailed as the model citizen, and is therefore given a credible platform for his words. Ironically, however, it turns out that Robert is responsible for the sexual assault and Skelly actually tried to stop it. Skelly's 'watching' led to him witnessing Robert trying to rape Eva, a fourteen-year-old crippled girl, and his attempts to help her are what gets him killed, as a neighbour comes out after hearing her screaming, assumes Skelly is attacking Eva, and shoots him.

Balm in Gilead is set in an all-night coffee shop on the Upper West Side in New York City, as the nighthawks gather to kill time, do 'business' or just wait for something to happen. These characters – reminiscent of Shepard's wanderers or the characters in Mamet's *American Buffalo* in their rootlessness and alienation – are individuals living outside society's rules, but forming their own version of community with its own codes (see Chapter 5). In his notes to the play, Wilson specifies that the characters' 'language, their actions, their reading of morality is individual but strict'.[3] The staging is essentially realistic, but Wilson's device of overlapping the characters' dialogue and having them talk simultaneously and over each other, while more 'real' than conventional realistic dialogue, functions anti-realistically in that the audience is unable to follow one coherent, consistent narrative. Speeches to the audience and comments on the action which break the fourth wall are common, as when Dopey and Fick step out of character and discuss the plot's unfolding:

Dopey [still to audience]. So now they're gonna kill him.
Fick. Joe?
Dopey. Yeah.
Fick. We ain't seen this, have we?

With that, they turn to the stage to watch the action (p. 67).

In the production of *Balm in Gilead* that I saw in the late 1980s at the George Street Playhouse, a regional theatre in New Brunswick, New Jersey, the director positioned the characters throughout the theatre as the audience filed in. They were in the hall, in the seats, in the aisles, and even in the restrooms – one tough 'lesbian' character sitting on the sink in the ladies restroom seemed particularly threatening – as the line between truth and illusion was blurred and audience members were not sure if these were 'characters' or actual 'people'. This staging is not included in the script and was a creative gesture that enhanced the production, bringing the audience into 'world' of the play, but clearly making the audience think about the boundaries between reality and representation.

Finally, the play's anti-realism is highlighted by the repetition of a key scene in which Joe gets stabbed, emphasising the importance of the scene and asking the audience to look again. By the end of the play, all is as before, and Fick wanders about the stage 'as at the beginning' (p. 72). In a sense, the ending mocks a realistic sense of closure. In realistic drama, the ending, after a series of conflicts and climaxes, marks a revelation of the truth of the play and a return to the order we saw at the beginning. In *Balm in Gilead*, there is a return to the beginning, but no truth is revealed, nothing has changed – it is a return to disorder, much like the 'sea of junk' at the end of *True West*, commenting on the chaos of postmodern culture.

The new honesty in the theatre after the 1960s and 1970s that Tennessee Williams hailed (see Chapter 2) allowed playwrights to explore issues such as race, gender and sexuality during the latter half of the twentieth century at a level that had not been previously done. In 1988, David Henry Hwang combined all these issues in his play about the relationship between gender roles and imperialism in Western and Eastern culture, *M. Butterfly*, which ran on Broadway for two years and won the 1988 Tony Award. *M. Butterfly* draws upon Puccini's 1904 opera, *Madame Butterfly*, which was based on the 1900 play by David Belasco. Hwang's work focuses on the cultural and political experiences of Asian-Americans in the United States. His first play, *F.O.B.* ('fresh off the boat') won an Obie Award in 1980, followed by *The Dance of the Railroad* (1981), *Rich Relations* (1986), *Bondage* (1991) and *Trying to Find Chinatown* (1996).

Hwang's brilliant presentation of the complexity of identity in *M. Butterfly* deals the issue of power in relation to sexist and racist stereotypes. Hwang takes the mythical figure of Puccini's Madame Butterfly, the submissive, self-sacrificing Japanese geisha girl, who ultimately commits suicide after she is deserted by the American naval officer who married and impregnated her, and turns her into 'M.' Butterfly – neither Madame nor Monsieur – an ambiguous symbol of gender complexity, political resistance and empowerment. Hwang transfers the action from Japan to China, with the character Song Liling as an opera singer who attracts the attention of a French diplomat, Rene Gallimard, while singing the death aria from *Madame Butterfly*. Gallimard falls in love with Song, claiming her as his 'Butterfly'; he is, however, duped by the fact that Song is actually a male spy for the Chinese government who is playing a woman's role in order to form a relationship with Gallimard and gain access to political information. The two engage in a twenty-year love affair, and the play – which shifts back and forth in time mainly from the 1960s to 1988 (the 'present day') in Beijing and Paris, with one scene recalling Gallimard's school days in 1947 – opens in the present with Gallimard in his French prison cell, jailed for treason, narrating the plight that brought him there.

The form of the play is anti-realistic in terms of its time shifts, moments of narration, and breaking of the 'fourth wall' by having characters address the audience. In Brechtian fashion, actors play multiple roles with minimal costume change, resisting any realistic illusion of unity between character and actor, and maintain audience awareness of the play as a performance. Moreover, Hwang's shift in the setting from Japan (in Puccini's opera) to China – two quite different national cultures – signifies a blurring of Asian cultural identity in the Western mind. Gallimard tells Song that she is 'convincing' as a Japanese woman, and Song replies that she assumes the 'irony is lost' on him.[4]

The complexities of identity, specifically in terms of gender, are brought to the surface in this play, and the essence of being is questioned along with the nature of 'love'. Erotic and political desire for domination are fused in Gallimard's desire for Song, and the politics behind the 'beauty' of 'Oriental submissiveness' in *Madame*

Butterfly – what Song calls a 'favorite fantasy' of Western men – are brought to the surface:

> Song: Consider it this way: what would you say if a blonde homecoming queen fell in love with a short Japanese businessman? He treats her cruelly, then goes home for three years, during which time she prays to his picture and turns down marriage from a young Kennedy. Then, when she learns he has remarried, she kills herself. Now, I believe you would consider this girl to be a deranged idiot, correct? But because it's an Oriental who kills herself for a Westerner – ah – you find it beautiful. (p. 1066)

Ultimately, however, when Song reveals herself to be a man, the power relations shift, and in the play's central moment of irony Song and Gallimard reverse roles, as Song dons a suit and addresses Gallimard as 'Butterfly', a label that he initially rejects. Song sheds the illusion of passive object (which, of course, was always an 'act') and occupies the position of desiring subject, revealing not only her biological sex, but the social implications – domination and control – that correspond to it.

Another irony in the play is that the same government that asked Song to pretend to be a woman in order to seduce Gallimard and spy for them later rejects her on the basis of her sexual identity. In communist China, Comrade Chin tells Song, 'there is no homosexuality' (p. 1073). The question remains, however, as to what constitutes sexual identity: desire, action, intention, or a combination of these. Song was posing as a woman to do her job, her national duty, but do her sex acts with Gallimard qualify her as a homosexual, or would that label apply only if she enjoyed the union? While Gallimard had sexual relations with a man, he did *believe* she was a woman, or at least he was able to convince himself that she was: 'Did I not undress her because I knew, somewhere deep down, what I would find? Perhaps. Happiness is so rare that our mind can turn somersaults to protect it' (p. 1076). Song claims that Gallimard never had to face the reality of her male body because she 'did all the work' sexually while '[h]e just laid back'; she 'was always on [her] stomach', never undressing completely because of her claim to shyness and modesty (p. 1081). She insists that she was able to fool Gallimard because she is a trained actor, an expert in the art of creating illusion. Her identity as a man made her even more skilful, as 'only a man knows how a woman is supposed to act' (p. 1077) according to the patriarchal codes and stereotypes of gender behaviour.

Gallimard's 'perfect woman' turns out to be a Western male imperialist *idea* of a woman, what a woman should be according to the male imagination, rather than who or what she actually is. When Song reveals himself to be a man, he remains the same person with whom Gallimard lived and made love for twenty years: 'Under the robes, beneath everything,' Song tells him, 'it was always me. Now, open your eyes and admit it – you adore me' (p. 1083). Yet Gallimard rejects the reality, preferring instead the lie: 'You showed me your true self. When all I loved was the lie. A perfect lie' (p. 1083). To Song's realisation that he only loved her when she was 'playing a part', Gallimard replies: 'I'm a man who loved a woman created by a man. Everything else – simply falls short' (p. 1083). The play ends with Gallimard 'crawling' towards the wig and kimono (p. 1082), clutching at the fantasy of 'a date with [his] Butterfly' (p. 1083), as desire and identification – wanting and being – merge. Gallimard becomes what he desires, as he puts on the wig and kimono and stabs himself to death, declaring that his name is 'Rene Gallimard – also known as Madame Butterfly' (p. 1084).

Five years after Hwang's exploration of the relationship between power and sexual identity, Tony Kushner would shake the very foundations of this relationship with his 'Gay Fantasia on National Themes', *Angels in America: Parts One and Two*, which opened on Broadway in 1993 and won, among other awards, the Pulitzer Prize for Drama and the Tony Award for Best Play of 1993 and 1994. Presented in two separate parts that each run approximately three hours long, the play is highly unrealistic in its staging, with fantasy sequences, actors playing multiple characters who share a connection, juxtaposed 'split scenes' that exhibit relationships in the action, ghosts who represent the main character Prior's ancestors and visit him at his bedside (reminiscent of *A Christmas Carol*), and an Angel with 'great opalescent gray-silver wings'[5] floating above the bed on stage. Even the name of the main character, 'Prior', is allegorical, signifying a connection to the historical past, what has come 'prior'. In a note on the staging, Kushner writes, 'The play benefits from a pared-down style of presentation, with minimal scenery and scene shifts done rapidly (no blackouts), employing the cast as well as stagehands' (p. 5). At one point in the play, the actor playing Prior, who is deathly ill, rolls his own bed onto the fully lit stage and climbs in to begin the scene, emphasising the Brechtian ideal of maintaining awareness of the performance as a perform-ance rather than as an illusion of 'reality'. Kushner continues, 'The moments of magic – the appearance and disappearance of Mr. Lies, the Book hallucination, and the ending – are to be fully realized, as bits of wonderful *theatrical* illusion – which means it's OK if the wires show, and maybe it's good that they do, but the magic should at the same time be thoroughly amazing' (p. 5). This is, after all, a 'fantasia'.

The play's postmodernism comes across most strongly in its acknowledgement of the place of the past in the present, its announcement that we are always recycling the old in order to create the new: 'It's All Been Done Before' (p. 33). Self-conscious references to canonical texts, especially central texts of American gay culture – Tennessee Williams's *A Streetcar Named Desire*, for example – and punning language: 'you know you've hit rock-bottom when even drag is a drag' (p. 31), also signify a postmodern awareness and playfulness. The acknowledgement of a historical past is evident from the play's title, as Kushner's Angel was inspired by the German-Jewish cultural critic Walter Benjamin's 'Theses on the philosophy of history' (1940). In his piece, Benjamin describes the angel in Paul Klee's 1920 painting, *Angelus Novus*, that he had purchased in 1921. For Benjamin, the movement of history is not one of steadfast forward motion intent on progress, but a messier intersection of past and present:

This is how one pictures the angel of history. His face is turned toward the past. Where we perceive a chain of events, he sees one single catastrophe which keeps piling wreckage upon wreckage and hurls it in front of his feet. The angel would like to stay, awaken the dead, and make whole what has been smashed. But a storm is blowing from Paradise; it has got caught in his winds with such violence that the angel can no longer close them. The storm irresistibly propels him into the future to which his back is turned, while the pile of debris before him grows skyward. This storm is what we call progress.[6]

The Angel of history who greets Prior at the end of *Angels in America, Part One* is not only an overtly anti-realistic device in this play's 'fantasia', but a reminder that the future bears the past along with it.

Another strong anti-realistic aspect of the play is its interaction between fictional characters and characters who represent key figures from various decades, such as Roy Cohn and Ethel Rosenberg, who appears as a ghost. Kushner sets the play in 1985–6 during the Reagan era (with an Epilogue set in 1990).[7] By the time President Reagan had acknowledged AIDS in 1987, believing it to be a disease that only affects the marginalised – gay men – over 20,000 Americans had died. Reagan's view of AIDS as a 'homosexual disease' and the moral condemnation associated with it is powerfully addressed in *Angels*. When Prior's ancestors – a '13th-century British squire' and 'an elegant 17th-century Londoner' – appear, they both announce how they had each died of different 'plagues', one that originated from fleas on rats, the other from the water supply. They understand AIDS as just another plague, one that is 'the lamentable consequence of venery' (p. 87). This view de-moralises and de-politicises AIDS, connecting it to the history of disease and illustrating its reality, rather than isolating it as the moral punishment against gay men, as the New Right often claimed during the 1980s. In *Angels*, the public merges with the private and the political is the personal.

Like Arthur Miller's *The Crucible*, *Angels in America* illustrates links to McCarthyism during the 1950s (see Chapter 2) in order to examine issues of power and exclusion in the history of America. In his 1953 play, Miller uses the seventeenth century witch trials in order to show parallels between this dark period in history and McCarthy's attack on alleged communists. In *Angels in America, Part One: Millennium Approaches* (world premiere 1991) and *Angels in America, Part Two: Perestroika* (world premiere 1992), Kushner more directly employs characters from the McCarthy era – Roy Cohn and the ghost of Ethel Rosenberg – to explore the complexities of how the political is related to the personal during the AIDS crisis of the 1980s and 1990s. Kushner claims that he picked Roy Cohn as a character because he was a closeted gay man who persecuted gays, and because of his close political connections to Senator McCarthy (who was also most likely a closeted homosexual). Cohn's homosexuality did not become public until after his death from AIDS in 1986. Ethel Rosenberg, her husband Julius Rosenberg, and her brother David Greenglass were Americans accused of being communist spies and selling secrets to the Soviets during the late 1940s. Ethel and Julius were convicted at their highly controversial trial in 1951, and executed in 1953. Roy Cohn's role in the trial is significant because he illegally influenced the selection of the judge and pushed him to impose the death penalty on the Rosenbergs in order to further his career and fuel McCarthy's anti-communist campaign. His actions were especially heinous with regard to Ethel, as there was no hard evidence against her. In 2001, David Greenglass, who was spared execution in exchange for his testimony against Ethel, admitted that he had falsely testified against his sister in order to protect his wife and children.

An overtly political dramatist and gay rights activist, Kushner's other works include *Slavs*, which is set during the collapse of the Soviet empire and won a 1995 Obie Award, and *Homebody/Kabul* (2001), a play about Afghanistan that was written before but produced just after the US invasion. In an interview for the *New York Times*, Kushner said that he wanted *Slavs* 'to speak to the particular dilemma that we're faced with now, those of us who believe that there's still a necessity for the collective, as well as the individual'.[8] This tension between the individual and the collective in America is one that marks Kushner's socialist politics and his plays, and is certainly a central dilemma in *Angels in America*.

Angels in America begins with a sermon on the American dream, and the problematic nature of American identity in this 'melting pot where nothing melted' (p. 10). Throughout the play, Kushner makes references to the idea of individuality that is valued in America versus a collectivism that is necessary to maintain a humane and democratic society. In *Angels*, these lines are often

drawn politically – through Republican or Democratic identifications, issues of race, religion and, at the centre, sexuality and the
growing AIDS epidemic. The complicated identities constructed
in the play bring up contradictions regarding the myth of America
and the 'dream' of inclusion and opportunity that it stands for, as
opposed to its reality. Difficult moral questions surrounding obligation and guilt are addressed through two pairs of characters – Louis
and Prior, a homosexual couple, and Joe and Harper, a 'heterosexual' Mormon couple. The play opens with Prior's admission that he
has contracted AIDS and Louis's dilemma surrounding whether he
is able to stay with his lover and support him, as 'he isn't so good
with death' (p. 25). Joe and Harper, a young married couple from
Utah, have just moved to New York for Joe's political career. Harper
has taken to heavily medicating herself because she feels alienated
by her husband, who turns out to be a homosexual struggling with
his identity and trying to resist his attraction to men.

As in *M. Butterfly*, the question of desire versus action becomes
important in the play. Joe believes that if he simply acts according
to the laws of the Mormon Church, acts as he is supposed to rather
than as he wants to, then that is all Harper can ask of him: 'As long
as my behavior is what I know it has to be. Decent. Correct. That
alone in the eyes of God' (p. 40). Louis is similarly struggling with
questions of desire versus obligation, freedom versus responsibility. If he does not want to take care of Prior, if he simply is not able
to face the reality of disease, is he morally obligated to stay? The two
religious identifications of the characters, Jewish and Mormon, are
significant in that both these religions teach that right *action*, what
one *does* rather than what one thinks or feels, is ultimately what
counts. The play, however, complicates these moral lines. The characters are politically identified as well; Louis is a socialist-minded
Democrat and Joe is a Republican. Ideology, morality, power,
action, and their connection to identity all come together in the
play. In *Angels in America, Part Two: Peristroika*, Joe and Louis
become lovers united by feelings of guilt and worthlessness, but
wind up parting in the end.

The connection between sexual identity and power is most
clearly revealed in the character of Roy Cohn. When Roy is
informed that he has AIDS, he refuses to admit he has the disease,

since it affects mostly 'homosexuals and drug addicts' (p. 43), and insists that he has 'liver cancer' (p. 46). Even though Roy admits to having sex with men, he rejects the label 'homosexual' as part of his identity. In a key speech to his doctor that reveals the politics of identity, he denies the common notion that sexual labels signify 'who someone sleeps with', pointing out instead: 'Like all labels they tell you one thing and one thing only: where does an individual so identified fit in the food chain, in the pecking order? Not ideology, or sexual taste, but something much simpler: clout' (p. 45). He continues:

> Now to someone who does not understand this, homosexual is what I am because I have sex with men. But really this is wrong. Homosexuals are not men who sleep with other men. Homosexuals are men who in fifteen years of trying cannot get a pissant antidiscrimination bill through City Council. Homosexuals are men who know nobody and who nobody knows. Who have zero clout. Does this sound like me, Henry?
> (p. 45)

Roy's position of power in society allows him to declare: 'Roy Cohn is not a homosexual. Roy Cohn is a heterosexual man, Henry, who fucks around with guys' (p. 46). Ultimately, however, social 'clout' turns out to be useless in a battle with disease, with the realities of the body, and Roy Cohn dies of AIDS, while Prior survives both physically and emotionally. *Angels in America, Part Two: Perestroika* ends with Prior's insistence on visibility: 'We won't die secret deaths anymore. The world only spins forward. We will be citizens. The time has come.'[9]

The question of the relationships among sexuality, death, identity and social visibility was the subject of much work in the theatre during the late 1980s and 1990s, as the AIDS epidemic grew into an international pandemic. Larry Kramer's *The Normal Heart* (1985) was the first major play after William Hoffman's *As Is* (1985), which opened a month before, to deal with AIDS. Kramer followed *The Normal Heart* with *The Destiny of Me*, its companion piece, in 1992; both plays are essentially realistic in their staging and mode of representation, marking a central difference from *Angels in*

America. While this chapter has so far focused on male playwrights' contributions to the exploration of the politics of American identity and the cultural issues surrounding sexuality, legitimacy, truth and visibility, women playwrights were certainly dealing with these issues as well and presenting them in complex dramatic forms. In 1992, Paula Vogel won the Obie Award for *The Baltimore Waltz*, a play about the death of her brother Carl, who died of AIDS in 1988, and the homophobia that haunted him. Vogel's plays often deal with sexualities and the body, and, while she understandably resists the limitations that come with the facile social categorisations of identity, her self-identification as a lesbian and a feminist playwright does inform her work. One of her early plays, *And Baby Makes Seven* (1984), deals with lesbians who parent several children, and another, *The Oldest Profession* (1981), addresses ageing prostitutes. *Hot 'n' Throbbing* (1992) explores the question of the distinction between 'dirty' pornography and 'harmless' adult entertainment and their effect on the imagination, using a hybrid of dramatic forms that weave expressionistic theatre conventions with realistic crime drama. *The Mineola Twins* (1997) was written two years before Vogel achieved success with *How I Learned to Drive*, but produced later, in 1999. It plays with what Vogel sees as the 'schizophrenia' of American cultural identity and the political split between conservatives and liberals, with its connection to sexual identity/action, particularly for women, that dramatically rose to the surface following the Clinton–Lewinsky scandal. One of Vogel's more recent plays, *The Long Christmas Ride Home* (2003), uses a flash-forward technique to look into the future, and casts puppets in the roles of children. The play revisits one of Vogel's earliest concerns, the damaging homophobia in America that is as fatal as AIDS.

Vogel's first major commercial success, *How I Learned to Drive*, was first performed off-Broadway in 1997, winning the Pulitzer Prize and the New York Drama Critics' Circle Award, Drama Desk Award, and Obie Award for best play. The play is about a young girl who is sexually molested by her uncle beginning at age eleven and continuing through her teenage years, but ultimately it takes on the themes of survival and the 'growing pains' of developing strength in character and becoming an adult. Vogel uses the driving lessons between the young girl 'Li'l Bit' and her Uncle Peck as a metaphor for sexual initiation, treating the subject of sexual seduction by an older relative as complex and not simply a predator/prey scenario. Uncle Peck is not Li'l Bit's blood relation, but the trust that is simultaneously compromised and intensified by the physical relationship remains a central issue. Stylistically, *How I Learned to Drive* makes use of three separate incarnations of a 'Greek Chorus' – a Male Greek Chorus, a Female Greek Chorus, and a Teenage Greek Chorus – who play multiple and shifting roles as well as comment on the action. Li'l Bit is both character and narrator in her play, and voice-overs announce each scene with a lesson on driving that also refers metaphorically to sexual negotiation. Finally, Vogel suggests that slides be shown at critical moments in the play to emphasise the impact of the scenes, but these slides were not used in the original New York production.

The construction of identity, especially female identity, in terms of sexuality and the body is key in this play. Li'l Bit explains that in her family 'folks tend to get nicknamed for their genitalia. Uncle Peck, for example. My mama's adage was "the titless wonder".'[10] Li'l Bit was named because when she was born her mother 'whipped [her] diapers down' and saw that there was '[j]ust a little bit' between her legs (p. 1753). When Li'l Bit appears in the play as a teenager, dinner table conversations regarding her large breasts abound, culminating in her grandfather's remark, 'If Li'l Bit gets any bigger, we're gonna haveta buy her a wheelbarrow to carry in front of her' (p. 1753). Her identity as a women lies in her sexuality. Even though she received a full college scholarship, her grandfather questions the usefulness of her education: 'How is Shakespeare going to help her lie on her back in the dark?' (p. 1753). The lack of sexual boundaries in the family fuels the action in this play, and for Li'l Bit the moral dilemma lies more in Peck's adultery, in a betrayal of her family – 'It's not nice to Aunt Mary' (p. 1757) – rather than in the seduction of his young niece.

The scenes between Uncle Peck and L'il Bit resist a reductionist interpretation as abuse, and for that reason they can be uncomfortable. Vogel plays with the audience's expectations and predetermined conceptions. Uncle Peck's character is presented sympathetically, even as sensitive to women; he helps Aunt Mary with the housework and insists that 'men should be nice to women' (p. 1767). He makes sure to let Li'l Bit know that he has not 'forced [her] to do anything' (p. 1757), even though his language is highly manipulative and seductive. He pleads that he thought Li'l Bit 'understood [him]' (p. 1757) when she expresses guilt about what they do. Her complicity in their sexual relationship remains questionable, and Uncle Peck is not seen as a villain, despite the clear portrayal of him as an older relative who seduces a child. When Li'l Bit returns from her first year at college and meets with Uncle Peck for the last time in order to break off their relationship, she is reluctant to lose the closeness they shared, despite her need to cut ties with him. The issue is further complicated by the suggestion that Li'l Bit is a lesbian, and while her new relationship can be seen as the catalyst for breaking things off with Uncle Peck, it ultimately remains separate from her decision. Simplistic labels and motives fail to completely identify character in this play. As Jill Dolan writes in her review of the New York production, 'Vogel's play is about forgiveness and family, about the instability of sexuality, about the unpredictable ways in which we learn who we are, how we desire, and how our growth is built on loss.'[11]

Like Vogel, other playwrights who have staged the complex construction and social maintenance of female identity during the last thirty years, such as Maria Irene Fornes[12] and Lisa Loomer, employ various dramatic conventions to convey their visions. What they have in common, however, is that they make use of an anti-realistic vision that distorts and moves past superficial appearance in order to access a truth beyond what ordinary experience tells us, and to emphasise connections, particularly among women, that are not readily apparent.

Fornes, one of the most innovative playwrights of the twentieth century, began her career in the 1960s, and continues to contribute to the canon of contemporary American drama through her complex presentations. Her plays make use of highly fragmented and even surrealistic dramatic structures. Because most of her work is experimental in style, however, she has not achieved the mainstream audience she deserves; her work has, however, been highly successful off-Broadway and with feminist audiences, as it is often concerned with revealing the uneven and violent treatment of women across cultures, the role of power in romantic relationships, and the various identifications that women embrace in order to cope and survive. She achieved her first successes with *Promenade* (1965) and *The Successful Life of 3* (1965), which won Fornes the first two of her Obie awards, and she has since received several awards for both playwrighting and directing. Three of her best-known works, *Fefu and Her Friends* (1977), *Conduct of Life* (1985) and *Abingdon Square* (1987), have also won Obies, and more recently her *Letters from Cuba* (2000) was honoured with an Obie Special Citation. A prolific writer, Fornes's other significant plays include *Eyes on the Harem* (1979), *Mud* (1983), *Sarita* (1984) and *Oscar and Bertha* (1991).

As both writer and director of several of her plays, Fornes controls the spectator's eye, offering radical new ways of seeing. Her first work to find a major audience, *Fefu and Her Friends*, is a feminist play in that it deals with the social forces that silence and destroy women, both psychically and physically. The limiting patriarchal construction/destruction of female identity, the self-imposed internalised oppression that women experience, and the need for new, self-determined identities are central issues in the play, as the distinction between acting and being, theatre and life, dissolves:

Sue: I had no idea we were going to do theatre.
Emma: Life is theatre. Theatre is life. If we're showing what
    life is, can be, we must do theatre.
Sue: Will I have to act?
Emma: It's not acting. It's being.[13]

For Emma, both the presentation of social identity and the forging of new ways of being involve the creation of character, in life as well as in the theatre.

Fornes's innovations in staging are probably most evident in *Fefu and Her Friends*, which is set in New England in 1935 and involves eight women who gather at Fefu's house for the common purpose of preparing a fundraising project related to education. The psychic and emotional fragmentation that the women experience is reflected in the fragmented staging, which reconfigures the traditional performance/performer relationship. In the play's first production in a Soho loft space in downtown New York, the audience was taken out of the auditorium and divided into four groups for Part Two of the play. Each group had to physically move to another part of the theatre, rotating through four spaces that represented rooms in Fefu's house in order to see four separate yet related scenes that the actresses performed simultaneously, repeating the action until all four groups had seen all four scenes. The audience came together again for Part Three. Rather than writing the play this way and then searching for a space that could accommodate it, Fornes found the space first and finished the play to take advantage of the space. Although she has since rewritten *Fefu* so that it could be performed in more conventional theatre spaces, the original staging demanded that the spectator see the same action from both a literal (physical) and, consequently, figurative point of view, challenging the very concept of 'realistic' vision. Fornes has claimed kinship with the writers of the avant-garde, asserting in an interview that 'if you call writers like Beckett and Ionesco and Genet a tradition, that is the tradition I belong to. I belong to the Off-Off-Broadway movement, which was the idea of doing art. And doing something that we loved doing.'[14]

Fornes's experiments with both style and content greatly influenced the next generation of women playwrights such as Lisa Loomer, who co-wrote the screenplay for the 1999 film *Girl, Interrupted* (starring Winona Ryder and Angelina Jolie), and is probably best known for her plays *The Waiting Room* (1994), *Expecting Isabel* (2000) and *Living Out* (2003). Much of her work focuses on the commonality of female experience across history, race, nationality and social class. *The Waiting Room* opens with women from three different historical periods and cultures – Victoria, a tightly corseted nineteenth-century English woman waiting for a hysterectomy, Forgiveness From Heaven, a wealthy eighteenth-century Chinese woman with bound feet, and Wanda, a contemporary American woman who has had multiple plastic surgeries, including three breast implants – sitting in a doctor's waiting room, discussing the reason for their visits. All three women are physically mutilated, or about to be mutilated in some way, in order to conform to patriarchally imposed social standards of beauty or 'health', as they deal with the condescending attitudes of the medical profession.

While the cultural dictates that oppress them are historically specific, the women are united not only by oppression but by their desire to comply with the social authority that creates and enforces it. In the play, sexuality and the body become the focus of the women's oppression. Victoria is waiting to have her ovaries removed because her husband believes that she is 'hysterical' due to 'too much education'.[15] The concept of female hysteria is connected to the ancient Greek concept, one which retained credibility through the Middle Ages, that the womb, or 'hystera', had to be kept moist through regular sexual intercourse or else it would wander around the body in search of moisture, causing physical symptoms in the body parts where it came to rest. The nineteenth-century understanding of hysteria was obviously more sophisticated than this notion but not unrelated, and the removal of the uterus was often seen as a 'cure' for hysterical symptoms. Forgiveness From Heaven has been experiencing trouble with her tiny bound feet, which make her desirable to men, but one of her toes has just fallen off. Wanda has been experiencing severe problems with her breast implants, a 'present' from her father, and she now finds that she has breast cancer. The play deals not only with the oppression of women, but with how one culture judges the practices of another and the politics of conventional versus orthodox medicine.

In Brechtian style, some actors play multiple roles that are thematically connected, and, like Kushner in *Angels in America*, Loomer specifies that scene transitions

> should be seen; [t]hink of them as bleeds, moments for characters to pass through each other's lives as they set props or move into or out of a scene, often carrying the concern of the previous scene. The transitions are extensions of the collage of time and locale . . . (p. 31)

Loomer highlights the complicity of women in their own physical and psychic mutilation throughout history, as they seek to be 'good' and are socially coerced into moulding their identities to fit specific models of appearance and behaviour.

In a different manner, *Living Out* also deals with the boundaries and consequences of good behaviour, focusing on the lives and experiences of immigrant Latina women who work as housekeepers and nannies to explore issues of race, class, power and citizenship. The terms 'living out' and 'living in' are ones that apply to the employment situation of nannies who live either outside or inside the employer's home, yet the term 'living out' has wider implications of identity and exclusion in America. Loomer is concerned with the notion of identity as 'illegal' or 'alien' – excluded from official citizenship – and the marginalisation of those who remain invisible in American culture and do not officially count. Loomer's play is based on interviews with actual nannies in the Los Angeles area, as she presents their stories on the stage and makes their lives 'visible'.

The staging of *Living Out* emphasises the human connections between the Latina nannies and their Anglo employers, despite cultural and economic differences. One of the central themes in this play is the notion that 'what a person perceives about someone else is what they already believe'.[16] Both the nannies and the employers have their own social and racial stereotypes; neither group is immune, and this connection is highlighted in the staging as each group of women alternately gathers in the same park to have similar conversations. The central employee–employer relationship centres around the characters of Ana, a woman from El Salvador who has two children of her own (one in El Salvador and one in the US) and is seeking work as a nanny, and Nancy, an entertainment lawyer who has just given birth to a daughter and hires Ana. Both women are married, and their complex negotiations of marriage, motherhood and work are more similar than they would seem at first. *Living Out* employs several 'split scenes', where Ana and her husband Bobby engage in similar conversations as Nancy and her husband Richard, in order to juxtapose the couples and illustrate connections. Often they are all on stage together engaging in overlapping conversations that signify 'a collage of time and space over [several] weeks', as 'lighting and a few costume changes indicate the passage of time' (p. 214).

Both husbands, while culturally different, experience similar feelings of resentment towards their wives' careers, yet they realise that two incomes are financially necessary. The issue is further complicated by the fact that both women admit to each other that they 'like to work' (p. 231), that their careers are not simply based on financial necessity, a secret they are reluctant to share with their husbands. Both Bobby and Richard are understanding men who want to accommodate their wives and negotiate the roles of childcare and working outside the home, but both are also influenced by cultural gender roles and feelings of neglect. The play's staging employs one set for both couples' living rooms, one that must be 'flexible enough so that the play can go back and forth between an expensive home on the Westside of Los Angeles and a modest apartment on the Eastside' (p. 185). The actors cross each other on the stage; as one husband leaves the couch, for example, the other occupies his place. In one scene, the men are even watching the same baseball game, but one in Spanish and the other in English (p. 204).

Ana and Nancy also share distinct similarities; they are essentially moral human beings who want to do a professional and honourable job, but both wind up lying to their employers in order to keep their positions. Ana is driven to lie in interviews and pretend that both her sons are in El Salvador in order to get a job, as her potential employers do not want her obligation to her own children to get in the way of making theirs a priority. Nancy too must deceitfully cover up her duties as a mother in order to avoid seeming pre-occupied or not committed to her career in a competitive business that, while making feminist claims, is overtly unsympathetic to motherhood. Yet ultimately it is social class that determines whose child will be more important, as Nancy does expect her daughter to remain Ana's priority.

Despite class differences, however, the two women develop a friendship, but one that winds up in tragedy for Ana. Foregoing her responsibility to her own family in order to do Nancy a favour '[a]s a . . . friend' (p. 233) and watch her daughter when Nancy has a work emergency, Ana allows her sister-in-law to take her son, Santi, to his soccer game. Through a complex series of events that lay ambiguous blame, he winds up in the hospital, and when Ana rushes to him, taking Nancy's daughter with her, Nancy mistakenly believes it is her daughter who was injured. Nancy quickly finds out the truth, but the scare makes her realise that she wants to stay home from now on and take care of her child. Through these events, Nancy finds out that Ana's son is actually in the US, and has gone to the hospital. Santi winds up dying of an asthma attack from a disease that he most likely would not have had if he lived on the more exclusive side of town, one where 'the air is better' (p. 205). When Nancy calls Ana to ask how Santi is, however, Ana allows her to believe that he has recovered. Ironically, the very child that Ana had to erase from the official narrative of her life in order to get a job is now actually gone. Whether Ana misled Nancy because she did not want her to feel guilty for asking Ana to watch her daughter, or because she did not want to seem like a failure as a parent, or simply because she did not want to further complicate the employer/employee relationship now that it was over, the result is that not only does she suffer the ultimate tragedy of losing a child, but it remains unspoken and does not even count. Ana's own son and his death remain 'invisible'.

NOTES

1. See Chapter 4. Similar laws were also revoked in 1968 in Britain. The first openly gay play was Mart Crowley's *The Boys in the Band*, produced in New York in 1968, and in London in 1969.
2. Lanford Wilson, *The Rimers of Eldritch and Other Plays* (New York: Hill and Wang, 1976), p. 3. Subsequent references appear parenthetically in the text.
3. Lanford Wilson, *Balm in Gilead and Other Plays* (New York: Hill and Wang, 1965), p. 3. Subsequent references appear parenthetically in the text.
4. David Henry Hwang, *M. Butterfly*, in *The Harcourt Brace Anthology of Drama*, 3rd edn, p. 1066. Subsequent references appear parenthetically in the text.
5. Tony Kushner, *Angels in America, Part One: Millennium Approaches* (New York: Theatre Communications Group, Inc., 1992), p. 118. Subsequent references appear parenthetically in the text.

6. Walter Benjamin, 'Theses on the philosophy of history', in *Illuminations*, ed. Hannah Arendt, trans. Harry Zohn (New York: Harcourt Brace Jovanovich, 1968), pp. 257–8.

7. Ronald Reagan (1911–2004) was President of the United States from 1981 to 1989.

8. Tony Kushner, quoted in Michael Cadden, 'Introduction' to *Slavs*, in *Political Stages* (New York: Applause Theatre and Cinema Books, 2002), p. 188.

9. Tony Kushner, *Angels in America, Part Two: Perestroika* (New York: Theatre Communications Group, Inc., 1992), p. 146. Critics such as Charles McNulty, for example, have pointed out the irony of Kushner's anti-Benjaminian optimism in the conclusion to *Angels in America, Part Two*. See Charles McNulty, '*Angels in America:* Tony Kushner's theses on the philosophy of history', *Modern Drama*, 39 (Spring 1996).

10. Paula Vogel, *How I Learned to Drive*, in *The Bedford Introduction to Drama*, 4th edn, ed. Lee A. Jacobus (New York: Bedford/ St Martin's, 2001), pp. 1752–3. Subsequent references appear parenthetically in the text.

11. Jill Dolan, 'Review of *How I Learned to Drive*', in *The Bedford Introduction to Drama*, p. 1782.

12. The playwright's name has also appeared as María Irene Fornés, but since the publication of her first anthology, Fornes has dropped the use of accents in her name.

13. Maria Irene Fornes, *Fefu and Her Friends*, in *Word Plays: An Anthology of New American Drama* (New York: Performing Arts Journal Publications, 1980), p. 17.

14. Una Chaudhuri, 'Maria Irene Fornes', in *Speaking on Stage*, ed. Philip Kolin and Colby Kullman (Tuscaloosa: University of Alabama Press, 1996), p. 112.

15. Lisa Loomer, *The Waiting Room*, in *American Theatre* (December 1994), p. 32. Subsequent references appear parenthetically in the text.

16. Lisa Loomer, *Living Out*, in *New Playwrights: The Best Plays of 2004*, ed. D. L. Lepidus (Hanover, NH: Smith and Kraus, Inc., 2005), p. 240. Subsequent references appear parenthetically in the text.

CHAPTER 7

Fragmented Representations of American Identity in the Theatre of the Vietnam War

Professor: Sometimes I feel like one of Pirandello's characters.
John DiFusco et al., *Tracers* (1983)

Because of its live and collaborative nature, as well as its ability to combine the verbal and the nonverbal, theatre is often the first to struggle publicly with complex political issues, and is a useful medium through which to examine culturally shared dramatic experiences that shatter a sense of certainty and reveal contradictions of acting and being. Nowhere was this contradiction more apparent in the United States during the 1970s and 1980s than in the aftermath of the Vietnam War. The New York theatre was the first to explore the ambivalence surrounding the Vietnam War, in much the same way as it would be the first to deal with the onset of AIDS – another morally complex national phenomenon where the body is the source of experience, knowledge and identity – during the mid-1980s.[1]

During the early years of the war in the late 1960s, plays dealing with the effects of the draft on America's youth were being produced, beginning with the first plays about the Vietnam War – the Open Theater's productions of Megan Terry's *Viet Rock* (1966) and Jean Claude van Itallie's *America Hurrah* (1966) – followed by the James Rado/Gerome Rasni counterculture musical *Hair* (1967). But it was during the 1970s and early 1980s especially, when the full impact of the war's aftermath was more immediate, that several plays dealing with the mythology of the Vietnam War on American life began to appear. H. Wesley Balk's *The Dramatization of 365 Days* (1972), an episodic dramatisation of Ronald J. Glasser's Vietnam memoir, *365 Days* (1971) and Amlin Gray's *How I Got That Story* (1979), about journalists during the war, were written by veterans who centred mainly on the consequences of combat. Significant Vietnam plays by non-veterans were also emerging during this time, such as Terrence McNally's one-act, *Botticelli* (1968), Lanford Wilson's *5th of July* (1978) and Stephen Metcalfe's *Strange Snow* (1983). In this chapter, I choose to focus on plays written by Vietnam veterans in order to highlight the dramatic transition from experience to art, reality to imagination. Among the most significant of these plays by veterans are David Rabe's trilogy, *The Basic Training of Pavlo Hummel* (1969, 1971), *Sticks and Bones* (1969, 1972) and *Streamers* (1970, 1976),[2] David Berry's *G.R. Point* (1980) and John DiFusco's collaborative psychodrama *Tracers* (1980), produced in Los Angeles at the Steppenwolf Theatre before being presented in New York in 1985.

In *The Great War and Modern Memory* (1975), Paul Fussell claims: 'The Great War was perhaps the last to be conceived as taking place within a seamless, purposeful "history" involving a coherent stream of time running from past through present to future.' This war

> took place in what was, compared with ours, a static world, where the values appeared stable and where the meanings of abstractions seemed permanent and reliable. Everyone knew what Glory was, and what Honor meant. It was not until eleven years after the war that Hemingway could declare in *A Farewell to Arms* that 'abstract words such as glory, honor, courage, or hallow were obscene beside the concrete names of villages, the number of roads, the names of rivers, the numbers of regiments, and the dates.' In the summer of 1914 no one would have understood what on earth he was talking about.[3]

But by 1975, the year Fussell published his exploration of the ways in which soldiers fighting in the First World War framed their experiences through familiar literary terms, over two million Americans who had fought in the Vietnam War knew exactly what Hemingway was talking about, and the fragmentation of indescribable experience left over from the war needed an outlet: not simply a catharsis, but a way of making some kind of meaning, if not quite making sense, of the psychic visions, physical sensations and atrocious actions of being a soldier in Vietnam.

In 'The recreation of Vietnam: the war in American fiction, poetry, and drama' (1990), Richard Sullivan suggests that in the literature of the war, 'Vietnam is represented as a place where ordinary experience merged with extraordinary experience to create a new world of meaning.'[4] Vietnam is arguably the American war most vulnerable to 'revisionism' in the areas of politics and media, but the theatre points to another very key form of revisionist mythmaking in this context. While war may always have been a part of American society, representations of the Vietnam War – not only in the theatre, but also in films, television, novels, poetry, photography, documentaries and biographical accounts – incorporated war into America's modern cultural psyche as a permanent scar on American life, illustrating the fragmented and contradictory sense of national identity that resulted.

In the Vietnam plays written during the 1970s and 1980s, the American soldier's 'performance' and actions in Vietnam are explored alongside the fantasy of an 'authentic' identity, or stable self, that existed before the experience of the war. In these works acting and being, myth and reality, become blurred to the point where they become indistinguishable, and therefore unreliable places to search for truth. History is revealed as myth, a narrative too inadequate to recreate experience. Language, too, is arbitrary and intangible, unable to capture the essence of the real. The only potential access to reality is rooted in the body. The close contact with the sights and smells of death, blood, vomit, dismembered body parts – in short, the unspeakable – become the experiences through which new identities for Vietnam veterans are formed. The violence of the American soldier's experience in Vietnam, the awareness of the physical body, therefore becomes the primary source of identity and knowledge in these Vietnam plays as they attempt to express the inexpressible.

Yet while the body is *perceived* as a stable marker of the real, it too is an unreliable place to search for truth, as it can certainly lie. The phenomenon of 'phantom limb' pain, for example – pain appearing to come from where an amputated limb used to be – was an experience common to Vietnam veterans who returned home from the war crippled and disfigured.[5] And even the comparatively ordinary experiences of the body such as race and gender cannot, of course, necessarily reflect any authentic 'essence'. Therefore, with no stable sense of identity and no stable sense of identification – as it is not only individual but national identity, what it means to 'be an American', that is called into question – the American Vietnam veteran in these plays is rootless and lost, left with a sense of dislocation that arises from both physical and psychic fragmentation.

In *Long Time Passing: Vietnam and the Haunted Generation*,[6] Myra MacPherson refers to the war zone in Vietnam – which also included Laos, Cambodia, and adjacent sea and air space – as the 'Vietnam theatre', evoking a common metaphor for modern war. On 13 April 2004, President George W. Bush also employed this parallel in a speech he gave in defence of his decision to invade Iraq, asserting that 'Iraq . . . is a theatre in the war on terror.' Fussell articulates that the 'most obvious reason why "theatre" and modern war seem so compatible is that modern wars are fought by conscripted armies, whose members know they are only temporarily playing their ill-learned parts'.[7] This factor was especially true of the Vietnam War, where the tour of duty was only 365 days. After completing one full year, a soldier knew that if he survived, he was home, but there was no national sense of closure, unlike other wars where soldiers fought together until the war was either lost or won. The fact that soldiers were rotated and did not train, fight and return with the same group of men (not only was there a fixed tour of duty, but soldiers were sent into Vietnam piecemeal and returned piecemeal) made this war seem even more like a 'coup de theatre' than previous wars, and led the soldiers to feel as if they were actors playing temporary parts. Fussell elaborates further on the comparison between war and theatre:

The wearing of 'costumes' not chosen by their wearers augments the sense of the theatrical. So does the availability of a number of generically rigid stage character-types [. . .] the hapless Private, the vainglorious Corporal, the sadistic Sergeant, the adolescent, snobbish Lieutenant [. . .] If killing and avoiding being killed are the ultimate melodramatic actions, then military training is very largely training in melodrama [. . .] It is thus the very hazard of military situations that turns them theatrical.[8]

Historically, the transformation of war experience into theatre has sought to calm fears about the uncertainty of wartime situations and translate the strange, the uncanny, into more familiar terms. Still referring to the First World War, Fussell continues:

> the dramaturgic provided a dimension within which the unspeakable could to a degree be familiarized and interpreted. After all, just as a play must have an ending, so might the war; just as an actor gets up unhurt after the curtain falls on his apparent murder, so might the soldier. And just as a play has a structure, so might a war be conceived as analogous to a play have a structure – and with it, a meaning.[9]

In addition to serving as a way to come to terms with and give meaning to temporal, excessive situations that were traumatic and unfamiliar, the metaphor of war as theatre had a tremendous social and psychological impact on negotiations of identity during and shortly after the Vietnam War. For the soldiers, seeing themselves as actors playing the parts of characters who act in a capacity that is separate from the values, morals and cultural identifications of the self was a psychological survival tactic. As Fussell argues, 'Seeing warfare as theater provides a psychic escape for the participant: with a sufficient sense of theater, he can perform his duties without implicating his "real" self and without impairing his innermost conviction that the world is still a rational place.'[10]

Yet the psychic fragmentation that this splitting of 'real' self and theatrical 'character' created fuelled the need for representations of a newly negotiated American identity that had to be formed and expressed by and for Vietnam veterans after the war. In the line from the Vietnam psychodrama *Tracers* that I quoted at the head of this chapter, the Professor states that he 'feel[s] like one of Pirandello's characters',[11] confused as to the boundaries between actor and character, being and performing, while the separation between 'authentic self' and soldier becomes blurred. This was especially true in the case of the Vietnam War. Whereas in the case of past wars, veterans had come home to warm receptions and parades – signs of national recognition and approval – for Vietnam veterans there was usually only hostility. The antiwar movement enforced feelings of guilt and purposelessness towards the war and denied the veterans the welcome that may have helped justify their experiences. Such national guilt, of course, often augmented whatever initial guilt veterans had felt. Once they returned home to an unwelcoming, accusatory, and what they perceived as ungrateful America, one that referred to these former soldiers as criminals and 'baby killers' rather than as heroes, the acknowledgement that self and other were one and the same, and that the self was responsible for the actions of the actor, blurred the boundaries between acting and being that needed to be explored.

For Vietnam veteran David Rabe, writing was a way for him to 'force some inner fog of feeling into thought', to give those feelings 'a shape in language that made them ideas [he] understood instead of shifting phantoms possessing [him]'.[12] Other authors writing about Vietnam identify the same sort of need to shape experience into language, to express the inexpressible. In 1986, John DiFusco revealed to me: 'For any of us who had gone to Vietnam, it's probably the most important thing in our lives. Especially for someone in the arts – painting, acting, writing – there is no way to get away from dealing with the war in your art.'[13]

In *The Basic Training of Pavlo Hummel*, the army becomes a metaphor for life, as the 'basic training metaphor, meaning "essential" training' was 'intended to include more in this case than the training given by the army' (p. xiii). The fragmented structure of *Pavlo Hummel*, as well as that of *Sticks and Bones*, echoes the fragmented experience of the Vietnam veteran. Not only is the structure of the play dreamlike and chaotic at times, but the fragmentations of the body are represented on stage as an unwavering reminder of a loss of wholeness and coherency, a psychic as well as physical castration. Rabe points out in the Introduction to *Pavlo*

Hummel the importance of the fact that 'the man with one arm and everything amputated below the waist was on stage while Pavlo visited the whorehouse' (p. xv), a constant reminder of physical, psychic and spiritual impotence.

In the Author's Note, Rabe says that it is 'Pavlo's body that changes. His physical efficiency, even his mental efficiency increases, but real insight never comes' (p. 110). In this play, identities marked by performances of nation, race or gender are all external illusions, unrelated to a primary, internal, essential identity. This 'essence' of identity, however, cannot be located or pinned down in the real, and is relegated to the place of myth. The body initially appears to be the only 'true' reality, but it too can mask truth. Ardell, the black soldier who appears and disappears throughout the play like an apparition or part of Pavlo's imagination (p. 9), tells him:

> The knowledge comin' baby. I'm talkin' about what your kidney know, not your fuckin' fool's head. I'm talkin' about your skin and what it sayin', thin as paper. We melt; we tear and rip apart. Membrane, baby. Cellophane. Ain't that some shit. (p. 96)

While there may be some truth in 'what your kidney know', Ardell further claims that Pavlo's essence does not correspond to his racial identity, his external body. He observes that Pavlo is 'black on the inside. In there where you live, you that awful hurtin' black so you can't see yourself no way. Not up or down or in or out' (p. 46).

Throughout the play, the physical and the psychological are united in the act of violence, and the boundaries between self and other are blurred, as Ardell tells Pavlo: 'When you shot into his head, you hit your own head' (p. 101). Similarly, Pavlo's brother is named Mickey, a nickname for 'Michael', which is, as we find out, Pavlo's original name. And when Mickey talks about his 'psychotic' wife, it is clearly her lack of identity boundaries that marks her as insane: 'she's pregnant again, she thinks, or you are or me or somebody' (p. 65).

Pavlo Hummel presents a nightmare cycle of death in which Pavlo, a soldier in the United States Army who is killed at the beginning by a Vietcong grenade, must return to basic training and then to Vietnam. Once again, he fails to gain understanding, and is finally killed again, this time by an American grenade. Even his death, the ultimate experience of the body, is presented as unstable and impermanent, failing to end the chaos and bring meaning. The play opens with Pavlo and Yen, a Vietnamese prostitute, momentarily exchanging identity by exchanging languages:

Yen: Creezy, creezy.
Pavlo: Dinky Dow. (p. 8)

Language is arbitrary and fluid, a false marker of identity that has no substance. Moreover, Pavlo had already transformed his identity before the play began by transforming his name. He confesses to his fellow soldier, Pierce, that he had his name 'legally changed' from Michael Hummel to Pavlo Hummel (p. 45), apparently to shield himself from his father's abandoning: '. . . someday, see, my father's gonna say to me, "Michael, I'm so sorry I ran out on you," and I'm gonna say, "I'm not Michael Asshole. I'm not Michael anymore" ' (45–6). For Pavlo, changing his external identity, his name, changes the essence of his identity. The two are blurred, and although Michael may have been hurt by his father's betrayal, this betrayal did not happen to Pavlo.

Back home, Pavlo asks his mother who his father was, and she answers his quest for a tangible identity by telling him that he 'had many fathers, many men, movie men, filmdom's great . . . they were your father' (p. 75). To Pavlo's enraged insistence that he wants to know who his 'real father!' is, she suggests he substitute image and metaphor for reality: 'He was like them, the ones I showed you in the movies . . .' (p. 75). His history, his origins, are presented as myth.

Racial and gender identity too are ultimately presented as myths. For the soldiers, Yen's identity is already suspect, a condition which seems to stem solely from the fact that she is Vietnamese, not from her status or actions as a prostitute. Her 'essence' comes from her racial or national marker, not from her actions or what she does. Jones tells Yen that she is inevitably diseased, her 'insides are rotten', not because she is a prostitute but because 'You Vietnamese, ain't you? Vietnamese same-same V.D.' (p. 80). He warns Pavlo of the dangers of Vietnamese women, telling him that they have no essence: 'They got no nature. . ... They got no nature, these women' (p. 80). For Jones, Vietnamese women are all artifice, all performance. Yen's racialised body and her national identity are therefore illusions, unreliable markers of her 'nature', and so the women of Vietnam are all myth. And, like its people, Vietnam itself is characterised as myth, as 'Vietnam don't even exist' (p. 66), except as a realm of nightmares.

Similarly, *Sticks and Bones* begins by immediately dismantling the perception of a 'seamless, purposeful "history" involving a coherent stream of time' that Fussell attributed to the Great War in the beginning of this essay. *Sticks and Bones* is a retelling of *The Adventures of Ozzie and Harriet* television series (1952–66), as David Nelson comes home from Vietnam blinded and changed, no longer the ideal 'American boy'. An attempt to fuse the historical with the personal opens the play. It begins with a series of slides – frozen images, fictions – that seem to be family photos from the early 1900s. But the time frame is confused, as images from both past and present merge together, and no one can firmly agree on whom the people in the slides are. Identity is called into question, and history becomes a fragmented fiction, a series of images that are unrecognisable and suspect. When the Sgt Major brings David home, he insists that he has the 'evidence' of David's identity – 'papers, pictures, prints' – but beyond that the Sgt Major 'know[s] . . . his blood' (p. 127). David is so unrecognisable that Ozzie and Harriet want to confirm his dental records and fingerprints; the body is the only possible reliable source of identity. David's own personal narrative, an eight millimetre film that he took in Vietnam as evidence of his experience, is equally unrecognisable, and appears only as a green blur to his family. In a familiar trope, David's blindness gives him insight. Left incapacitated, he knows that the body is the only truth, but Ozzie ultimately denies even this, failing to accept his son and declaring: 'Flesh is lies' (p. 217).

Rabe's final play in the Vietnam trilogy, *Streamers*, continues the themes presented in *Pavlo Hummel* and *Sticks and Bones* – the exploration of national, racial, gender and sexual categories as markers of identity, the blurred boundaries between acting and being, the instability of reality, and the unreliability of language. The play begins with Richie's insistence that '[w]e've got to make up a story' to cover up Martin's suicide attempt, but throughout the play they are all making up stories, war stories, in an attempt to define themselves and their actions.[14] Vietnam is again presented as a myth, a place that 'didn't even exist' (p. 11) until they got there.

One of the central actions in the play revolves around Richie's sexual identity/actions, as his fellow soldiers refuse to believe that he is 'really' a homosexual. Roger even goes so far as to insist that 'maybe you think you've tried it, but that don't make you it' (p. 29), creating a definite split between acting and being, performance and essence, that questions the location of character. But Richie is not convinced, and fuses acting and being, claiming, 'I don't know how else to be' (p. 28). Billy warns him that if he continues to act like he's homosexual, 'you're gonna have us all believin' you are just what you say you are' (p. 78), as action and being will merge. Yet while actions are not necessarily the final determinant of character, for Carlyle, one of the black men in the barracks, character is not to be found in the body either. In fact, he believes that the 'black man's problem' is that he is 'too close to his blood, to his body. It ain't that he don't have no good mind, but he BELIEVE in his body' (p. 67), and the body can be as much a source of deception as the mind.

The issue of where character ultimately lies is further complicated in Billy's sense of discrepancy between his impression of his former identity – the markers of who he was back home in American society – and his actions in Vietnam. His acknowledgement that he is 'a twenty-four-year-old goddamn college graduate – intellectual goddamn scholar type' and yet he has 'got a razor in [his] hand . . . thinkin' about comin' up behind one black human being and . . . thinkin' nigger this and nigger that' (p. 87) disorients him, and his actions shock him: 'I wanna cut his throat. THAT IS RIDICULOUS. I NEVER FACED ANYBODY IN MY LIFE WITH ANYTHING TO KILL THEM. YOU UNDERSTAND ME?' (p. 88). Ultimately, however, he is worried about the public reception of his performance – his 'reputation' – not the action itself: 'Jesus Christ, I got sweat all over me when I think a what I was near to doin'. I swear it. I mean, do I think I need a reputation as a killer, a bad man with a knife?' (p. 88).

The final disorientation of identity occurs at the end, with Sergeant Cokes, drunk and dying of leukemia, recounting his war stories, which he describes as 'like a goddamn Charlie Chaplin movie, everybody fallin' down and clumsy' (p. 108). But while the enemy soldier 'was Charlie Chaplin', Cokes '[doesn't] know who he was' (pp. 108, 109) in this script. Aware that he is close to death, he is not even a character in his own story, and he is left with only the experience of the dying body. The play ends with the collapse of language, as Cokes sings gibberish in 'a makeshift language imitating Korean, to the tune of "Beautiful Streamer"' ' (p. 109).

David Berry's *G.R. Point*, first presented as a staged reading at the Eugene O'Neill Playwrights' Conference in 1976, then later produced in 1977 and 1979 in New York City, focuses on the place where bodies are taken for identification: the 'Graves Registration Point'. Berry describes the play as a 'play of reconciliation',[15] a bringing together, a making whole. The play, which takes place in 1969, begins with the character Straw, who is in charge of bringing bodies to the G.R. Point, pointing out that there was 'hardly nothin'' left of' the latest addition; he 'looks like a jig-saw puzzle' (p. 10), while Deacon, completing the paperwork, exclaims: 'You frag 'em, we bag 'em!' (p. 11). Once again, the physical fragmentation reflects a psychic fragmentation and a severe sense of dislocation.

Micah, the new guy on the scene, has his first experience of psychic disorientation when, in an attempt to defend Mama-san from being coerced into sex with Deacon, he realises that he 'could have killed him. That didn't come out of my head!' (p. 22). Zan insists that Micah was just performing a role, wanting to play 'John Asshole Wayne and be a hero' (p. 22), but warns him that '[t]he Nam hasn't got any heroes' (p. 22), and the important thing is to stay alive. Physical survival is key, as abstract concepts such as virtue and honour become meaningless. Zan tells Micah to '[g]et out of your head. Try livin' in your belly' (p. 22), but neither pro- vides stability, and Micah ultimately 'feel[s] like [he's] nowhere' (p. 22). Instability is ubiquitous in the play, and while Shoulders is referring to Micah's urgency to get to the latrine when he asks him whether '[t]he place got your insides loosened up . . .?' (p. 12), the question could certainly describe a psychic 'loosening' as well. By the end of the play, Micah is so aware of the disparity between the role he plays as a soldier and the sense of his authentic identity back in 'the World', between action and being, that all he can desire is 'to be . . . whole!' (p. 46).

Micah clings to the markers of his identity back home, his family's three-hundred-year-old historical roots in Maine, and regularly writes his mother 'everything that happens here and everything going on in my head' (p. 27). Objective physical reality and subjective internal reality are presented as equivalent and eventually cancel each other out, as Zan questions the validity of Micah's accounts: 'What truth?! *Your* truth? Maybe your truth isn't everybody's . . .' (p. 27). Later on in the play, however, he tries to write home, but '[c]an't find the words', wanting to simply let her 'know who I am' (p. 40). But when Zan asks who that is, there is no answer. The self cannot be located in language, and even photographs, which Deacon presents as '*history*' (p. 38) and offers up for sale, are not reliable, as representation simply supports 'all your lies' (p. 39).

Like the work of Rabe and Berry, *Tracers*, a docudrama about the Vietnam War experience, aims to recreate the struggle with identity and the real that faced American soldiers returning from the war. When *Tracers* opened at the Odyssey Theater in Los Angeles in October 1980, it was very well received by both critics and audiences, going on to successful productions in San Francisco, New York, London and Sydney. The play was written and originally performed by seven actors,[16] all actual Vietnam veterans. *Tracers* was first conceived and directed by John DiFusco out of a series of veterans' discussions and psychodrama workshops which took place over a six-month period, beginning in April 1980, and was eventually produced by Joe Papp's New York Shakespeare Festival in conjunction with Tom Bird's organisation VETCo. (Vietnam Veterans Ensemble Theatre Company) at the Public Theatre.[17] The non-profit theatre ensemble company VETCo. was founded by Bird in 1978 as the first theatre in the United States designed by and for Vietnam veterans. An actor, director and Vietnam War veteran himself, Bird initially formed VETCo. in order to 'utilize the stage as a means of exploring, reflecting upon, and evaluating the American experience in Vietnam,' and its aims now extend to examining contemporary issues of war and peace.[18]

The form of *Tracers* is unmistakably Brechtian, with episodic scenes, 'fragmented costuming . . . and a minimum of props' (p. 3) reflecting the veterans' fragmentation of experience/identity. The soldiers have taken on the names of 'characters' – Dinky Dau, Baby San, The Professor, Scooter, etc. – which have become their new identities for the tour of duty. John Wayne again comes up as a reference for the soldier who is conscious of playing a prescribed role (pp. 17–18), and dreamlike imagery is used to illustrate the merging of reality and illusion (p. 25).

There is clearly a sense of fragmentation and alienation through-out the play, as characters struggle to make sense of their new identities in Vietnam. To the Professor's observation that he 'never smoked dope before [he] came to this green suck', Doc replies, 'I bet you never killed anyone before you came to this green suck, either' (p. 83). In this scene titled 'Professor and Doc' (pp. 76–85), the two bond over their interest in philosophical discussion and enquiries into the nature of reality. They see identity as fictitious; they are characters in a book, actors in a drama. Doc sums up this feeling of psychic dislocation typical of veterans of the Vietnam War, both on and off the stage, and claims to rely on the physical as the only stable reality: 'Sometimes I feel like I'm reading a book about this dude in Vietnam, but it isn't a book – it's real, it's me, and I'm here' (p. 79).

Their attempts to locate stability, however, shift between the external and the internal, the physical and the psycholinguistic, and their conversations initially point to a reliance on a solipsistic, insular reality. The Professor's sense that he feels 'just like one of Pirandello's characters' (p. 80) leads him to the conclusion that Pirandello's

> basic premise is that thought has more stability to it than reality, because reality is constantly changing, and because of that, concepts, ideas, things that exist only within the realms of thought, actually have more stability to their reality than the ever-decomposing three-dimensional objects that surround us. (p. 81)

Objective, external reality is rejected as unstable, and stability is sought in the subjective mind. But this escape from the real proves unsatisfactory, as the temporary connection between the Professor and Doc quickly turns back to the reality of physical violence and death. At the end of the scene, the Professor explains that he and Doc eventually became close, until one day when he was told that Doc had killed himself, putting a .45 to his head. All that was left was a note, but the Professor 'didn't read the damn note,' insisting, 'I can't converse with a note, I can't relate to a fuckin' note, I can't be friends with a note.' Language fails him, but physical release proves just as unlikely: 'I sat down and tried to cry. But, as hard as I tried, I could not shed one tear for my friend who had just killed himself' (p. 85).

Emotional and intellectual connection in Vietnam War drama, when it happens at all, is temporary, replaced by the reality of the fragmented body that also fails to make sense of experience, forcing the characters to turn back to a fragmented psycholinguistic experience that ultimately fails them as well. In the scene titled 'Fun and Games' (pp. 59–62), Dinky Dau and Baby San sit together, apparently having a conversation about their own particular problems, but neither one is listening or responding to the other. There is a stark lack of human connection in this scene, since, as Doc and the Professor demonstrate, connections prove to be fleeting and dangerous.

The scene in *Tracers* that most directly confronts the centrality of the body in the Vietnam experience is 'Blanket Party', where '[e]ach character is frozen in a position that is a physical manifestation of each actor/veteran's response to seeing dead bodies all over the stage,' but in typical Brechtian fashion, '[n]o bodies or props should be used' (p. 69). The designation of 'actor/veteran' in this scene illustrates the fluidity of identity and the merging of representation and the real. Just as in Pirandello's plays, the boundaries between actor/character/actual person, or fiction and life, are blurred to the point of complex and arbitrary distinction. The 'blanket party' involves clearing out the fragments of dead bodies after a battle and attempting to identify them. The soldiers have difficulty matching body parts with the bodies to which they belong, and even though Little John does not think it makes a difference since '[y]ou can't tell 'em apart anyway!' (p. 73), Dinky Dau reminds him, 'That's a human being you're fuckin' around with!' (p. 74). Physical reality matters, and being human means living in/with the body.

In the above plays, the American soldier's experience in Vietnam points to the body as an orienting force, the only place that can begin to stabilise the conflicts between reality and illusion. But the experience of the body is one of violence and fragmentation, not of reconciliation and wholeness. As Carlyle states in *Sticks and Bones*, the body cannot be relied on for the location of truth, and so, like Micah in *G.R. Point*, these veterans are ultimately left with no sense of self, no sense of place, feeling like they're 'nowhere'.

NOTES

1. New York's first major AIDS play, William Hoffman's *As Is*, was produced by the Circle Repertory Theater and opened in March 1985 in a small theatre space called The Glines, eventually transferring to a brief run on Broadway, where it was nominated for three Tony awards. *As Is* was followed by Larry Kramer's seminal work, *The Normal Heart*, a month later.

2. Drafts of *The Basic Training of Pavlo Hummel* and *Sticks and Bones* were both finished during 1969. *Pavlo Hummel*, however, was not given its first production until 1971 by Joe Papp at the Public Theater, and while *Sticks and Bones* was done at Villanova in 1969, it did not reach Broadway until 1972. *Streamers* was first copyrighted in 1970, but not performed until 1976. Rabe served in Vietnam from 1965 to 1967, and began writing his cycle of Vietnam plays roughly six months after his return. It was during the 1970s, therefore, that these plays were given major productions.

3. Paul Fussell, *The Great War and Modern Memory* (New York: Oxford University Press, 1975), p. 21.

4. Richard A. Sullivan, *The Legacy: The Vietnam War in the American Imagination*, ed. D. Michael Shafer (Boston: Beacon Press, 1990), p. 165.

5. For more on the notion of the 'phantom limb', see Elaine Scarry, *The Body in Pain: The Making and Unmaking of the World* (New York: Oxford University Press, 1985).

6. Myra MacPherson, *Long Time Passing: Vietnam and the Haunted Generation* (New York: Doubleday and Company, 1984).
7. Paul Fussell, *The Great War and Modern Memory*, p. 191.
8. Ibid. p. 191–2.
9. Ibid. p. 199.
10. Ibid. p. 192.
11. John DiFusco et al., *Tracers* (New York: Hill and Wang, 1986), 80. Subsequent references appear parenthetically in the text.
12. David Rabe, *The Basic Training of Pavlo Hummel / Sticks and Bones: Two Plays by David Rabe* (New York: Penguin Books, 1978), p. xi. Subsequent references appear parenthetically in the text.
13. John DiFusco, in a conversation with the author, 13 November 1986.
14. David Rabe, *Streamers* (New York: Alfred A. Knopf), p. 4. Subsequent references appear parenthetically in the text.
15. David Berry, *G.R. Point* (New York: Dramatists Play Service, 1980), p. 7. Subsequent references appear parenthetically in the text.
16. The original cast of *Tracers* included John DiFusco, Vincent Caristi, Richard Chaves, Eric Emerson, Rick Gallavan, Merlin Marston and Harry Stephens, and was conceived by these seven actors along with writer Sheldon Lettich, also a Vietnam veteran.
17. Joe Papp initially wanted to present *Tracers* in repertory with the new play about AIDS, Kramer's *The Normal Heart*, reasoning that both were plays about young men dying and how they deal with the experiences they encounter. Bird and DiFusco were completely against the idea, however, so the concept was scrapped.
18. VETCo. informational flyer.

CHAPTER 8

The 'NEA Four' and Performance Art: Making Visible the Invisible

There is a religious war going on in this country, a cultural war as critical to the kind of nation we shall be as the Cold War itself, for this war is for the soul of America.
Pat Buchanan, 1992 Republican National Convention speech

We don't have the communists to go after, they need an enemy within and they've decided it's us.
John Fleck, in an interview for *The Drama Review*, 1991

I believe that performance art may contribute to a significant change in culture. A change that allows a bigger 'we'.
Anna Deavere Smith, *Talk to Me: Listening Between the Lines* (2000)

At the 1992 Republican National Convention in Houston, Texas, insurgent candidate for President, Pat Buchanan, argued that a battle between socially conservative and socially liberal values was taking place in America. His declaration that the identity of America as a nation, its 'soul', was at stake spurred what came to be known throughout the 1990s as the 'culture wars', a term generally attributed to sociologist James Davison Hunter. Hunter's 1991 book, *Culture Wars*, divided American citizens into culturally 'orthodox' and culturally 'progressive', and explored the issues surrounding 'the struggle to define America'.[1] These revolved around topics that intersected complex social, religious and political lines – abortion, homosexuality, the separation between Church and State, and public schooling, to name a few. While the recognition of a 'culture war' was officially announced in a political forum, the events that led to Buchanan's 1992 comments were rooted in a controversy over public funding for artistic expression in America.

The controversy over the role of public funding for the arts was fiercely brought to public attention in 1989 when the work of two photographers, Robert Mapplethorpe and Andres Serrano, became the subject of debates on the issue of artistic accountability. In July 1989, the Corcoran Gallery in Washington, DC planned to open a retrospective exhibition of Mapplethorpe's photographs, a show that was partly funded by a $30,000 grant from the National Endowment for the Arts (NEA). The grant was not for the making of the photographs, which employed homoerotic imagery and the iconography of sadomasochism, but for their display. Between the time of the Corcoran's agreement with Mapplethorpe and the actual mounting of the exhibition, however, the museum decided to cancel the show. They cited a variety of vague and unconvincing reasons, and finally claimed that the 'political climate' in Washington – the rise of the New Right and its ultraconservative politics – made the show and the museum a target that could be used to denounce the NEA and possibly jeopardise future funding for the Corcoran.

The hostility towards the NEA had already been set in place by the controversy over Andres Serrano's piece, *Piss Christ* (1987), a cibachrome print of a wood and plastic crucifix submerged in a splashing of Serrano's urine. Serrano had been awarded a $15,000 fellowship from the Southeastern Center for Contemporary Art Awards for the Visual Arts, which had juried a contest under the NEA. Serrano's photograph had been attacked by fundamentalist religious organisations such as the American Family Association, which read it as an offensive image that equated Christ with excrement. While the provocative title of the photograph opens it up to a host of (mis)interpretations, it can more reasonably be interpreted from an artistic and social point of view as a comment on religious alienation in society or the tension between religion and the 'dirty', alienated body in the age of AIDS. In any case, Serrano's photograph was denounced by politicians as 'vulgar' and 'shocking', with Republican Senator Jesse Helms leading the attack on using public funding to promote 'obscene or indecent materials'. Religious leaders such as Pat Robertson attacked Serrano and the NEA on his Christian Broadcasting Network, and urged viewers to pressure Congress to eliminate public funding for the arts until it could assure the American people that such 'patently blasphemous' art would not be supported.

What was at stake, ultimately, in this battle over 'offensive' art is the suppression of sexual difference and religious freedom in America. The issue is not the 'obscene' depiction of sexuality in Mapplethorpe's work or the 'blasphemy' of Serrano's image, but the *type(s)* of sexualities that Mapplethorpe's work renders visible and the commentary on religious hypocrisy, or at least complexity, in America that Serrano's work reveals. At issue here is a battle over *visibility*: who and what will be allowed expression in American culture, who will 'count' and who will be erased. The multiplicity that these artists represented was one that embraced the spirit of diversity in terms of American identity, yet one that the New Right felt completely justified in denying.

This is the climate in which four performance artists were awarded, then denied, NEA grants in the summer of 1990, fuelling a national debate that would be battled out in the court system for eight years. While the NEA theatre panel voted unanimously to award grants to eighteen solo performance artists, the NEA chairman at the time, John Frohnmayer, vetoed the decision and denied grants to Karen Finley, Holly Hughes, Tim Miller and John Fleck – later known as the 'NEA Four' – citing 'political realities' and maintaining that their work was 'indecent'. This indirect form of censorship – denying funding to American artists once their work has been validated by a community of their peers – was seen by the artistic community as rooted in a pernicious homophobia, and dangerously parallel to Senator Joseph McCarthy's tactics in the 1950s.[2] Three of the artists denied grants are openly gay/lesbian – Hughes, Miller and Fleck – and Finley's work is sexually explicit, using various discourses of sexuality to reveal, among other things, the hidden violence and hypocrisy surrounding the construction of female identity in American culture. These artists sued the US

Government and won in 1993, having their grants reinstated. In 1998, however, the Clinton administration appealed the decision, taking it to the Supreme court, and won, with the court ruling that the NEA could use 'general standards of decency' – a decidedly vague concept – in making funding decisions. As a result of the years of controversy surrounding public funding, the NEA, under pressure from Congress, has since stopped funding individual artists.

The attack on artists, particularly the increasingly visible and controversial solo performance artists who were gaining legitimacy during the 1980s and 1990s, that took place during the 'culture wars' is crucial to any discussion of the struggle for American identity on the contemporary stage. While performance texts contain significant differences in terms of theme, style and intent, what they tend to have in common is that they occur in real time and place (as opposed to creating some fictional illusion) and embrace an improvisational, often conversational or even confessional tone with the audience: the 'fourth wall' is not only broken but nonexistent. Performance art may certainly include several 'characters' or performers, but often it involves a solo performer addressing an audience. These performance monologues usually maintain an autobiographical focus and contain fragmented narratives, or several stories woven together, as opposed to a single developed story line. Through a combination of performance genres (stand-up comedy, vaudeville, striptease, dance, the visual arts) and a blurring of the boundaries between representation and the real, performance art attempts to express the inexpressible and articulate that which cannot be articulated directly through language: the gaps and inconsistencies in rational expression.

Politically, these performances serve to reveal what is hidden, make visible what is invisible, and expose the subtle power relationships that function in our culture. To this end, performance artists often embrace and celebrate excess – that which is 'too much' – to shock the audience members and remove them from their comfort zones in order to destabilise sensibilities and allow them to see differently. Feminist performance art especially uses this technique of exaggeration to defamiliarise the all-too-familiar power relations that seem natural, so as to challenge the relationship of women to the dominant system of representation within patriarchal constructs. Performance art's relationship to postmodernism can be seen in the above conventions (fragmented narratives, a combination of artistic styles, and blurring of boundaries between fiction and reality), as well as in its focus on the multiplicity of truth(s). Philip Auslander refers to the 'antirepresentational strategies of postmodernist theatre and performance art, strategies that overtly questioned the truth-value of any and all representations'.[3]

In the late 1960s and early 1970s, women's performance art evolved in conjunction with the feminist movement, positioning women as speaking subjects in the theatre as opposed to passive objects. By both foregrounding and subverting their status as sexual objects to be looked at, women performance artists subverted expectations and played with patriarchal ways of constructing the role of 'woman' on stage. When Carolee Schneemann performed her piece 'Interior Scroll' in 1975, standing nude in front of her (mostly female) audience in ritualistic body paint and slowly pulling out a rope-like 'text' from her vagina that she began to 'read', she was commenting on the different ways in which men and women are constructed to experience the world differently, 'writing' from their 'sex' as a point of departure. Probably the most controversial of the performance artists in this chapter, Karen Finley, challenges the hegemonic models of patriarchy by initially appearing to participate within them. In other words, in many of Finley's performances, she presents her (often naked and covered in chocolate, egg, glitter or honey) female body as a conventional object for the male gaze, then promptly proceeds to subvert these expectations through her monologues, resisting the dominant power structures, language and values set up by a male-dominated system. As Lynda Hart points out, 'Finley's work excites a multiplicity of spectatorial identifications that illuminate the complexities of seeing. She is both susceptible to assimilation and co-optation by the dominant gaze that decries her representations and a model for subversive transgressions.'[4]

Finley's work plays with this 'dominant gaze' and seeks to expose what we are unable or refuse to see as a society. Her principle subject is the abasement and abuse of women in a male-dominated society, as she addresses 'unsafe' political topics such as abortion, moral hypocrisy, AIDS, violence against women, the sexual abuse of children, the commodification of art(ists), and other political power struggles, in unapologetic language and graphic images. Finley is infamous for using food ritualistically in her work, but as outrageous as her performances can be, her use of nudity and food in her work has often been grossly exaggerated, misunderstood and sensationalised in the media. In 1986, her performance of 'Yams Up My Granny's Ass' turned her into an overnight scandal after a cover story, 'Unspeakable Practices, Unnatural Acts', appeared in the *Village Voice*, claiming that she had actually sodomised herself with an uncooked yam onstage. She had not, but that charge stuck, drawing increasing attention to Finley and her work. *The Constant State of Desire* (1986) continued to explore how women not only are victimised by society but learn to degrade and victimise themselves as they are alienated from their own bodies.

Finley's work often appropriates the male point of view and male language in her performances in order to expose its assumptions and violence towards women, as in *I'm an Ass Man* (1984), which focuses on sexual violence. In *We Keep Our Victims Ready* (1989), Finley smeared chocolate all over herself as a metaphor for how women are 'treated like shit', then covered herself with red candy hearts because 'after a woman is treated like shit, she becomes more lovable'.[5] This performance led to her being called 'The Chocolate Smeared Woman' in the press, which both trivialised her use of chocolate out of context and added to her fame. She responded to this portrayal, as well as to the NEA controversy, with her piece *The Return of the Chocolate Smeared Woman* (1998), where she declares that she has 'been in an eight-year, sexually abusive relationship with Jesse Helms'.[6]

In *Shut Up and Love Me* (2001), a piece 'about sex, and about the need to connect, the need for intimacy', Finley moved from chocolate to honey, rolling around naked in 'the golden goo. This time it isn't about violence,' she explains. 'It is the simple pleasures of the flesh. Honey has so many meanings, but it is also just sweet.'[7] And in *Make Love* (2003), she dealt with reactions to 9/11 using the 'icon/New Yorker' Liza Minnelli as an 'imaginary creature, a goddess, diva to project onto and live through . . . Liza, as a parody, as an artistic device to make information less threatening' when her own persona as Karen Finley seemed to get in the way of the audience's ability to transfer the emotional burden onto her performance. With a cast featuring multiple Liza impersonators (and Finley as 'Liza 3'), *Make Love* became a safe place 'to throw our pathos, hilarity, mockery, and taboos about 9/11 [. . .] while trying to process this national tragedy and the current political climate'.[8] Her latest work, *George and Martha* (2006), imagines an affair between George Bush and Martha Stewart as a comment on the American political climate and the connections between war and sexuality, with a sly reference, of course, to American founders George and Martha Washington.

Although her methods are strikingly different from Finley's, Holly Hughes similarly foregrounds sexuality in her performances and challenges expectations of what it means to be a woman on stage:

> Just because men have exploited and colonized the female body onstage doesn't mean that we cannot put on our own versions. A lot of feminist theatre critics and academics feel that female sexuality can never be represented onstage without it becoming a peep show. I really disagree. You have to take the risk.[9]

Hughes began her career at New York's WOW ('Women's One World') Café, run by a collective of women with an interest in performing alternative theatre. There she developed and performed in her first play, *The Well of Horniness* (1983), whose title puns a controversial 1928 novel by Radclyffe Hall, *The Well of Loneliness*, now a classic of lesbian literature. Full of irony and naughty puns, Hughes's piece parodies the film noir genre, adding her own lesbian twist and playing with stock phrases from these detective films to produce her particular style of 'Dyke Noir Theatre'. *The Well of Horniness* self-consciously explores the instability of sexual identity and opens up a space for alternative representations of sexuality. Throughout the 1980s, Hughes continued to write and perform in plays such as *The Lady Dick* (1985), which similarly foregrounds an overt lesbian sexuality, and *Dress Suits to Hire* (1987), a mixture of erotic fantasy and pulp drama, where two women, one who exhibits a predatory sexuality, and her more repressed 'sister', who struggles against her lesbian desires, live in a clothing shop and try on different outfits as different facets of their personalities. In her later solo performances – *World Without End* (1989) and *Clit Notes* (1990), for example – Hughes deals with intimate topics such as her relationship with her parents and a sense of alienation growing up lesbian. In 1999, Hughes's promotional material for her new solo piece, *Preaching to the Perverted*, featured her draped in an American flag, as the performance playfully recounted her appearance in front of the Supreme Court during the NEA Four controversy, using rubber ducks to represent the Supreme Court Justices.

Politics and performance come together most directly in Tim Miller, who is as widely known for his political activism with the AIDS coalition ACT UP as he is for performances such as *Buddy Systems* (1985), *Some Golden States* (1987), *Stretch Marks* (1989), *My Queer Body* (1992), *Naked Breath* (1994), *Fruit Cocktail* (1996) and *Us* (2003). Like several of the artists discussed in this chapter, Miller's performances are highly interactive with the audience, and often centre on the body as a site of emotional and political conflict. His work 'strives to find an artistic, spiritual, and political exploration of his identity as a gay man'.[10] In *Spilt Milk* (1997), Miller weaves personal storytelling with political agenda, recounting the experiences of a young gay man arriving in San Francisco, where Harvey Milk – 'a fag like [him]'[11] who had been elected to city office – was 'changing the world',[12] but his hopes are crushed when he hears that both Milk and the mayor, Moscone, had been murdered. In *Glory Box* (1999), he explores the topic of same-sex couples and their struggle for marriage and immigration rights, an issue Miller has personally dealt with in trying to keep his Australian partner of several years in the United States. Rejecting what he considered the 'boring' realistic theatre (with 'all these people being characters') because it did not draw enough on what he 'liked about theatre or the theatrical, which was ritual, humor, body,' Miller developed solo performance work that was 'identity based'.[13] Unlike conventional Western realism, 'performance is ready to draw on anything – from vaudeville to ritual suicide'. Miller maintains 'a deep belief in autobiography and in creating identity and representation'. For him, 'It's the main job of theater.'[14]

The political pitfalls of solo performance work that, as Jo Bonney explains, 'finally made room for the previously marginalized, diverse voices of this society',[15] were evident in John Fleck's use of Christ imagery in his 1989 performance piece, *Blessed Are All the Little Fishes*. This piece was attacked by right wing conservatives as immoral and blasphemous for Fleck's use of a toilet as a baptismal font and container of holy water, with candles and a picture of Jesus floating in it. Fleck – who claims that he was devoutly Catholic in his youth and even wanted to be a priest – challenged this reductive interpretation, however, and explained the performance's imagery in terms of symbolism, moral confusion, and the irony of self-serving biblical interpretation:

> I've been criticized for peeing on Jesus Christ, but I never did that. It was very innocent. This man really believed that Jesus was speaking to him through his bodily functions – through his vomit and his urine *and* while he was reading the Bible. [. . .] Another side is that I didn't do it innocently and you also have to be careful. In a way, this man was interpreting the Bible to suit his ends. The Bible has been reinterpreted so many different times by so many different people. In a way this man is off his rocker and it's blasphemous and he's deluded.[16]

Fleck's discussion of *Blessed* points to a commentary on the complexities of religious epiphany versus delusion, and the hypocrisy of corrupt religious leaders who interpret the Bible to suit their own ends, particularly in terms of the scandals surrounding televangelists Tammy Faye and Jim Bakker and Jimmy Swaggart at the time.

The works that followed later – *DiRT* (1999) and *Mud in Your Eye* (2001), for example – were similarly confrontational, taking on culture's hypocrisies and playing with audience expectations. In *DiRT*, Fleck comments on the commodification of both art and the artist's body in a consumer culture: 'And this body, please, I could buy better than this,'[17] as he employs dirt both literally and metaphorically. At one point he comes out and makes a self-conscious reference to the NEA controversy, which was essentially all about 'dirty' language and images: '. . . there's no more funding for this kinda stuff anymore – so we've gotta fund each other – that's right – you pay for my dirt, I pay for yours, and then you pay for somebody else's and now it's my turn to pay for *yours* [. . .] you see, it's the Farming Theory of Free Market Economics.'[18] In *Mud in Your Eye*, Fleck enters through the audience to finally reach the bar on stage – draped with red, white and blue foil with an American flag in its centre – and have a cocktail before he performs a dance number on how George W. Bush was supposed to have been born a girl, and acts out an adolescent trauma with the use of a hand puppet. Ultimately, however, the piece is about finding identity and negotiating both the labels that we choose and the ones that are thrust upon us.

It was not only the artists known as the 'NEA Four', of course, who were fusing performance with the politics of identity during the 1980s and 1990s. The experimental feminist performance group Split Britches, founded in 1980 by Lois Weaver, Peggy Shaw and Deborah Margolin (who joined in 1981), wrote and directed pieces such as *Split Britches* (1981), *Beauty and the Beast* (1982), *Upwardly Mobile Home* (1984), *Little Women* (1988) and *Lesbians Who Kill* (1992), works which centred on recreating the past in order to more clearly see possible future(s). Vivian Patraka describes *Split Britches* as a piece that gives voice to 'women too old, too poor, too dumb, too lesbian, or too insistent on controlling their own lives to be visible,' characters 'outside the public (male) gaze of history who challenge its standard determinants of class, age, gender, and sexual preference'.[19] Split Britches was instrumental in founding the WOW Café, which became a prominent venue for lesbian and feminist performance, and Peggy Shaw received an Obie Award in 1988 for her role in Holly Hughes's *Dress Suits to Hire*.

In 1991, Lois Weaver and Peggy Shaw collaborated with members from the performance group Bloolips to present *Belle Reprieve*, a gender-bending deconstruction of Tennessee Williams's *A Streetcar Named Desire*. Employing anti-realistic theatrical devices such as vaudeville, drag, torch singing and tap dancing, *Belle Reprieve* puns the name of Blanche's lost family estate, 'Belle Reve', or 'Beautiful Dream', and comments on the underlying sexual politics of Williams's play. Deb Margolin is also well known for her solo performance work in pieces such as *Of All the Nerve* (1989), which began her solo career, *970-DEBB* (1990), *Gestation* (1991), *Of Mice, Bugs, and Women* (1993), *Cartheives! Joyrides!* (1995), *O Wholly Night and Other Jewish Solecisms* (1996) and *Critical Mass* (1997). Many of these shows were developed at the performance art space Dixon Place in New York, one of the most pioneering venues for theatrical experimentation in the downtown theatre world. In *Bill Me Later* (1998), Margolin takes on the Bill Clinton-Monica Lewinsky scandal, playing Lewinsky as, in Lynda Hart's words, 'a woman in love, with the only power that the dominant order allows women – the seduction of a powerful man'.[20] In 2001 she presented *Three Seconds in the Key* (2001), which she wrote and performed, fusing television advertisements, professional basketball and her own battle with Hodgkin's Disease. The piece maintains a storyline through a collage of images: Margolin's character and her son cope with her illness by displacing their anxieties onto the basketball heroes who come out of the TV and into their world, as she struggles with the beauty of life in the face of death.

Another influential feminist performance group in the tradition of Split Britches is The Five Lesbian Brothers, a theatre collective founded by Mo Angelos, Babs Davy, Dominique Dibbell, Peg Healy and Lisa Kron, which grew out of the WOW Café in 1989. Their works, such as *The Secretaries* (1994) and *Brave Smiles* (1993), are known for the playful disbanding of sexist stereotypes. Their more recent production, *Oedipus at Palm Springs* (2005), is a contemporary lesbian take on the tragedy of *Oedipus* that deals with the timeless themes of denial and repression, exploring how what we do not know, or will not see, eventually comes back to haunt us. Lisa Kron has also had a very successful solo career, with pieces such as *101 Humiliating Stories* (1994) and *2.5 Minute Ride* (1999), where she juxtaposes her family's trip to Auschwitz with their annual outing to an Ohio amusement park, using the image of the 2.5 minute roller coaster ride as a symbol for facing one's demons. Kron examines her relationship with her family, moving back and forth from the intensity of Auschwitz to the triviality of the amusement park, finding challenging and revealing emotions in both places. The triumphant joy that her father experiences when he insists on trying the roller coaster is seen alongside a different kind of triumph as he/they confront the collective historical trauma of

Figure 8.1 As her mother Ann (Jayne Houdyshell) observes, Lisa Kron addresses the audience in the American Conservatory Theater's 2005 production of *Well*. (Source: American Conservatory Theater.)

the Holocaust. Most recently, Kron was nominated for a Tony Award for her performance in her latest piece, *Well*, which ran on Broadway to rave reviews in 2006.

In the early 1990s, Anna Deavere Smith pioneered a different kind of performance, one that blended journalism/documentary with theatre, in her series of pieces called *On The Road: A Search for American Character*, which explores issues of race, community and identity in America. Smith would interview people and then perform their words herself, employing minimalistic settings and onstage costume changes to merely suggest character transformations in the tradition of Brechtian theatre. She relied instead on language and gesture, as her goal was 'to find American character in the ways that people speak'.[21] These performances were not simply about mimicry, however, but about using language to 'become the other'.[22] 'I knew that by using another person's language,' Smith explains, 'it was possible to portray what was invisible about that individual' and, on a social level, language could 'also be a photograph of what was unseen about society'.[23]

Her first major piece to come out of *On the Road, Fires in the Mirror* (1992), explored the 1991 conflict between blacks and Jews that took place in Crown Heights, Brooklyn, after a rabbi's motorcade on the way to religious services ran a red light and accidentally hit two Guyanese-American children, killing one of them. Three hours later, a group of young black men fatally stabbed a Hasidic history professor from Australia, who was walking a few blocks from the accident, in an act of apparent retaliation. These events fueled riots that lasted for three days. Smith went into the community to interview both prominent individuals who were directly involved in the conflict as well as those who experienced it from the margins. Her performance recreated the 'characters' she interviewed as well as some public speeches, but while she took down exact words, the final product was edited and rearranged in order to focus on the essence of each character sketch and compose a series that came together as a play. Smith has said that she chose Crown Heights because, as a multi-ethnic, multi-religious community, 'everyone wears their beliefs on their bodies – their costumes', so that identity and difference are visibly marked.[24]

In her next piece, *Twilight Los Angeles, 1992* (1993), Smith explored the 1992 Los Angeles riots that followed the verdict of the first Rodney King trial, after four LAPD police officers were caught on tape beating the unarmed King and then acquitted. Smith used the same technique for *Twilight*, interviewing those in the community and performing their words in an effort create understanding and identification with the other. Sandra L. Richards writes that in Smith's work, 'The speaker is given back his or her own words and rhythms in a body that is clearly Other. In that a female body is seen at times executing "male" movements, gesture becomes paradigmatic of gendered, social constructions.'[25] In other words, as in all the performances discussed in this chapter, prime markers of social identity such as gender and race are removed from their naturalised contexts and revealed as constructions, as performances. Smith won Obie Awards for both her solo performances in *Fires* and *Twilight*, and was nominated for two Tony Awards in 1994 for *Twilight* as Best Actress and Author of Best Play.

Fires in the Mirror was also a runner-up for the 1992 Pulitzer Prize in Drama, and while *Twilight Los Angeles* was nominated for the 1993 Pulitzer Prize, it was disqualified on the grounds that it was not fiction and could only be performed by Smith as the play-wright (or interviewer), leading to important debates on what constitutes a 'play'. Smith has continued to write and perform insightful pieces on American character with plays such as *House Arrest* (2000), which explores the history of the American presidency and came out of her involvement in the 1996 presidential elections that she covered for *Newsweek* magazine. Smith's 'sense is that American character [. . .] lives not in what has been fully articulated, but in what is in the process of being articulated, not in the smooth-sounding words, but in the very moment that the smooth-sounding words fail us. It is alive right now. We might not like what we see, but in order to change it, we have to see it clearly.'[26] In 1996, she was the recipient of the MacArthur Foundation 'genius' grant, and credited with creating 'a new form of theater – a blend of theatrical art, social commentary, journalism, and intimate reverie'.[27]

The solo character sketches that Danny Hoch brings to life in his pieces, such as *Some People* (1994) and *Jails, Hospitals and Hip Hop* (1998), reveal character through language along the same lines as Smith's performances do, but are not based on any interviews or 'journalistic' material. Instead, Hoch creates and performs is characters from social observation: 'This is my world! These are my inner monologues, layered composites of stories and voices from me, my family, my neighborhood, my people.'[28] His work is strongly influenced by hip hop tradition; he sees hip hop as 'the future of language and culture in the multicultural society'[29] and uses it in his work 'as an art of reclamation, turning the less-than-zero poor kid into something better', someone visible and worthy of attention.[30] His characters struggle with the performance of American identity, subtly aware of the tensions between acting and being. In *Jails, Hospitals and Hip Hop*, an inmate on Riker's Island knows that a police officer automatically sees his appearance as his essence, and complains, 'He don't like the way I look. I live in 163rd Street, I got a certain look. People in Park Avenue, *they* got a certain look [. . .] he see somebody that appears – I don't even know – *unprofessional*, or whatever, he automatically think criminal.'[31] Hoch's performances reveal character most interestingly in his 'race drag', or performance of another race to reveal race itself as a performance. Like Smith, he portrays multiple characters in his work, and 'every figure is desperate to speak – language is a soul print and way of busting through isolation. It can also be a stamp of dislocation, as throats choke on alien words.'[32]

The varied projects that could be identified as 'performance art' have developed a rich and diverse history in the American theatre, from the early success of Lily Tomlin and Jane Wagner's *The Search for Signs of Intelligent Life in the Universe* (1985) on Broadway, or the fusion of storytelling and song that marks Laurie Anderson's prolific body of work, to the ubiquity of Eve Ensler's *The Vagina Monologues* (1996) and the powerful monologues of Eric Bogosian and John Leguizamo, who continually cross the lines that divide performance styles, fusing stand-up comedy, social commentary and theatre. What these pieces stylistically have in common, however, is that they blur traditional genre boundaries and perform a repetition of social and historical conventions in order to expose them as conventions – not natural states – and therefore alterable, up for negotiation. As Sandra L. Richards writes:

> By beginning to understand how we are necessarily seduced into thinking and feeling certain aspects of identity as an irreducible category of existence, we become aware of the limits of our own discourse and may be more open to entertaining different modes of being that address some of those limitations. Theater, because it deploys multiple sign systems within a public arena, can serve as a particularly powerful realm for the renegotiation of identity(ies).[33]

NOTES

1. James Davision Hunter, *Culture Wars: The Struggle to Define America* (New York: Basic Books, 1991).
2. For a discussion of McCarthyism see Chapter 2.
3. Philip Auslander, 'Postmodernism and performance', in *The Cambridge Companion to Postmodernism*, ed. Steven Connor (Cambridge: Cambridge University Press, 2004), p. 110.

4. Lynda Hart, Introduction to *Acting Out: Feminist Performance*, ed. Lynda Hart and Peggy Phelan (Ann Arbor: University of Michigan Press, 1993), p. 8.

5. Karen Finley, *The Return of the Chocolate Smeared Woman*, in *A Different Kind of Intimacy* (New York: Thunders Mouth Press), p. 84.

6. Ibid. p. 258.

7. Ibid. p. 286.

8. Karen Finley, Introduction to *Make Love*, in *TDR: The Journal of Performance Studies* (Winter 2003), 53.

9. Holly Hughes, quoted in *Out From Under*, ed. Lenora Champagne (New York: Theatre Communications Group, 1990), p. 6.

10. Tim Miller biography in *Extreme Exposure*, ed. Jo Bonney (New York: Theatre Communications Group, 2000), p. 414.

11. Tim Miller, *Spilt Milk*, in *Extreme Exposure*, p. 157.

12. Ibid. p. 163.

13. Tim Miller, quoted in Steven Durland, 'An anarchic, subversive, erotic soul: an interview with Tim Miller', *TDR: The Journal of Performance Studies*, 35: 3 (1991), 176.

14. Ibid. 176.

15. Jo Bonney, Preface to *Extreme Exposure*, p. xiv.

16. John Fleck, quoted in Linda Frye Burnham, 'An unclassified number: an interview with John Fleck, *TDR: The Journal of Performance Studies*, 35: 3 (1991), 195.

17. John Fleck, *DiRT*, in *Extreme Exposure*, p. 224.

18. Ibid. 226.

19. Vivian M. Patraka, 'Split britches in *Split Britches*: performing history, vaudeville, and the everyday', in *Acting Out: Feminist Performance*, p. 217.

20. Lynda Hart, Introduction to Deb Margolin in *Extreme Exposure*, p. 324.

21. Anna Deavere Smith, Introduction to *Fires in the Mirror* (New York: Bantam Doubleday Dell, 1993), p. xxiii.

22. Ibid. p. xxx.

23. Ibid. pp. xxxii–xxxiii.

24. Anna Deavere Smith, quoted in Carol Martin, 'The word becomes you: an interview with Anna Deavere Smith' [1993], in

A Sourcebook for African-American Performance, ed. Annemarie Bean (London: Routledge, 1999), p. 268.

25. Sandra L. Richards, 'Caught in the act of social definition: on the road with Anna Deavere Smith', in *Acting Out: Feminist Performance*, p. 42.

26. Anna Deavere Smith, Introduction to *Fires in the Mirror*, p. xli

27. MacArthur grant quote from www.pbs.org/now/shows/232/index.html [accessed 15 February 2007].

28. Danny Hoch, Introduction to *Jails, Hospitals and Hip Hop and Some People* (New York: Villard Books, 1998), p. xiv.

29. Ibid. p. xvii.

30. Laurie Stone, Introduction to Danny Hoch in *Extreme Exposure*, p. 355.

31. Danny Hoch, *Jails, Hospitals and Hip Hop and Some People*, p. 11.

32. Ibid. p. 354.

33. Sandra L. Richards, 'Caught in the act of social definition', in *Acting Out: Feminist Performance*, p. 50.

Conclusion

I might not look the same, but I am your mirror. If you don't
see yourself, somebody done stole your soul.

Sarah Jones, performing Miss Lady in
Bridge and Tunnel (2004)

Thom Pain: Or – to employ the popular phrase we use
today to express our brainless and simpering tolerance of
everything, the breakdown of distinction, our fading national
soul – 'whatever.'

Will Eno, Thom Pain (2005)

Is Thom Pain correct? Is our 'national soul' fading, and what does
that say about American identity? What does that even say about
the need to identify a national soul, that is to say, a stable, unified
and essential core of being? Is there indeed a 'tolerance of everything, the breakdown of distinction'? If so, have we somehow lost
a distinct character that once existed, or are we constantly and
continuously forming new ones? Perhaps the 'mirror' that Martin
Esslin presents to us in the Introduction is cracked, reflecting back
to us an image in multiple fragments that are nonetheless still connected at the cracks, coming together as a whole. These are some of
the issues surrounding the performance of American identity that
the playwrights and theatre troupes in this volume have explored.
I began the Introduction with Carol Martin's question to Anna

Deavere Smith, 'What experience constitutes being an American?' and set out to explore how this experience has been represented in the contemporary American theatre. Yet perhaps it is not 'an experience' we should look for, not a 'soul' in the sense of a singular entity, but a multiplicity of experiences represented by the diversity of authors and styles. As the twenty-first century dawns, it seems appropriate to think about what *is* particular about our national soul and how it will continue to be reflected in the theatre. For Smith, 'American character lives not in one place or the other, but in the gaps between the places, and in our struggle to be together in our differences.'[1]

While traditional theatre that employs essentially realistic frameworks continues to flourish and tell complex, thoughtful stories, alternative performance styles, such as the solo character sketches of Will Eno's Pulitzer Prize finalist *Thom Pain (based on nothing)* and Doug Wright's *I Am My Own Wife*, which won the 2004 Tony Award for Best Play, or irreverent subversions such as *Avenue Q*, which took the 2004 Tony for Best Musical, are moving rapidly into the mainstream, and play with subjectivity, race, gender and sexuality in creative ways. Along these lines, the performance of characters who serve as constructed types, representative of certain cultural, moral or social identities rather than psychologically consistent individual personalities, is marked by the growing prominence of solo performers such as Sarah Jones in *Bridge and Tunnel*. Jones's portrayal of fourteen characters apparently defied traditional categorisation, receiving a 'special' Tony Award in 2006. Performer Lisa Kron blurs the line between actor/character/author and plays herself in *Well* (2004), a full-length play which features an additional cast of five characters – an ensemble of four who portray different figures from Kron's past, and Jayne Houdyshell, who played Kron's mother. *Well* brilliantly fuses autobiographical solo performance, memory play and traditional theatre to create a complex net of identifications and disrupt the boundaries between representation and reality. The play moved from New York's Public Theater to Broadway, and both Kron and Houdyshell were nominated for Tony Awards in 2006.

The construction of reality and the negotiation of identity in America continue to be salient topics for playwrights in the twenty-first century. Especially since 9/11, Arab-American playwrights such as Betty Shamieh, Heather Raffo and Leila Buck have been emerging to provide complex representations of social identity and religious identification in a new world order, while more established Jewish-American playwrights such as Israel Horovitz, Tony Kushner and David Mamet are addressing the complexities of contemporary Jewish identity as simultaneously tied to religion, culture, politics, and both the long history and present reality of anti-Semitism. The instability of identity has also been a major topic for playwrights such as Diana Son, author of the award-winning *Stop Kiss* (1998), which explores shifting sexual identities, and Daniel Beaty, who wrote and performed his solo piece *Emergence-See* (2006), which shifts back and forth from monologue to slam poetry as he portrays approximately 40 different African-American characters, at New York's Public Theater. Centred around a common historical experience, particularly slavery, *Emergence-See* confronts what Beaty believes is contemporary African-Americans' inability to come to terms with their shared racial past in America. Son's *Satellites* (2006) tells the story of Nina, a Korean-American architect and new mother, and her husband Miles, an African-American who was adopted by a Caucasian family and grew up in a white neighbourhood; both feel disconnected from their ethnic identities. While *Satellites* is Son's most realistic work to date in terms of style, *Stop Kiss* was much more fantastical, and Son has claimed to be heavily influenced by Brecht and other European writers in her work.

For African-American dramatists, there still remain too few mainstream opportunities in the theatre, despite the recent revival on Broadway of Lorraine Hansberry's *A Raisin in the Sun* in 2004 (starring hip hop performer, producer and entrepreneur Sean Combs) and the success of August Wilson's work. African-American culture is now, more than ever, dominated by hip hop and rap, and in the twenty-first century we should be looking at the popularity of hip hop as a postmodern form of dramatic expression that relies on the history of African-American performance. The hybrid style of 'hip hop theatre', which performer/writer Will Power has described as 'a contemporary form that fuses hip hop culture with contemporary forms of theatre',[2] is increasingly on the rise. His production of *The Seven*, a reimagining of Aeschylus' *Seven Against Thebes* in the tradition of hip hop theatre, was first performed on 19 January 2006 and ran for a month in February 2006 at the New York Theatre Workshop in downtown Manhattan. According to Power, hip hop theatre tells a story using the four basic elements of 1970s urban hip hop – DJing, MCing, graffiti art and break dancing – and developed out of the styles of 'spoken word' and slam poetry being performed in artists' collectives such as the Nuyorican Poets Cafe in New York City (which Sarah Jones came out of) and Urban Poets Society in London. Power believes, 'There is an evolution of a new culture . . . Hip hop theatre is theatre for today,' but it is also 'theatre that reinvents ancient theatrical relationships and ancient theatrical questions . . . Hip hop was able to bring the generations together.'[3]

This continuous reinvention of traditional forms and artistic relationships in the theatre to comment on a cultural identity that is always in flux, constantly recreated through time, is what contemporary American drama celebrates. Smith reminds us, 'the mirrors of society do not mirror society,'[4] so we must look for our 'soul', our cultural meaning(s), in the cracks, in the gaps. 'In America,' she emphasises, 'identity is always being negotiated. [. . .] There is an inevitable tension in America. It is the tension of identity in motion.'[5] In *Marxism and Literary Criticism*, Terry Eagleton writes, 'The task of theater is not to "reflect" a fixed reality, but to demonstrate how character and action are historically produced . . . The play itself, therefore, becomes less of a reflection *of*, than a reflection *on*, social reality.'[6] The explorations in this volume have revolved around the issue of how anti-realistic theatre deconstructs the very idea of theatre as mimesis, or a static 'reflection of' social reality, in favour of new 'mirrors' that offer audiences alternative perspectives or 'reflections on' the social and historical realities of contemporary American identities and their performance on the stage. In the tradition of anti-realistic theatre, these reflections are often deliberately fragmented or distorted in order to illustrate a more complex reality that exists beyond the surface. As Miss Lady reminds us, 'I might not look the same, but I am your mirror.'

NOTES

1. Anna Deavere Smith, Introduction to *Fires in the Mirror*, p. xli.
2. Will Power, in a presentation at the New School in New York City, 2 December 2005.
3. Ibid.
4. Anna Deavere Smith, Introduction to *Fires in the Mirror*, p. xxviii.
5. Ibid. pp. xxxiii–xxxiv.
6. Terry Eagleton, *Marxism and Literary Criticism* (Berkeley: University of California Press, 1976), p. 65.

Student Resources

Anti-realism

A form of theatre that resists the conventions of realism, eschewing representations of superficial reality in favour of more abstract presentations of the subjective realities that exist beyond the surface. In anti-realistic theatre, which may encompass expressionism, surrealism, minimalism, Epic Theatre, Theatre of the Absurd, and other anti-mimetic forms, stage settings are usually not specific of any particular time or place, characters exist as symbols for particular ideas rather than as complex representations of 'actual' human beings, narrative plot is rejected in favour of more general themes, and the dialogue (which is often fragmented or minimalistic) exists to further the action rather than to provide discursive meaning.

Epic Theatre

An anti-realistic form of theatre associated most famously with Bertolt Brecht. Brecht's Epic Theatre resisted mimetic or realistic illusion, and instead employed an 'episodic' style of presentation that distanced, or 'alienated', the audience members from a performance in order to appeal to their critical thinking facilities rather than to their emotions. Epic Theatre espoused Marxist convictions and saw the theatre as a catalyst for social change.

Fourth wall

The invisible wall that separates the stage action from the audience in realistic theatre. The 'fourth wall illusion' is the notion that the proscenium theatre space represents a room or house with four 'walls', and the front wall is invisible, or has been removed, so that the audience can peer into the 'lives' of the characters as voyeurs and eavesdroppers.

Mimesis

Aristotle's notion of dramatic action as an imitation or 'mirroring' of reality/nature, which was fundamental to his conception of the function of the theatre.

Performance art ('live art' in Britain)

Performances that occur in real time and place, usually maintain an autobiographical focus, and combine performance genres such as stand-up comedy, vaudeville, striptease, dance, theatre and the visual arts in order to blur the line between the representation and the real. While differing widely in terms of theme, style and intent, performance art pieces directly address the audience and use unconventional and sometimes controversial techniques to expose the politics surrounding identity.

Postmodern

A term that refers to both a particular historical era that is generally considered to have begun after the Second World War and the cultural or artistic products that mark this era. Critics often make a distinction between the terms **postmodern*ity*** and **postmodern*ism*** on the basis that the first implies the social or historical period that involves a transition from modernism, while the second is associated with the specific ideas, styles and cultural formations that came out of this historical period. Characteristics of postmodern literature and drama include: a focus on the instability of meaning, along with an irony and playfulness in the treatment of linguistic constructs; an acknowledgement of the past and a sense that literary creation is never truly original, but owes a debt to what has come before; a lack of any hierarchy or boundaries in the treatment of 'high' and 'low' culture; and an eschewing of the notion of an origin or essential 'core' in terms of identity, as identity becomes a series of layers or 'masks' with no distinction between the artificial and the real.

Realism

The form of theatre based on Aristotelian theories of representation that dominated the American stage during the 1940s and 1950s. Realism as a dramatic style sought to reproduce the surfaces of reality, with stage settings that reflected a specific place and time, and characters who aimed to mirror the speech, dress and behaviour of their middle-class audiences engaging in readily believable social and domestic situations.

Slice of life

The notion in realistic theatre that the audience is watching a 'slice' of someone's real life on the stage.

Theatre of the Absurd

A term coined by Martin Esslin in 1961 to describe what he saw as a new movement primarily in the European and British drama of playwrights such as Beckett, Ionesco, Genet and Pinter during the 1940s and 1950s, which attempted to present the existential anguish and absurdity of the human condition.

GUIDE TO FURTHER READING

Alexander, Robert, *I ain't yo' uncle*, in *Colored Contradictions: An Anthology of Contemporary African-American Plays*, ed. Harry J. Elam, Jr and Robert Alexander (New York: Plume, 1996).

Algarin, Miguel and Lois Griffith (eds), *Action: The Nuyorican Poets Cafe Theater Festival* (New York: Touchstone, 1997).

Artaud, Antonin, *The Theater and Its Double*, trans. Mary Caroline Richards (New York: Grove Press, 1958).

Auslander, Philip, 'Postmodernism and performance', in *The Cambridge Companion to Postmodernism*, ed. Steven Connor (Cambridge: Cambridge University Press, 2004).

Barnett, Claudia, 'A prison of object relations: Adrienne Kennedy's *Funnyhouse of a Negro*', *Modern Drama*, 40: 3 (1997).

Bean, Annemarie, *A Sourcebook for African-American Performance* (London: Routledge, 1999).

Beckett, Samuel, *Endgame* (New York: Grove Press, 1958).

Benjamin, Walter, 'Theses on the philosophy of history', in *Illuminations*, ed. Hannah Arendt, trans. Harry Zohn (New York: Harcourt Brace Jovanovich, 1968).

Berkowitz, Gerald M., *American Drama of the Twentieth Century* (New York: Longman Publishing, 1992).

Berry, David, *G.R. Point* (New York: Dramatists Play Service, 1980).

Bigsby, C. W. E., *Modern American Drama 1945–1990* (Cambridge: Cambridge University Press, 1992).

Boal, Augusto, *Theatre of the Oppressed*, trans. Charles A. and Maria-Odilia Leal McBride (New York: Theatre Communications Group, 1985).

Bonney, Jo (ed.), *Extreme Exposure* (New York: Theatre Communications Group, 2000).

Bottoms, Stephen J., *The Theatre of Sam Shepard: States of Crisis* (Cambridge: Cambridge University Press, 1998).

Brecht, Bertolt, *Brecht on Theatre*, trans. John Willett (New York: Hill and Wang, 1964).

Bullins, Ed, *Clara's Ole Man*, in *Five Plays by Ed Bullins* (New York: The Bobbs-Merrill Company, 1968).

Bullins, Ed, *Goin' a Buffalo*, in *Five Plays by Ed Bullins* (New York: The Bobbs-Merrill Company, 1968).

Bullins, Ed, 'Black theatre 1998: a thirty-year look at Black Arts Theatre', in *A Sourcebook for African-American Performance*, ed. Annemarie Bean (London: Routledge, 1999).

Burnham, Linda Frye, 'An unclassified number: an interview with John Fleck', *TDR: The Journal of Performance Studies*, 35: 3 (1991).

Carroll, Dennis, *David Mamet* (New York: St Martin's Press, 1987).

Chadhuri, Una, 'Maria Irene Fornes', in *Speaking on Stage*, ed. Philip Kolin and Colby Kullman (Tuscaloosa: University of Alabama Press, 1996).

Champagne, Lenora (ed.), *Out From Under* (New York: Theatre Communications Group, 1990).

Connor, Steven, *Postmodernist Culture: An Introduction to Theories of the Contemporary* (Oxford: Blackwell Publishers, 1997).

Connor, Steven (ed.), *The Cambridge Companion to Postmodernism* (Cambridge: Cambridge University Press, 2004).

Curb, Rosemary, 'Fragmented selves in Adrienne Kennedy's *Funnyhouse of a Negro* and *The Owl Answers*', *Theatre Journal*, 32: 2 (1980).

Day, Christine R. and Bob Woods (eds), *Where I Live: Selected Essays by Tennessee Williams* (New York: New Directions, 1978).

Devlin, Albert J. (ed.), *Conversations with Tennessee Williams* (Jackson: University Press of Mississippi, 1986).

Diamond, Elin, 'The shudder of catharsis in twentieth century performance', in *Performance and Performativity*, ed. Andrew Parker and Eve Kosofsky Sedgewick (New York: Routledge, 1995).

DiFusco, John et al., *Tracers* (New York: Hill and Wang, 1986).

Dolan, Jill, 'Review of *How I Learned to Drive*', in *The Bedford Introduction to Drama*, 4th edn, ed. Lee Jacobus (New York: Bedford/St Martin's, 2001).

Durland, Steven, 'An anarchic, subversive, erotic soul: an interview with Tim Miller', *TDR: The Journal of Performance Studies*, 35: 3 (1991).

Eagleton, Terry, 'Capitalism, modernism, and postmodernism', in *Against the Grain: Essays 1975–1985* (London: Verso, 1986).

Eagleton, Terry, *Marxism and Literary Criticism* (Berkeley: University of California Press, 1976).

Elam Jr, Harry J. and Robert Alexander (eds), *Colored Contradictions: An Anthology of Contemporary African-American Plays* (New York: Plume, 1996).

Esslin, Martin, *The Theatre of the Absurd* (New York: Penguin Books, 1961).

Esslin, Martin, *An Anatomy of Drama* (New York: Hill and Wang, 1976).

Finley, Karen, *A Different Kind of Intimacy* (New York: Thunders Mouth Press, 2000).

Finley, Karen, *The Return of the Chocolate Smeared Woman*, in *A Different Kind of Intimacy* (New York: Thunders Mouth Press, 2000).

Finley, Karen, *Make Love, TDR: The Journal of Performance Studies* (Winter 2003).

Fleck, John, *DiRT*, in *Extreme Exposure*, ed. Jo Bonney (New York: Theatre Communications Group, 2000).

Fornes, Maria Irene, *Fefu and Her Friends*, in *Word Plays: An Anthology of New American Drama* (New York: Performing Arts Journal Publications, 1980).

Fussell, Paul, *The Great War and Modern Memory* (New York: Oxford University Press, 1975).

George, Nelson, *Hip Hop America* (New York: Penguin, 1998).

Hart, Lynda and Peggy Phelan (eds), *Acting Out: Feminist Performance* (Ann Arbor: University of Michigan Press, 1993).

hooks, bell, 'Performance practice as a site of opposition', in *Let's Get It On: The Politics of Black Performance*, ed. Catherine Ugwu (Seattle: Bay Press, 1995).

Hutcheon, Linda, *The Politics of Postmodernism* (London: Routledge, 1989).

Ionesco, Eugène, *The Bald Soprano and Other Plays* (New York: Grove Press, 1958).

Innes, Christopher, *Avant-Garde Theatre (1892–1992)* (London: Routledge, 1993).

Jones, LeRoi (Amiri Baraka), *The Slave*, in *Dutchman and The Slave: Two Plays by LeRoi Jones* (New York: William Morrow and Company, 1964).

Jones, LeRoi (Amiri Baraka), 'The Revolutionary Theatre', in *The Harcourt Brace Anthology of Drama*, 3rd edn, ed. W. B. Worthen (Orlando: Harcourt, 2000).

Jones, LeRoi (Amiri Baraka), *Dutchman*, in *The Harcourt Brace Anthology of Drama*, 3rd edn, ed. W. B. Worthen (Orlando: Harcourt, 2000).

Hoch, Danny, *Jails, Hospitals, and Hip Hop and Some People* (New York: Villard Books, 1998).

Hunter, James Davison, *Culture Wars: The Struggle to Define America* (New York: Basic Books, 1991).

Hwang, David Henry, *M. Butterfly*, in *The Harcourt Brace Anthology of Drama*, 3rd edn, ed. W. B. Worthen (Orlando: Harcourt, 2000).

Kennedy, Adrienne, *A Movie Star Has to Star in Black and White*, in *Adrienne Kennedy in One Act* (Minneapolis: University of Minnesota Press, 1988).

Kennedy, Adrienne, *Funnyhouse of a Negro*, in *Adrienne Kennedy in One Act* (Minneapolis: University of Minnesota Press, 1988).

Kitwana, Bakari, *The Rap on Gangsta Rap: Who Run It? Gangsta Rap and Visions of Black Violence* (Chicago: Third World Press, 1994).

Kolin, Philip C. (ed.), *The Undiscovered Country: The Later Plays of Tennessee Williams* (New York: Peter Lang, 2002).

Kolin, Philip C., *Understanding Adrienne Kennedy* (Columbia: University of South Carolina Press, 2005).

Kolin, Philip C. and Colby Kullman (eds), *Speaking on Stage* (Tuscaloosa: University of Alabama Press, 1996).

Kushner, Tony, *Angels in America, Part One: Millennium Approaches* (New York: Theatre Communications Group, Inc., 1992).

Kushner, Tony, *Angels in America, Part Two: Perestroika* (New York: Theatre Communications Group, Inc., 1992).

Kushner, Tony, *Slavs!*, in *Political Stages* (New York: Applause Theatre and Cinema Books, 2002).

Loomer, Lisa, *The Waiting Room*, in *American Theatre* (December 1994).

Loomer, Lisa, *Living Out*, in *New Playwrights: The Best Plays of 2004*, ed. D. L. Lepidus (Hanover, NH: Smith and Kraus, Inc., 2005).

Ludlum, Charles, *Ridiculous Theatre: Scourge of Human Folly*, ed. Steven Samuels (New York: Theatre Communications Group, 1992).

McGowan, John, *Postmodernism and Its Critics* (Ithaca: Cornell University Press, 1991).

McNulty, Charles, '*Angels in America*: Tony Kushner's theses on the philosophy of history', *Modern Drama*, 39 (Spring 1996).

MacPherson, Myra, *Long Time Passing: Vietnam and the Haunted Generation* (New York: Doubleday and Company, 1984).

Mamet, David, *American Buffalo* (New York: Grove Press, 1976).

Mamet, David, *Glengarry Glen Ross* (New York: Grove Press, 1983).

Martin, Carol, 'The word becomes you: an interview with Anna Deavere Smith', in *A Sourcebook for African-American Performance*, ed. Annemarie Bean (London: Routledge, 1999).

Miller, Arthur, *Death of a Salesman* (New York: Viking Penguin, 1949).

Miller, Arthur, *The Crucible* (New York: Penguin, 1953).

Miller, Tim, *Spilt Milk*, in *Extreme Exposure*, ed. Jo Bonney (New York: Theatre Communications Group, 2000).

Ntozake Shange, *for colored girls who have considered suicide when the rainbow is enuf* (New York: Macmillan Publishing Company, 1977).

Paller, Michael, *Gentlemen Callers: Tennessee Williams, Homosexuality, and Mid-Twentieth Century Drama* (New York: Palgrave Macmillan, 2005).

Parks, Suzan-Lori, *The America Play*, in *The Harcourt Brace Anthology of Drama*, 3rd edn, ed. W. B. Worthen (Orlando: Harcourt, 2000).

Parks, Suzan-Lori, *The Death of the Last Black Man in the Whole Entire World*, in *The Bedford Introduction to Drama*, 4th edn, ed. Lee Jacobus (New York: Bedford/St Martin's, 2001).

Patraka, Vivian M., 'Split britches in *Split Britches*: peforming history, vaudeville, and the everyday', in *Acting Out: Feminist Performance*, ed. Lynda Hart and Peggy Phelan (Ann Arbor: University of Michigan Press, 1993).

Pinter, Harold, *The Caretaker and The Dumb Waiter* (New York: Grove Press, 1961).

Potter, Russell, *Spectacular Vernaculars* (Albany: SUNY Press, 1995).

Rabe, David, *Streamers* (New York: Alfred A. Knopf, 1977).

Rabe, David, *The Basic Training of Pavlo Hummel/Sticks and Bones: Two Plays by David Rabe* (New York: Penguin Books, 1978).

Reed, Ishmael, *The Preacher and the Rapper*, in *Action: The Nuyorican Poets Cafe Theater Festival*, ed. Miguel Algarin and Lois Griffith (New York: Touchstone, 1997).

Reinelt, Janelle G. and Joseph R. Roach (eds), *Critical Theory and Performance* (Ann Arbor: University of Michigan Press, 1992).

Richards, Sandra L., 'Caught in the act of social definition: on the road with Anna Deavere Smith', in *Acting Out: Feminist Performance*, ed. Lynda Hart and Peggy Phelan (Ann Arbor: University of Michigan Press, 1993).

Rose, Tricia, *Black Noise: Rap Music and Black Culture in Contemporary America* (Hanover, NH: University Press of New England, 1994).

Roudané, Matthew C. (ed.), *The Cambridge Companion to Tennessee Williams* (Cambridge: Cambridge University Press, 1997).

Ryan, Steven, '*Oleanna*: David Mamet's power play', *Modern Drama*, 39 (Fall 1996).

Saddik, Annette J., 'The (un)represented fragmentation of the body in Tennessee Williams' "Desire and the Black Masseur" and *Suddenly Last Summer*', *Modern Drama*, 41 (Fall 1998).

Saddik, Annette J., *The Politics of Reputation: The Critical Reception of Tennessee Williams' Later Plays* (London: Associated University Presses, 1999).

Scarry, Elaine, *The Body in Pain: The Making and Unmaking of the World* (New York: Oxford University Press, 1985).

Shepard, Sam, *Buried Child*, in *Sam Shepard: Seven Plays* (New York: Bantam, 1981).

Shepard, Sam, *La Turista*, in *Sam Shepard: Seven Plays* (New York: Bantam, 1981).

Shepard, Sam, *The Tooth of Crime*, in *Sam Shepard: Seven Plays* (New York: Bantam, 1981).

Shepard, Sam, *True West*, in *Sam Shepard: Seven Plays* (New York: Bantam, 1981).

Shewey, Don, *Sam Shepard* (New York: Da Capo Press, 1997).

Smith, Anna Deavere Smith, *Fires in the Mirror* (New York: Bantam Doubleday Dell, 1993).

Smith, Michael, 'The good scene: off-off Broadway', *Tulane Drama Review*, 10: 4 (Summer 1966).

Spoto, Donald, *The Kindness of Strangers: The Life of Tennessee Williams* (New York: Ballantine Books, 1985).

Starkey, Marion L., *The Devil in Massachusetts* (New York: Alfred A. Knopf, 1949).

Sullivan, Richard A., 'The war in American fiction, poetry, and drama', in *The Legacy: The Vietnam War in the American Imagination*, ed. D. Michael Shafer (Boston: Beacon Press, 1990).

Ugwu, Catherine (ed.), *Let's Get It On: The Politics of Black Performance*, ed. Catherine Ugwu (Seattle: Bay Press, 1995).

Vogel, Paula, *How I Learned to Drive*, in *The Bedford Introduction to Drama*, 4th edn, ed. Lee Jacobus (New York: Bedford/ St Martin's, 2001).

West, Cornell, *Race Matters* (New York: Vintage Books, 1994).

Williams, Megan, 'Nowhere man and the twentieth-century cowboy: images of identity and American history in Sam Shepard's *True West*', *Modern Drama*, 40 (Spring 1997).

Williams, Tennessee, *Camino Real* (New York: New Directions, 1953).

Williams, Tennessee, *The Theatre of Tennessee Williams*, 8 vols (New York: New Directions, 1971–1992).

Williams, Tennessee, *Stairs to the Roof*, ed. Allean Hale (New York: New Directions, 2000).

Wilson, Lanford, *Balm in Gilead and Other Plays* (New York: Hill and Wang, 1965).

Wilson, Lanford, *The Rimers of Eldritch and Other Plays* (New York: Hill and Wang, 1976).

Wright, Glenn and Raul Santiago Sebazco, *The Crime*, in *Action: The Nuyorican Poets Cafe Theater Festival*, ed. Miguel Algarin and Lois Griffith (New York: Touchstone, 1997).

Zola, Émile, 'Naturalism in the theatre', in *The Theory of the Modern Stage*, ed. Eric Bentley (Baltimore: Penguin Books, 1968).

Index

agitprop, 46, 67–8n, 117, 127n
AIDS, 123, 160, 161, 162, 163,
    164, 174, 188n, 189n, 191,
    195, 197
Albee, Edward, 9, 10, 29, 35, 36–7,
    66, 74, 80, 83, 148n
    The American Dream, 36–7
    The Zoo Story, 9, 36
    Who's Afraid of Virginia Woolf,
    37
Alexander, Robert, 11, 100
    I Ain't Yo Uncle, 101
Alienation Effect, 21
anti-realism, 2, 5, 67n, 155
anti-realistic, 68, 74, 88, 90, 121,
    154, 156, 160, 166, 199, 210
Aristotle, 3–4, 8, 17, 20, 29, 39n
Artaud, Antonin, 4, 7, 8, 9, 10,
    23–7, 66, 110, 129
Auslander, Philip, 194

Baraka, Amiri [LeRoi Jones], 11,
    72, 73–6, 78, 83, 89
    Dutchman, 73, 74–8
    The Slave, 74, 77, 78

Barnett, Claudia, 85
Baudrillard, Jean, 141
Bean, Annemarie, 93
Beaty, Daniel, 209
Beckett, Samuel, 8, 9, 10, 29,
    32–4, 35, 36, 37, 53, 65, 66,
    148n, 149n, 168
    Endgame, 32, 34, 149n
    Happy Days, 33, 34
    Krapp's Last Tape, 33, 34
    Waiting for Godot, 8, 32, 33, 34,
    35
Benjamin, Walter, 159, 173n
Berry, David, 14, 175, 184–5,
    189
    G.R. Point, 14, 175, 184–5,
    188
Bigsby, C.W.E., 61, 130
Black Arts Movement (BAM),
    11, 72, 73, 80
Blau, Herbert, 9, 26, 32
Boal, Augusto, 2–4
Bottoms, Stephen J., 133
Bread and Puppet Theater, 12,
    115–16

Brecht, Bertolt, 4, 7, 8, 10, 17–18, 20–3, 24, 26, 27, 30, 42, 47, 49, 66, 67n, 68n, 102, 110, 115, 116, 117, 120, 129, 153, 156, 159, 169, 186, 187, 201, 209
Bullins, Ed, 11, 72, 73, 78, 79, 83
Clara's Ole Man, 79–9
Goin' a Buffalo, 78, 79–80
Burroughs, William S., 125

Café Cino, 64, 131
Carroll, Dennis, 142
Chaikin, Joseph, 12, 108, 112, 113, 114
Chuck D, 94, 105n
Cohn, Roy, 160, 161, 162, 163
communism, 47, 49, 61
Connor, Steven, 25, 140, 141, 145
culture wars, 190, 193
Curb, Rosemary, 84

Diamond, Elin, 24
DiFusco, John, 14, 174, 175, 179, 185, 189n
Tracers, 14, 174, 175, 178, 185–8, 189n
Dr Dre, 95, 96, 97
Dolan, Jill, 166

Eagleton, Terry, 68n, 139, 210
El Teatro Campesino, 12, 116, 117–18
Eno, Will
Thom Pain (based on nothing), 207, 208
environmental theatre, 12, 118–19
Epic Theatre, 17, 18, 21, 23, 110

Esslin, Martin, 1, 2, 7, 27, 28, 29, 35, 36, 207

Finley, Karen, 15, 192, 194–6
George and Martha, 196
Make Love, 195–6
Shut Up and Love Me, 195
The Return of the Chocolate Smeared Woman, 195
We Keep Our Victims Ready, 195
First World War, 5, 17, 45, 175, 178
Fleck, John, 15, 190, 192, 198–9
Blessed Are All the Little Fishes, 198
DiRT, 198–9
Mud in Your Eye, 198, 199
Foreman, Richard, 12, 124, 127
Fornes, Maria Irene, 13, 166, 167, 168
Fefu and Her Friends, 167–8
fourth wall, 12, 21, 22, 109, 110, 154, 156, 193
Fussell, Paul, 175, 177, 178, 182

gangsta rap, 97–9, 100, 105
Gelber, Jack, 9, 12, 110
Genet, Jean, 8, 9, 10, 25, 27, 28, 29, 37, 66, 71, 119, 168
George, Nelson, 95, 97, 98
Gray, Spalding, 119, 120, 127
Greenglass, David, 161
Grotowski, Jerzy, 12, 114, 121

Hansberry, Lorraine, 10, 90, 209
Hart, Lynda, 194, 200
Harvey, David, 68n

hip hop, 11, 12, 93, 94, 95–101,
    103, 105n, 106n, 203, 209–10
Hoch, Danny, 15, 100, 203
Hoffman, William, 163, 188n
House Un-American Activities
    Committee (HUAC), 48, 49,
    50, 63
Hughes, Holly, 15, 192, 196–7,
    199
Hunter, James Davison, 190
Hwang, David Henry, 13, 151,
    155, 156, 158
    M. Butterfly, 151, 155, 156–8,
    162

Ibsen, Henrik, 5, 18, 19
Ice Cube, 11, 72, 94–6, 98, 99
Innes, Christopher, 28
Ionesco, Eugène, 8, 9, 10, 17,
    29–31, 37, 66, 168
    The Bald Soprano [*The Bald
    Prima Donna*], 8, 30

Jameson, Fredric, 68n, 140
Jones, Sarah, 207, 208, 210

Kennedy, Adrienne, 11, 72, 77, 80,
    81, 82, 83, 84, 85, 86, 87, 89
    *A Movie Star Has to Star in
    Black and White*, 83, 86
    A Rat's Mass, 81, 82, 83
    Funnyhouse of a Negro, 72, 77,
    80, 83–5, 87
Kolin, Philip, 83, 86
Kramer, Larry, 163, 188n,
    189n
Kron, Lisa, 15, 200, 201, 208;
    see also The Five Lesbian
    Brothers

Kushner, Tony, 15, 151, 158,
    159–61, 169, 173n, 209
    Angels in America, 151, 158,
    160–3, 169

La MaMa E.T.C., 23, 24, 64, 81,
    82, 112, 131, 136
LeCompte, Elizabeth, 119, 120,
    121
Living Theatre, 9, 12, 109–12,
    114, 122
Loomer, Lisa, 13, 166, 168, 169,
    170
    Living Out, 168, 170
    The Waiting Room, 168–9
Ludlum, Charles, 101, 121, 122–3,
    124, 127
Lyotard, Jean-François, 139

McCarthy, Joseph, 10, 47, 48–9,
    50, 56, 60, 61, 62, 160, 161,
    192
McCarthyism, 47, 49, 53, 56, 70n,
    160
McGowan, John, 141
McNulty, Charles, 173n
MacPherson, Myra, 177
Malcolm X, 72, 73
Mamet, David, 13, 64, 79, 103,
    130, 137, 138–44, 154, 209
    American Buffalo, 79, 140,
    142–3, 148, 154
    Glengarry, Glen Ross, 140,
    141–2, 143, 146
Mapplethorpe, Robert, 191, 192
Margolin, Deb, 15, 199–200; *see
    also* Split Britches
Martin, Carol, 1, 207
Method acting, 2, 113

Miller, Arthur, 10, 40, 41, 50, 56,
    60, 61, 62, 63, 90, 120, 138,
    150n, 160
    All My Sons, 50, 56
    Death of a Salesman, 40, 50,
        56–60, 90, 150n
    The Crucible, 56, 60, 61, 62–3,
        120, 160
Miller, Tim, 15, 192, 197
    Glory Box, 197
    Spilt Milk, 197
Milner, Ron, 11, 72, 73, 80
mimesis, 1, 3, 129, 210
modernism, 5, 139, 146

National Endowment for the Arts
    (NEA), 15, 109, 190, 191,
    192, 193, 195, 197, 198, 199
naturalism, 19–20
'NEA Four,' 15, 190, 192, 197,
    199
Nuyorican Poets Cafe, 99, 100,
    210

off-Broadway, 9, 11, 15, 51, 64, 80,
    108, 110, 112, 131, 164, 166,
    168
Ontological-Hysteric Theatre, 12,
    124
Open Theater, 12, 108, 112–15,
    116, 174

Paller, Michael, 66, 111
Parks, Suzan-Lori, 11, 72, 86,
    87–8, 89
    The America Play, 87, 88
    *The Death of the Last Black
        Man in the Whole Entire
        World*, 87, 88–9

Patraka, Vivian, 199
performance art, 15, 190, 192,
    193–4, 200, 204
Performance Group, 12, 118, 119
Pinter, Harold, 9, 10, 29, 34, 35,
    36, 37, 38n, 39n
    The Dumb Waiter, 34–5
Pirandello, Luigi, 28, 174, 179,
    186, 187
postmodernism, 6, 7, 46–7, 68n,
    121–2, 139, 159, 194
Power, Will, 209–10

Rabe, David, 14, 175, 179, 180,
    182, 185, 188n
    Sticks and Bones, 175, 179, 182,
        188, 188n
    Streamers, 175, 182–4 188n
    *The Basic Training of Pavlo
        Hummel*, 175, 179–82, 188n
realism, 2–3, 5, 7, 8, 13, 18–20, 21,
    23, 26, 27, 30, 40, 67, 74, 75,
    76, 102, 109, 116, 118, 137,
    197
Reed, Ishmael, 11, 100
Richards, Lloyd, 90
Richards, Sandra L., 202, 204
Ridiculous Theatrical Company,
    12, 121, 122, 123
Roach, Joseph, 142
Rose, Charlie, 72, 94, 96
Rose, Tricia, 105n
Rosenberg, Ethel, 160, 161
Rosenberg, Julius, 160
Roudané, Matthew, 137, 149n
Ryan, Steven, 140

San Francisco Mime Troupe, 12,
    116–17

Scarry, Elaine, 188n
Schechner, Richard, 12, 118–19, 120
Sebazco, Raul Santiago, 11, 99
Second World War, 1, 5, 6, 7, 10, 17, 26, 28, 29, 35, 40, 41, 43, 45, 46, 47, 52, 56, 58, 63, 90, 92, 131, 138
Serrano, Andres, 191, 192
Shange, Ntozake, 11, 72, 86, 87, 89
  for colored girls who have considered suicide when the rainbow in enuf, 86–7
Shaw, Peggy, 199
Shepard, Sam, 9, 13, 34, 64, 114, 119, 129, 130–2, 136, 137, 138, 139, 140, 145, 147, 148–9n, 154
  Buried Child, 34, 131, 137, 149n
  The Tooth of Crime, 119, 131–7
  True West, 129, 131, 132, 133, 137, 145–8, 150n, 155
slice of life, 15
Smith, Anna Deavere, 1, 15, 190, 201–3, 204, 207–8, 210
  Fires in the Mirror, 202
  Twilight Los Angeles, 1992, 202, 202–3
Son, Diana, 209
Split Britches, 15, 199, 200
Starkey, Marion, 61
Stewart, Ellen, 64
Stonewall Riots, 151–2
Strindberg, August, 18, 19, 25

Terry, Megan, 12, 112, 174
The Five Lesbian Brothers, 15, 200
Theatre Genesis, 9, 131

Theatre of the Absurd, 7, 9, 28, 29, 31, 38, 39, 83

Valdez, Luis, 12, 116, 117, 118
Van-Itallie, Jean-Claude, 12, 112, 174
VETCo., 185
Vietnam, 185, 186, 187, 188, 188n
Vogel, Paula, 13, 164–5, 166
  How I Learned to Drive, 164–6
  The Baltimore Waltz, 164

Waits, Tom, 125
Weaver, Lois, 199
well-made play, 7, 18, 20, 23
West, Cornel, 103
Williams, Megan, 132, 146, 147
Williams, Tennessee, 9, 10, 25, 40, 41, 44, 45, 49–52, 55, 63–7, 148n, 150n, 155
  A Streetcar Named Desire, 41, 43–4, 49, 68–9n, 159, 199
  Cat on a Hot Tin Roof, 41, 44, 49, 68–9n
  Camino Real, 41, 47, 48, 49, 50–6, 69n
  In the Bar of a Tokyo Hotel, 64, 65
  Kirche, Küche, und Kinder, 65, 66–7
  Orpheus Descending, 41, 44
  Stairs to the Roof, 45–7, 67–8n, 68n
  Suddenly Last Summer, 41, 44, 64, 67n
  Sweet Bird of Youth, 41, 44
  The Glass Menagerie, 25, 41–3, 45, 50, 57, 58, 67n, 68–9n, 70n

The Gnädiges Fräulein, 64, 65
*The Remarkable Rooming House
of Mme. LeMonde*, 65, 66
*The Two-Character Play / Out
Cry*, 64–5, 70n, 149n
THIS IS (An Entertainment),
65, 66
Wilson, August, 11, 89, 90, 91, 93,
209
Fences, 90–3
Wilson, Lanford, 13, 152, 153, 154
Balm in Gilead, 152, 153, 154–5
The Rimers of Eldritch, 152–4

Wilson, Robert, 12, 112, 125,
127
Wooster Group, 12, 119,
120–1
*L.S.D. (...Just the High
Points...)*, 120
Workers' Theatre, 67–8n, 68n,
117; *see also* agitprop
Wright, Doug
I Am My Own Wife, 208
Wright, Glenn, 11, 106

Zola, Èmile, 18, 19